101 BEST
BUSINESSES FOR
PET LOVERS

101 BEST
BUSINESSES FOR
PET LOVERS

**What You Need to Know about Starting and
Succeeding in a Pet Business of Your Own**

Joseph Nigro and Nicholas Nigro

SPHINX® PUBLISHING
AN IMPRINT OF SOURCEBOOKS, INC.®
NAPERVILLE, ILLINOIS
www.SphinxLegal.com

First Edition: 2007

Published by: **Sphinx® Publishing, An Imprint of Sourcebooks, Inc.®**
Naperville Office
P.O. Box 4410
Naperville, Illinois 60567-4410
630-961-3900
Fax: 630-961-2168
www.sourcebooks.com
www.SphinxLegal.com

This publication is designed to provide accurate and authoritative information in regard to the
subject matter covered. It is sold with the understanding that the publisher is not engaged in
rendering legal, accounting, or other professional service. If legal advice or other expert assistance
is required, the services of a competent professional person should be sought.

*From a Declaration of Principles Jointly Adopted by a Committee of the
American Bar Association and a Committee of Publishers and Associations*

This product is not a substitute for legal advice.

Disclaimer required by Texas statutes.

Library of Congress Cataloging-in-Publication Data

Nigro, Joseph.
   101 best businesses for pet lovers / by Joseph Nigro and Nicholas Nigro. -- 1st ed.
      p. cm.
   ISBN-13: 978-1-57248-634-8 (pbk. : alk. paper)
   ISBN-10: 1-57248-634-1 (pbk. : alk. paper)
   1. Pet industry. I. Nigro, Nicholas J. II. Title. III. Title: One hundred one best businesses for pet
lovers.

SF414.7.N54 2007
338.4'76360887--dc22
                                                                              2007026787

Printed and bound in the United States of America.
   SB — 10 9 8 7 6 5 4 3 2

⚓ CONTENTS ⚓

INTRODUCTION
A Pet-pourri of Entrepreneurial Opportunities

I made my entrepreneurial debut at the tender age of 19. The year was 1979—a simpler snapshot in time. A peanut farmer with a toothy smile was the president. Bill Gates was an inconspicuous Windows® salesman. And the phrase *pet care* wasn't ever uttered in the same breath as *big business*.

As fate would have it, my fledgling business endeavor found me the co-owner with Rich Covello of a mom-and-pop shop called *Pet Nosh*. Located on a well-traveled boulevard in the New York City borough of Queens, the place sold pet food and supplies. The business soothsayers of the day deemed it a grungy way to earn a dollar; a monetary dead-end that catered to a small clique of *pet fanatics*.

Despite all the doomsday analysis and dire predictions about my chosen business path, I nonetheless set out after my slice of the American dream with confidence. My partner and I were hell-bent on carving out ours by servicing pet owners and their growing legions of pets. We sensed that the people/pet connection was on the cusp of something big—really big—and that Pet Nosh could share in its bounty if we played our business cards right. To make a long story short, the Pet Nosh ownership bid adieu to the retail sliver of the pet care trade in 1996. That is, we sold Pet Nosh's eight superstores in the tri-state area of New York, New Jersey, and Connecticut to retail behemoth

Petco for $19.1 million! And it's no stretch of the imagination for me to say that the relationship between people and their pets had evolved—and rather dramatically at that—during my seventeen years as a pet retailer.

The modern-day business of pets is a cradle-to-grave affair. Entrepreneurs of all ages, backgrounds, and talents are diligently working to fulfill every need and cater to every whim of the contemporary pet owner. But these aren't conventional pet owners that we are talking about, but pet *parents* who look upon their cats, dogs, and birds as *children*, albeit of the four-legged and feathery variety.

The astonishing by-product of this increasingly intimate people/pet relationship is an innovative and intriguing assortment of pet-specialty businesses that are at once omnipresent and multiplying in numbers. Long a malodorous footnote in the world of commerce, the pet care trade is currently a mega-billion dollar colossus that is forecast to reach even loftier heights in the coming years. The dollars spent on pets has more than doubled since 1994 (when pet care spending totaled *just* $17 billion)! The business of caring for—and, indeed, pampering—pets is now more potent than the human toy industry. It is sweeter than the candy trade. Believe it or not, more cat food is sold in the United States today than baby food!

The humanization of the present-day household pet—now called a *companion animal*—has fashioned a very lucrative industry. Cats, dogs, birds, and an assortment of other pets are indulged as never before. More and more of their diets are *premium* in ingredients and taste appeal. Everything from pets' choices of playthings, health and beauty products, and fashions are growing in numbers as well as varieties. There is a mammoth welcome mat out for existing and, of course, prospective businesspersons on the pet care frontier. There are infinite profitable avenues to venture down in satisfying today's incredibly devoted pet parents and their mollycoddled menageries of animal friends. Between the covers of ***101 Best Businesses for Pet Lovers*** is a cornucopia of business and career ideas on which you can pitch your entrepreneurial tent in this incomparable trade, which, by the way, exhibits no indications of grinding to a halt or reversing direction. In addition, you'll be supplied with information and incisive counsel on the things you need to know to at once initiate and prosper in a strikingly broad range of moneymaking possibilities.

Whatever your special talents, monetary circumstances, or dreams for the future, there is something for you in *101 Best Businesses for Pet Lovers*. In fact, many of the business and career prospects chronicled on the book's pages can be commenced on a shoestring budget or, in some instances, with no out-of-pocket investment at all. Potential pet entrepreneurs will learn everything from what a pet-sitting business entails to what you need to know to be a pet-parenting tutor to the legal and logistical ABCs involved in manufacturing premium pet foods and gourmet treats from the comforts of home. My brother, who labored in every conceivable capacity during Pet Nosh's existence—from teenage stock boy to store manager to editor of the customer newsletter called *Nosh News*—and I have put our combined decades of experience in the trade to work for you, unfurling an eclectic and entertaining mix of profitable pet-related undertakings for you to consider.

If you are in any way, shape, or form skeptical that the pet care trade is chock-full of genuine opportunities, here is a representative sampling of some of the pet business and career possibilities found in *101 Best Businesses for Pet Lovers*:

- ★ Pet food and supply retailer
- ★ Pet photographer
- ★ Doggie daycare
- ★ Doggie fashions designer
- ★ Cat furniture maker
- ★ Professional pooper scooping
- ★ Premium dog food maker
- ★ Pet-parenting tutor
- ★ Veterinary technician
- ★ eBay pet merchandise seller
- ★ Cricket farmer
- ★ Pet cemetery proprietor
- ★ Pet food sampler
- ★ Catnip farmer

★ Professional pet sitting
★ Pet party host
★ Doggie summer camp
★ Pet bakery
★ Professional dog groomer
★ Professional dog trainer
★ Dog washer
★ Pet relocation service
★ Pet artist
★ Pet writer
★ Pet greeting card maker
★ Online pet-dating network *for the two-legged*

★ Geese away
★ Pet candle making
★ Aquarium maintenance
★ Reptile breeder
★ Cat toy inventor
★ Pet masseuse
★ Pet minister
★ Aquarium plant farmer
★ Pet talk radio show host
★ Animal party choreographer
★ Perfect dog locating service

And there are many more where they came from....

—Joseph Nigro

The Pet Entrepreneur Profile

Regardless of the pet care business enterprise you ultimately choose as your own, it behooves you to do it right—*right from the start*. To increase your odds of realizing genuine business success, each and every pet entrepreneur needs to go into battle with four key guns ablazing:

★ Nerve
★ Brainpower
★ Resources
★ Passion

It's an indispensable quartet that combines formidable personality characteristics with access to ample financing (if required).

Nerve

For starters, inaugurating any kind of business in any field of endeavor brings with it a degree of risk, particularly if a sizeable investment of dollars is involved. There is no such thing as a sure thing on the entrepreneurial playing field. Entrepreneurs are called *risk takers* for very good reasons. And this is precisely where *nerve* comes in. The meek may in fact inherit the earth, but the strong will have to run businesses for them.

Beginning in the idea stage, your principal task as a pet entrepreneur in the making is to minimize this built-in risk. While risk comes with the business territory, you largely determine its magnitude. In other words, you shape your level of risk by the particular business you choose to call your own and by the decisions you subsequently make in both getting it off the ground and managing it on a day-to-day basis. You can't avoid decision-making in any kind of business—be it a pet shop on Broadway or a pet-sitting venture where you call on your clientele's homes. It comes with the territory.

Brainpower

Once you've exhibited the all-important resolve to launch a pet business, it's time to let your smarts assume center stage. Nerve meet brainpower! Let your intellect arm you with the most vital quality a businessperson can have: *good sense*.

No, you don't need a college degree to be a successful pet entrepreneur—except in a few select careers—nor a genius I.Q. What you do need—be you a high school dropout or a charter member of Mensa—is a genuine feel for the business or career landscape that you tread upon. That is, you want both your heart and your head firmly grounded in the reality of your particular sliver of the pet care market. You also want to be fully aware of the trends in the overall economy and consumer culture. Simply put, you have to appreciate what you are up against in both the short-term and the long-term.

Every single day is a new battle with new challenges. Nothing stays the same in business and you can't either. A successful businessperson is *always* a realistic and flexible individual. You have to combine a strong work ethic with an ability to make crucial decisions on a recurring basis and often at a moment's notice. In other words, you have to have a plan, but it has to be one that can change quickly if necessary.

Resources

Okay, we can safely say that business is neither for the fainthearted nor the dimwitted. But all the nerve and brainpower in the world can only take you so far without *resources—i.e.,* money in the bank. Under-capitalization is the bane of countless entrepreneurs—many with very good business ideas but very speculative and shortsighted business plans. If you doubt this cold hard fact of the business experience, call on the entrepreneurial graveyard, which is teeming with under-financed businesses that went belly-up before they knew what hit them. You need to have the requisite financing in place to simultaneously get your business off the ground and keep it afloat in the critical building years.

Passion

Very few businesses succeed without passionate ownership. Too many entrepreneurs establish businesses with serious doubts clouding their decision-making and without a genuine ardor for the task at hand. As baseball pitcher Tug McGraw once opined, "Ya gotta believe!" Is your pet business concept or career choice something you absolutely want to see through? Do you want to be your own boss and chart your own destiny? Are you ready for all the responsibilities that come attached to being your own boss?

Business Planning ABCs

If you are on the cusp of inaugurating a full-time enterprise in the pet care trade—or part-time venture where you'll be investing both time and money—it behooves you to research and write a thorough business plan. Business planning is not the sole prerogative of big shots jumpstarting multi-million dollar companies, as many aspiring entrepreneurs surmise. Business plans are desirable for all entrepreneurs—from the pet button maker to the dog trainer to the proprietor of a pet food and supply store on Main Street. The nuts and bolts of getting entrepreneurial endeavors off the ground—and making them long-term successes—are one and the same for Donald Trump and for you. Business success *always* amounts to individuals or corporations doing the same crucial things right—*i.e.*, prudent financial management, effective marketing, solid customer and employee relations, and so on.

If you absolutely believe that there is an ample market for the product or service that you intend on introducing to the pet consumer, you've completed step one. Then comes the all-important soul searching on your part. *Do you have the gumption and the wherewithal to provide this product or service to the marketplace (i.e.,* the requisite capital, marketing strategy, the right personality, etc., to make things happen)? If you categorically feel that the answer is yes, then put it in writing. Formulate a business plan that shows the world—and potential investors, if you need them—that you've done your homework and are sufficiently armed and ready for the challenge of operating a successful pet care business of your own.

Business Planning Basics

A business plan embodies the vision of your idea and of your firm. It is a document that should be replete with facts, figures, and projections that validate your confidence in your business concept. A business plan should function as a reference guide that choreographs your moves and anticipates eventualities, including the inevitable speed bumps on the road to riches.

Simply understood, your business plan should serve as a blueprint for your entrepreneurial success. Remember, though, that you are never bound by any strictures in it. Both the natures of business *and* business plans are flexible—always works in progress that can be adjusted with changing circumstances. Nevertheless, a business plan details what you anticipate accomplishing at various milestones in your business life and conveys exactly how you plan on attaining your various objectives. A business plan articulates your strategies in getting from point A to point B.

Consider a carefully scripted business plan your *reality barometer*. The overriding reason that the majority of start-up businesses implode is that they are born and function in a separate reality—*a false reality*. For most businesspersons, the human spirit is plainly willing, but it's the marketplace reality—the flesh, as it were—that is weak. To emerge triumphant out of the business scrimmage, you have to harmonize your dreams with your unique abilities, personality quirks, status in life, as well as the state of the economy, evershifting consumer tastes, and—most especially—market for your particular pet product or pet service.

Organizing a thorough business plan compels you to see your idea through and determine if it can pass muster in the bright light of day. And, when it does, the business plan then serves as an indispensable roadmap, enabling you to establish goals and timetables from which you can continually measure your progress.

The Business Plan Foundation

Anyone can write a business plan. With modern computer technology, you can produce a nice looking document brimming with charts and colorful graphics. But, bear in mind: business planning is not about glitz and packaging. You don't help yourself by inserting random numbers into market analysis, sales projections, and estimated cash flows. Many aspiring entrepreneurs fashion business plans that sparkle on the printed page, but are devoid of any real substance.

There are three key components that all business plans should include. They are:

1. A meticulous evaluation of the product or service that you will be offering consumers, and how it distinguishes itself from the existing competition.
2. An overview of your potential customer pool, how you are going to attract clientele, and what you plan to do to keep them in the fold over time.
3. A complete and honest assessment of your capital needs in both the short-term and the long-term, with a strict accounting of where that money will come from.

These three particulars tackle the most fundamental business concerns: the legitimacy of the product or service for sale, the size and nature of the customer base, and both today's and tomorrow's cash flow. If you can pinpoint a ready and solid audience for your product or service, bring them into your business tent, and develop a sufficient cash flow to sustain and grow your company, you are sitting in the proverbial catbird seat.

The Business Plan in Action

You've researched your market and know who your potential customers are. You know, too, where your investment dollars are coming from. You've settled on a most probable cash flow and have determined a break-even point. You've also looked into your soul and concluded that this is what you want to do with your life. It's time now to put it all down on paper. Remember that writing a business plan should never be approached as a press release or an advertisement. Keep hype and flowery superlatives to a minimum. Instead, let solid research do the talking—facts and more facts along with realistic assessments based on them.

There are nine areas that constitute most business plans:

1. **Executive Summary**. This is a one- to two-page abstract of the entire business plan. Make this synopsis short and sweet. Consider this your pithy sales pitch and make it compelling.

2. **Table of Contents**. List the sections of the business plan here. This should be a simple listing—and nothing more. No descriptions of the sections to follow are necessary.

3. **The Company**. A thorough description of the company that you are starting is made here. Describe the principal factors that will distinguish it from the competition. Demonstrate in this section exactly why you feel your success is probable.

4. **Market Analysis**. Here you describe the industry and customer base of your chosen business. Identify the markets that you'll be targeting and tapping into. Discuss where you see the markets heading in the future.

5. **Marketing Plans**. Be very specific in this section about how you intend to compete in the marketplace. Reveal your advertising plans. And discuss how long you feel it'll take before you attract customers and generate sustained business.

6. **Business Operations**. This is your opportunity to present an overview of exactly how your business will function. Describe your location and facilities in detail. Address the matter of employees and how many, if any, you will employ.

7. **Funding**. Here you address the fundamental question of how much money you need to open your business. Then, how many dollars you will require over the next one, two, and three years. Follow the money, as it were, and very precisely describe how it will be allocated along the way.

8. **Financial Data**. In this very key section, you will need to make quarter-by-quarter projections of profit and loss, until you determine a break-even point. Then, you should make annual projections for the five years after that. Back up your projections with fact-based assumptions and research, erring, if at all, on the conservative side of the ledger.

9. **Appendices**. Lastly, you can conclude your business plan with pertinent materials that will enhance it in some way. Articles from newspapers and magazines, for instance, about your industry or particular business.

This business plan foundation may be more formal and detailed than you require, particularly if you are self-financing your venture or if it's a part-time affair with minimal investment required. However, if you are going to a bank for a loan or trying to attract investors to your side, you have to complete a thorough business plan—there's no getting around it.

Making It All Legal

When you establish a legal business entity, you must select from one of the following forms of ownership:

★ Sole Proprietorship   ★ Corporation
★ Partnership   ★ Limited Liability Company

Sole Proprietorship

Each one of these distinctions has its plusses and minuses. Nevertheless, the preponderance of businesses exist as sole proprietorships. It's the simplest of setups because you, in essence, are the business. There are few distinctions made between your business earnings and your personal income. You own the business assets and all the profits that you generate (before the government gets its share). You can also become a sole proprietor with a minimum amount of paperwork and a pretty straightforward tax situation.

The downside of a sole proprietorship is that you are wholly responsible for any of your business liabilities and incurred debts. In addition, you cannot deduct various benefits as business expenses, which you could under a corporate structure. You are also without much flexibility at tax time. Corporations can plan for taxes vis-à-vis what salaries are taken by their shareholders—*i.e.*, you and your partners, if you have any.

Partnership

If you are entering into a pet care business with a partner, you can form a legal partnership, which is akin to the sole proprietorship, only there are two or more parties involved. The key in these arrangements is a *written partnership agreement* between or among the partners, spelling out in precise detail everything and anything that matters:

- ★ How decisions will be made
- ★ How profits will be shared
- ★ How disputes will be resolved
- ★ How one partner can buy out another
- ★ How additional partners can be brought into the business
- ★ How the partnership can be dissolved
- ★ What happens in the event that one partner dies

There are countless large enterprises with substantial assets—partnerships and incorporated businesses—that do not have vital contingencies in their legal arrangements. For instance, they do not specify exactly what happens upon the death of one partner. If you are young, in particular, the furthest thing from your mind is shuffling off this mortal coil. But it's been known to happen. So, make sure that every *i* is dotted and *t* is crossed the moment you become a legal partnership. One day, you might be very happy that you did.

Corporation

If you opt not to be a sole proprietorship or a partnership, then your remaining option is incorporation. Corporations are chartered by the individual states. Assorted laws, regulations, and tax situations apply from state to state, with some states more corporation-friendly than others (like Delaware). Both federal and state law recognize corporations as legal entities, separate and apart from their ownership. They can be taxed, sued, and enter into contractual agreements. Corporations' owners are shareholders, who have limited liability as individuals for debts incurred by the business—a big plus for entrepreneurs. However, corporations are more costly to initiate (fees, lawyers, etc.) and maintain (more complex accounting and legalities), and they come attached to additional bureaucratic red tape. They also put you in the position of possible double taxation—*i.e.*, your business gets taxed and so does your salary from the business. However, only your salary is subject to the self-employment tax, which is 15.3% on the first $90,000 of income, and not your profits. In a sole proprietorship or partnership, your profits are your income and hit with this very considerable self-employment tax. In other words, corporate structures enable you to take less in salary and do more intricate tax planning to possibly minimize your tax burden.

What form of business ownership you ultimately select should be based on the type of business you are in, what kind of profits you anticipate, and what assets you own (both business *and* personal). Talk with current businesspersons. Consult, too, with an accountant and lawyer to discuss what is right for you and your precise situation. You can always begin your business journey as a sole proprietorship or partnership and then incorporate down the road when it better suits your new circumstances. You may also consider the benefits of becoming an S Corporation, if you qualify, which enables you to be taxed like a sole proprietorship or partnership, but still receive the limited liability protection inherent in the corporate structure. There is also the Limited Liability Company (LLC), which provides its *members* limited liability for certain debts and actions in a less formal set-up than the traditional corporate structure.

Laws and Disorder

No matter what business field you choose to romp through, you won't ever be alone. Government bureaucrats are guaranteed to be there alongside you the whole time. There are all kinds of laws and regulations—federal, state, and local—that apply to businesses. Depending on the particular pet business you select, your form of ownership (sole proprietorship, partnership, corporation), or where you operate the business, these laws and regulations will vary. But, for sure, you will be at the mercy of bureaucratic edicts that run the gamut from tax responsibilities to building codes to insurance requirements to employment polices.

The exact nature of your pet care business will determine the licenses and permits—if any—that you may have to procure from government entities: federal, state, and local. Requirements for small business enterprises run a wide gamut, depending, of course, on what you are doing and where you are doing it. Before you make a big move, contact the requisite government institutions and get the scoop on what you need vis-à-vis licenses and permits to operate a completely aboveboard business. What follows is a roster of the kinds of governmental licenses and permits that you may be legally required to obtain before hanging out your "Open for Business" shingle or flying your "Grand Opening" bunting:

- ★ Business operation license
- ★ Federal employer identification number (EIN) or tax identification number (compulsory for most business setups)
- ★ "Doing Business As" permit
- ★ Zoning permit, applicable to some home-based businesses
- ★ Health department permit, applicable to any kind of food production
- ★ Sales tax license for retail and service businesses
- ★ Fire department permit, necessary for many retail and service businesses

The bottom line is that you have to know exactly what licenses and permits you need, and what laws and regulations you need to be in compliance with. The enormous hand of the government is interested—above all else—in getting dollars from you to keep it in business. As an entity, government is a cold-blooded animal and not particularly interested in your personal success. The laws and regulations on the books vary from the necessary, complicated, and fair to the excessive, trifling, and punitive.

Throughout our Pet Nosh retail years, we operated in quite a few municipalities and got a fair sampling of government's bearing on the entrepreneurial spirit. In New York City, home of the original Pet Nosh store, we experienced first-hand how the Big Apple—dynamic as it is—views its businesspeople. For instance, the city's Department of Sanitation once issued an edict that all shopkeepers in New York's five boroughs had to have their front sidewalks swept and pristine before eleven o'clock each morning, or risk a summons. In theory, this decree from on high seemed fair enough. After all, businesspersons operate in neighborhoods and have a responsibility to keep their places clean for the general good. For strictly business reasons, too, they should desire maintaining such tidiness. But the trouble with many bureaucracies is that even the most well-intentioned laws and regulations often become mere excuses to harass innocent people and write out tickets.

the Department of Sanitation used the bylaw as a way to fleece busi-
for bucks. Caught in the dragnet with guilty parties were countless
businesspersons who were in fact complying with the decree. That is,
businesses with gum wrappers deposited by Mother Nature or paper cups
dropped by inconsiderate passersby received summonses at all points
throughout the day. And these kinds of stories are legion. This red tape reality
is even more of a reason why you have to know what laws and regulations
you are operating under because the ticketing brigade awaits you without
sympathy for your entrepreneurial ignorance or financial straits.

A Checklist for Starting Your Business

What follows is a checklist of the key things you need to do when converting
a business idea into a business reality. Of course, some of the items may not
apply to your particular circumstances.

_____ Conduct a thorough personal inventory of your interests and talents.

_____ Review your life circumstances and assess how a business will fit
into it in both the immediate and long-term future.

_____ Appraise your financial situation and the financial risks involved in
starting a business.

_____ Determine exactly why you want a business of your own and what
you anticipate getting out of it.

_____ Conduct a market analysis of any business idea under consideration.

_____ Consult with businesspersons about what life as an entrepreneur
entails.

_____ Confer with businesspersons in your chosen field.

_____ Identify your customer base.

_____ Identify your competition.

_____ Find a location to operate your business.

_____ Ascertain start-up costs.

_____ Prepare a comprehensive business plan.

_____ Apply for a business loan or obtain requisite capital from other sources, if necessary.

_____ Consult with a lawyer about obtaining a lease.

_____ Sign a lease after consultation with a lawyer.

_____ Choose a business name.

_____ Select a form of ownership (sole proprietorship, partnership, or corporation).

_____ Register your business with government entities.

_____ Obtain any necessary business licenses or permits.

_____ Set up telephone service.

_____ Establish a business checking account.

_____ Procure a federal employer identification number, if needed.

_____ Procure a state employer identification number, if needed.

_____ Procure a state sales tax certificate, if applicable.

_____ Purchase necessary business insurance coverage.

_____ Obtain a credit card merchant account.

_____ Become acquainted with local business codes.

_____ Purchase furniture, fixtures, etc., for your business location.

_____ Contact needed vendors and place initial orders.

_____ Consult with an accountant.

_____ Determine a launch date for your business.

_____ Put out the welcome mat.

_____ Treat your customers well.

_____ Generate profits.

Pet Food for Thought

The sweeping pet food recall of recent times sent justifiable shockwaves through the vast and diverse community of pet parents. While the commonly accepted wisdom has long been that there are cosmic differences in pet food formulae, the recall trail led to the sullied doorstep of a solitary manufacturer. Yes, Menu Foods churns out a wide array of cat and dog diets for a breathlessly long roster of pet food companies, including many premium brands.

What this sorry but incredibly revealing episode augurs for both current and aspiring pet entrepreneurs is, believe it or not, more opportunities and open doors. It's true. The consequences of the intricately complex pet food scare are in fact an entrepreneurial boon and not a commercial setback for an industry bursting at the seams. This lucrative reality is evidenced by the immediate jump in sales of organic pet foods, which were already making serious inroads into the traditional pet food market long before the recall. Growing numbers of pet owners also cast their eyes on fare made from only *human-grade* ingredients. Again, this snippet of the pet food business was blossoming prior to the scare, but is now poised to fully flower in the coming years.

A human thread clearly runs through the pet care trade, but it is hardly limited to food products—not by a long shot. This book's sum and substance unmasks time and again how the contemporary household pet—as an integral part of the human family—is at the epicenter of an incredible commercial phenomenon. One, by the way, that isn't about to be derailed by a pet food scare. On the contrary. The recall merely contributed to a realigning of priorities for many pet parents who found safer and better alternatives to their pets' erstwhile diets.

However, this celebrated commercial pet food blunder didn't diminish in the least Americans' love for their pets. Rather, it underscored people's profound passion for the furry, feathery, and four-legged in their inner and intimate circles. For one, retailers of potentially contaminated products were quick to yank products from their shelves, as well as reassure anxious pet consumers of what was not impacted by the recall. By and large, manufacturers and retailers alike didn't experience any notable blows to their bottom lines.

Up and down and inside and out, the business of pets is incredibly fluid and perpetually innovative. This is precisely why there is so much opportunity within its expanding confines. Whether it's a food product, plaything, grooming tool, medicine, or a service—it doesn't matter—demand is on the upswing and not about to be squelched by even the most egregious of commercial missteps. The pet care industry is rock solid because it is built atop the strongest of foundations—the inviolable bonds between people and their multitudes of beloved pets. If there is one lesson for pet entrepreneurs that can be extracted from this pet food mess, it's that quality and safety must reign supreme over the agenda of every new business's founding and ensuing operating.

CHAPTER I
Services for the Four-legged

Professional Dog Groomer
☛ Mobile Dog Grooming

With all the hoopla that surrounds the modern pet care trade in its infinite splendor and perpetual innovation, we sometimes forget that the old reliable businesses in the industry are also flourishing and charting new territories with each passing day. For instance, today's mushrooming pet commerce has not bypassed one of its entrepreneurial pioneers: the professional dog groomer. As a matter of fact, pet grooming services are more accessible than ever before. More grooming businesses than ever before can be found on Main Street, USA. They are also located on the premises of some of the biggest pet food and supply superstores in the country. Mobile grooming services are available as well, where the groomer comes to the pet owner and pet in a specially-equipped vehicle, instead of the other way around. This powerful combination of greater visibility and a more painless availability has cracked wide open a whole new market for these old hands in the business of pets.

Indeed, the numbers of dogs getting professionally groomed these days is increasing at a rapid pace. And, not surprisingly, grooming businesses and individuals in grooming careers are growing commensurate with this broader demand. Nevertheless, there is still a shortage of qualified men and women to perform all of the grooming jobs that current pet-parenting consumers desire. In addition, when factoring in the multiple millions of canines in American households, the overall number of dog owners who patronize the services of professional groomers is relatively small. What all of this means is that more and more pet parents are seeking out professionals to groom their animal companions—but the demand is clearly outpacing the supply. In other words, there is a rather sprawling and highly profitable entrepreneurial space clamoring to be filled by qualified **professional dog groomers**.

If you are contemplating a career in dog grooming, a good place to begin your due diligence is the **Pet Groomer** website @ PetGroomer.com (800-556-5131). This cyber portal is chock-full of information on the ABCs of the grooming business. It is a gateway of knowledge with links aplenty to the many particulars surrounding a career or establishing a business in the fertile field of dog grooming. The folks at Pet Groomer consider themselves consultants for both current groomers and the groomers of tomorrow. They describe career opportunities in the trade as "limitless," citing the statistic that there are approximately 4,000 dogs and cats for every single grooming business.

How Much Does It Cost to Start This Kind of Business?

The investment required in this field largely depends on where you are and where you want to go. With both patience and perseverance, learning the ins and outs of the grooming trade can be accomplished on a shoestring budget. That is, if you follow the tried and true method of initially serving as an apprentice for a professional groomer, you won't be plunking down a lot of dollars to build a potentially exciting and lucrative career. In fact, many of today's successful groomers acquired their skills by first working alongside professionals in some capacity—often as compensated assistants. There are many grooming outfits looking for help. These are the ideal places to achieve your grooming wings.

On the other hand, if you are at the point where you want to open a grooming business in a brick-and-mortar building, you will need a sizeable investment—in the $25,000 to $50,000+ range. Grooming enterprises require serious monetary outlays for equipment from bathtubs to tables to clippers. There is insurance that must be purchased and operating permits that must be acquired. If you are traveling down the route of **mobile dog grooming** and considering the purchase of a specially equipped van, the initial investment costs will be on par with opening up a physical locale.

There is an emergent trend in the field of grooming that revolves around wheels; that is, of grooming services that call on pet owners and pets at their residences. Offering every kind of service from nail clipping to haircuts to aromatherapy to flea baths, mobile grooming is now just a proverbial phone call away.

Moviegoers got a glimpse of *mobile grooming* in the film *Dumb and Dumber*. Throughout the flick, intelligence-challenged Jeff Daniels drove around in a furry dog-shaped "Shaggin' Wagon," offering his pet-grooming services to interested parties. Rest assured, mobile grooming is not quite as it is depicted in this comedic farce. It is, in fact, an emergent pet-specialty service that is one of the most sought after entrepreneurial opportunities in the trade.

In a nutshell, mobile dog—and cat—grooming involves the groomer pulling into a customer's driveway in a fully outfitted van. These vans regularly include such features as heated bath water, large stainless steel washtubs, high-velocity blow dryers, hydraulic grooming tables, and central vacuum systems to keep the floors free from hair and dander. This mobile service meets the needs of both pet parents and pets—pets receive individual care, they are not in far-off shops for hours, and they are never in contact with other animals. It's a less stressful grooming alternative for pet and pet owner alike.

What Qualifications Do You Need for This Kind of Work?

You need to know what you are doing in this field—it's as simple as that. You determine how you reach this competence level. As previously noted, working with proven professionals and learning the grooming business inside and out is highly recommended. There are also invaluable professional membership associations in the field—the **National Dog Groomers Association of America (NDGAA)** and **International Professional Groomers (IPG)**—that provide both coursework and accreditation. Some community colleges offer two-year associate degree programs in the discipline of pet grooming, too. However, as with many other pet-specialty services, there are no laws that necessitate a degree or special accreditation to call oneself a groomer.

If you are contemplating a career as a dog groomer, or establishing a grooming business, there are two professional associations worth looking into. They are the **National Dog Groomers Association of America (NDGAA)** @ National DogGroomers.com (724-962-2711) and the **International Professional Groomers (IPG)** @ IPGCMG.org (847-758-1938). The latter awards qualified parties with the designation Certified Master Groomer (CMG). In fact, both organizations supply certification to individuals who satisfactorily complete their programs and meet their standards of excellence. On these two websites, glean the ABCs of all that professional grooming entails. There is a huge amount of information in this field that needs to be absorbed in areas ranging from the tools of the trade to the specialized know-how required for grooming a roster of particular breeds.

Grooming is nevertheless a business service that discerning consumers will carefully vet. They are going to want to know your credentials. And just because you aren't required to have any under the law isn't going to satisfy the people whom you want to attract as clients. Interested parties will only feel comfortable turning their animal friends over to you when you have demonstrated in some manifest way that you can do the job and do it well.

How Do You Find Customers?

If you have a pair of capable hands and the requisite knowledge to perform as a professional groomer, you can look for positions in the employ of others. There are many independent grooming outfits in need of qualified personnel to expand their current businesses. The retail superstores in the trade are increasingly on the hunt for professional dog groomers to work on their often profitable service sides.

If you want to establish your very own grooming enterprise, advertise in the usual places and via the usual methods—newspapers, direct mail, etc. Print up fliers and business cards, and distribute them to your target demographic—dog parents. Use the copious information available through the professional organizations in this discipline to your advantage. And remember: Word of mouth and testimonials to your competence are your best friends in this business.

Professional Dog Trainer 🦴 Mobile Dog Training

Any Tom, Dick, and Harriet can put up a shingle purporting to be a dog trainer. This is still the reality, even in the enlightened age of pet parenting. No rock-hard laws yet exist mandating prescribed credentials before calling oneself a **professional dog trainer**. There are no colleges or universities that award traditional degrees in the field.

Nevertheless, there are alternative educational institutions and organizations solely devoted to dog training and animal behavior that furnish accreditation in the discipline. Serious and accomplished dog trainers are more than just dog lovers who place ads in the Yellow Pages offering to right the behavior of unruly and neurotic canines for a fee. If you hope to someday be a sought-after and respected dog trainer, you must first demonstrate that you are qualified to get the job done.

How Much Does It Cost to Start This Kind of Business?

Since what makes a dog trainer *a dog trainer* is so subjective, the amount of investment in this career opportunity is purely up to you. You can largely self-educate yourself in this field for minimal out-of-pocket costs. Your biggest investment will be in your time—in learning all that goes into dog training and dog-training businesses.

What Qualifications Do You Need for This Kind of Work?

The key to unlocking career success in dog training revolves around *your* pedigree, not the dogs you will be training to be more refined four-legged citizens. Simply put, you have to know your stuff and prove that you know it. If you are contemplating a potentially rewarding career as a dog trainer, you should:

★ **Educate yourself on canine behavior**—even if you think you know all there is to know. Contact the **Association of Pet Dog Trainers (APDT)**, the **National Association of Dog Obedience Instructors (NADOI)**, or another organization in the field. Complete canine education courses where offered. Attend training seminars. Work with a professional trainer as an apprentice. And, of course, read books on the subject of training methods and animal behavior—there are multiple titles in print

★ **Understand that dog training, first and foremost, is a service business**. This means that—yes—you will be working with the furry and four-legged, but it's the two-legged animals that will make or break you. In other words, you have to please dog parents in order to get compensated, to get references, and to get more business. You must have people skills and a wealth of patience to be a successful dog trainer. This is not a career for people haters.

★ **Appreciate the width and breadth of dog training**. For instance, dogs enrolled in training classes must be properly vaccinated. You must know what inoculations are required. If you are going into the training business on your own, you must be properly insured, or if you are working for somebody else, make certain that your employer is insured. It is absolutely essential that dog trainers consider the health and well-being of all the dogs in their care, as well as protect themselves from any unfortunate events or mishaps.

You can procure vital information on the ABCs of life as a dog trainer via the **Association of Pet Dog Trainers (APDT)** @ APDT.com (800-PET-DOGS). This international organization furnishes an extensive trainer directory, too. By combing the APDT database by city, state, and zip code, you can locate trainers near you who are members in good standing. You can also ascertain what members must do to receive and maintain their APDT certification. If you are interested in this line of work, speak to as many professional trainers as possible. Learn from them what the occupation entails and all that goes into starting a training business or forging a career in the field.

The **National Association of Dog Obedience Instructors (NADOI)** @ NADOI.org is an organization dedicated to ensuring that individuals calling themselves "dog trainers" are—essentially—qualified to do the job. If you are contemplating a life as a dog trainer, you'll find copious information and counsel at this website.

How Do You Find Customers?

There is a budding consumer demand for qualified dog trainers. With increasing numbers of pets in households lorded over by devoted pet parents, more and more opportunities exist for experienced professionals in this vital behavioral province. In addition, with the national retail chains adding in-store services, such as training, to their menus, demand is generated that wouldn't otherwise exist.

The icing on the cake of this career is undeniably the rise of **mobile dog training** services. That is, dog trainers who make house calls. A new market for training services exists when dog and dog parent don't have to venture out into the intimidating wider world, but instead can remain in the familiar surroundings of home sweet home. There are many pet owners who would not—under any circumstances—consider bringing their companion animals to trainers, but who would consider having trainers come to their homes. The days of family doctors making house calls may be over—because it doesn't pay. The days of pet professionals making them has just begun—because it does.

Professional Dog Walking

Dog walking for a few bucks has been around since time immemorial or, at the very least, since the invention of the dog leash. **Professional dog walking**

as a profitable business entity, on the other hand, is a more a recent
enon. Years ago, a neighbor's boy or girl might walk your dog f
pocket change. Today, dog walking is a growing and legitimate serv
ness advertised in the Yellow Pages. Yes, dog walking is now in the entrepreneurial company of plumbers, florists, and pizza restaurants.

Before the advent of what is known as pet parenting, leaving your dog home
alone all day was common practice—the societal norm. After all, other than
having that neighbor kid come by to take your dog out for a stroll, what were
the alternatives? Nowadays, it's considered bad form to keep your dog
cooped up all day long, nervously awaiting your return. And the reality is that
many dog owners are working longer and longer hours, which means the
home alone clock sometimes chimes ten, twelve, or more hours. This is a
long stretch of time for your canine buddy to resist nature's call. And it's time
enough for your best pal to take out his snowballing frustrations on your
furniture, rugs, and any number of household items.

Dog walking as a full-time business or part-time job is therefore no longer
farfetched. Dog walkers can and do charge $15 to $25 per half hour of their
time. This business is ideal for those looking to supplement their already
existing incomes, or for retired persons with time on their hands seeking to
augment those meager Social Security checks. Of course, making dog
walking a full-time career is also possible, but this entails building up a
client base and often walking multiple pets at once. (There are multi-lead
dog-walking devices that enable you to do just that.)

Dog walking as a business is often confused with pet sitting, but they are not
one and the same. Often, pet-sitting entrepreneurs include dog walking on
their service menus, but what we are discussing right now is visiting clients'
homes or apartments—when they are at work or otherwise occupied—and
taking their canine friends for a walk in the great outdoors for a contractu-
ally specified period of time.

9

How Much Does It Cost to Start This Kind of Business?

Start-up costs for dog-walking businesses are minimal. Some initial spending on advertising—fliers and business cards—is really all that is required. What a dog-walking enterprise needs is a dog walker, and that's you. However, if you are looking at this as a bona fide business undertaking that you plan on growing and growing some more, you should purchase insurance and bonding. You would be wise to fully protect both yourself and your clientele by operating completely aboveboard.

What Qualifications Do You Need for This Kind of Work?

Legally, you don't need any special certification to walk somebody else's dog. No college diploma is required. However, your customers are going to expect that you have certain credentials and pose questions like these:

★ Do you have—or have you had—a dog?

★ Do you like dogs?

★ Do you have any experience in canine first aid or obedience?

In other words, your clientele will want to know if you are qualified to care for their beloved pets. As in so many pet-related service businesses, the most trusted are those that are adequately insured and bonded. Keep in mind that you will be entering people's homes when they aren't on the premises. If you are planning on building your dog-walking business into a real moneymaker, you might look into establishing a Limited Liability Company (LLC) or another formal corporate structure, rather than operating as a sole proprietorship in the eyes of the law. This route can personally protect you from a lawsuit if something goes awry, which is always a possibility.

How Do You Find Customers?

Make it known that you are offering a dog-walking service, and concentrate your initial promotional volleys—if possible—in pet-parenting hot spots. That is, put your business cards and fliers in veterinarian offices, kennels, and on cars in pet food and supply superstore parking lots, for example.

Your customers are going to want to know about your credentials for caring for their dogs. But you have to vet them as well. Any animal that you consent to walk should be—foremost—well-behaved and licensed. Secondly, all dogs in your care should be properly vaccinated against rabies, DHLLP (distemper, hepatitis, leptospirosis, parainfluenza, parvo virus), and Bordatella (kennel cough). During the flea season—especially if you are walking in grassy areas or in the company of other dogs—your canine clientele should be treated with flea preventatives of some kind.

If you have more capital to work with and are more ambitious, you could place a small ad in the Yellow Pages, or in local newspapers and penny savers. But you don't need any huge outlays of money to get this brand of business rolling. Your customers are responsible for providing their dogs' collars and leashes. You've just got to show up. If you call a big city home, you might not even require a mode of transportation; you could walk to all of your jobs. If you live in a rural or suburban area, a vehicle is obviously a must, but your own car will do.

Professional Pet Sitting
Fetch! Petcare Franchise

According to the Bureau of Labor statistics, nonfarm animal caretakers have increased by more than 40% since 1999. The federal government defines these folks as the men and women who "feed, water, groom, bathe, exercise or otherwise care for pets and other nonfarm animals." In other words, *not* the men and women who are milking cows, tossing feed into pens of squealing porkers, or plucking eggs out from under squawking chickens. No, these individuals are caring for *domestic pets* in quite a variety of ways—and getting recompensed for their services.

Prior to the pet care trade's dramatic upsurge of recent years, these so-called caretaker jobs belonged to relatively small numbers of groomers, dog trainers, and kennel personnel. There were very few persons operating pet-sitting businesses or anything resembling today's doggie daycares. If you fancy being in the company of cats, dogs, birds, et al.—and are a very responsible and trustworthy human being—you might want to sample **professional pet sitting** as a career. You could either look for employment in an up and running pet-sitting business or establish your very own company. Whether you go to work for somebody else as a hired hand, or decide to do it alone, you will be entering one of the fastest growing entrepreneurial endeavors in the pet care trade. Pet sitters are in great demand.

How Much Does It Cost to Start This Kind of Business?

On the surface, inaugurating a pet-sitting business seems rather straightforward. Come up with a catchy name, register your business with appropriate government agencies, and advertise your services. But life is never so simple, and neither is a business undertaking. For starters, legitimate pet sitters *must* be insured and bonded. After all, you are asking your prospective clientele to turn over their house keys to you and allow you into their homes. Then, on top of that, you are being entrusted with caring for their beloved pets. A business rooted in this depth of trust comes attached to colossal responsibilities. Your customers are going to want to know a little something about you. But you, too, must do your homework—screen all of your clients, both two-legged and four-legged, have contingency plans for emergencies, etc.—and be prepared for occasional rough waters.

Founded in 1989, the **National Association of Professional Pet Sitters (NAPPS)** @ PetSitters.org (856-439-0324) boasts an eclectic and growing membership. The association offers pet-sitter accreditation "to those who demonstrate professional experience, complete pet-care-related home study courses, attend professional conferences, and abide by a code of ethics." It also shows prospective pet sitters where and how to procure essential pet-sitting business insurance via **Business Insurance.** Interested parties can drop by PetSitterInsurance.com (800-962-4611) for all of the information. The bottom line is that entrepreneurs who visit clients' homes to feed, walk, medicate, exercise, and spend quality time with their cats, dogs, and birds are expected to purchase commercial liability insurance (in case of accidents or negligence) and be bonded as well (to cover theft by them or their employees).

What Qualifications Do You Need for This Kind of Work?

Highly qualified staffs run many of the biggest pet-sitting businesses. They champion their employees' stellar credentials to do the job. And why shouldn't they? Dog trainers, groomers, and veterinarians—or some combination of these pet professionals—operate some of the most successful pet-sitting outfits around. And although this may sound like a broken record: there are no laws that mandate professional credentials of any kind for the job of pet sitting. Still, it helps if you are exceedingly knowledgeable in the field of pet care. After all, pet sitters are called upon to do many things, including:

- ★ Feedings
- ★ Medicating
- ★ Dog walking
- ★ Grooming
- ★ Cat litter box maintenance
- ★ General care tasks

Although pet-sitting work responsibilities often include dog walking, one can be a professional in that role alone—and operate a business that just walks dogs. The focus here is on the "sitting" aspect. That is, you go to your clients' homes and spend quality time with their pet or pets while simultaneously performing a variety of tasks.

Pet Sitters International (PSI) @ PetSit.com (336-983-9222), which includes membership here and abroad, estimates that pet sitters are calling on more than ten million homes annually. To learn more about the roles and responsibilities of pet sitters—what is expected of you and what it takes to succeed in this kind of business—explore what this key organization in the field has to offer.

To get this business ball rolling in the right direction, you will have to invest money in its proper establishment. That is, you will have to purchase the requisite insurance and be suitably bonded. If you ignore these vital safeguards, you will not be taken seriously as a genuine and upstanding pet sitter. But, in the big picture, you can get this business off the ground with minimal capital outlays.

How Do You Find Customers?

Like most of the service businesses in the pet care trade, pet-sitting enterprises are built on reputation. You might first try to find customers who are friends and acquaintances—or friends of friends. If you do good work for them, you have instant references and testimonials to your talents and reliability. Then, promote yourself in pet-specific territories—*i.e.*, where pet parents are known to roam in great numbers. Leave business cards and fliers at pet-specialty retailers, veterinarian offices, and kennels. Put them on cars in parking lots. (Since most households have one or more family pet, pet parents are really everywhere.)

Pet-sitting businesses are always in need of a few good men and women. It's the only way they can grow their businesses. If you think you have what it takes to appeal to established pet-sitting outfits, and you'd rather work for somebody else than start your own venture, you can find pet sitters near you by calling the **Pet Sitter Locator** @ 800-296-PETS. Many pet sitters are listed in the Yellow Pages, too.

Depending on the size of your budget, you could place an ad in the Yellow Pages and local newspapers. But before you reach for the stars in this business, it cannot be overstated: It's best to have some real testimonials from truly satisfied customers under your business belt. Many prospective clients are going to want to see your references. Once you have folks singing your praises as a pet sitter, you are well positioned to expand your business.

Fetch! Pet Care is the largest pet-sitting business in the country. The company offers interested parties a chance to own a Fetch! Pet Care franchise. *Entrepreneur* magazine identified this franchise as among the lowest cost and lowest risk franchises around. To learn more about this business opportunity, visit FetchPetCare.com (866-338-2463).

Pet Masseuse

We most definitely reside in a new age. As portions of this book amply illustrate, the times we live in even transcend species. For instance, as pet parents we believe that our four-legged friends are entitled to aromatherapy and, when required, a few minutes on the proverbial couch with a therapist. And so it should come as no surprise to you that professional massages for the pet-set are both available and an accepted part of the culture. There is a demand for qualified **pet masseuses**. Generally speaking, visiting a pet masseuse is more of a canine than a feline thing. You probably don't need an explanation why.

The pet masseuse offers to let his or her fingers do the walking over your beloved animal friend. And just what are the benefits that come from this non-invasive treatment? The very same benefits that we purport to derive from a soothing massage:

★ Increased blood circulation and energy
★ Relief of pain
★ Strengthening of muscle tone
★ More rapid recovery from accidents or ailments
★ Reduction of anxiety

You get the picture. Just like we people, domestic pets get stressed now and again. In fact, horse massaging has a long and noble tradition. Thus, becoming a pet masseuse can prove very rewarding—financially, of course, but also spiritually on some higher plane. There's just something about an honest-to-goodness massage from somebody who knows what he or she is doing.

How Much Does It Cost to Forge This Kind of Career?

There are massage training schools and home study course that offer accreditation in this field. Check them out. Essentially, this is where any career investment comes into play—in your education. Then, when you have the right touch, you'll have to expend a few dollars promoting yourself as a qualified pet masseuse who is open for business. Start-up costs are nominal.

What Qualifications Do You Need for This Kind of Work?

Outside of medical and foodstuffs, the pet care trade is largely unregulated. That is, you can call yourself just about anything in the industry and not have to worry about running afoul of the law. But this doesn't mean that all businesspersons are created equal—they're obviously not. Just as in the fields of dog training and grooming, your clientele are going to want to know what your qualifications are as a pet masseuse. When you sport hands-on credentials, so to speak, you are armed and ready to perform this kind of work.

To jumpstart your due diligence, drop by the **International Association of Animal Massage Therapists** @ IAAMT.com. This outfit can fill you in on the many particulars involved in the massage business, including what makes a qualified masseuse a qualified masseuse. Also, check out **Massage Awareness** @ MassageAwareness.com (561-383-8205). Here you will encounter information on massaging practices, as well as available home study courses. A venerable trainer of animal therapists is **Equissage** @ Equissage.com (800-843-0224). Indeed, there is a cornucopia of material on the Internet for aspiring entrepreneurs in this line of work. Check out, too, the many practicing masseuses—what they do, what they charge, etc.

17

How Do You Find Customers?

There is always a market for just the right touch. Not only are more and more men and women hanging out their pet masseuse shingles, but they are also going to work for others in pet-specialty shops and veterinarian practices, as well as plying their trade alongside groomers and trainers. You will repeatedly encounter throughout this book evidence that the business of pets is interwoven. Wherever possible, pet entrepreneurs of all stripes are feathering one another's nests.

Pet service careers or businesses are very profitable frontiers in which to tread. For instance, the leading pet food and supply retailers are placing greater emphasis on the service sides of their businesses. This is where their profit margins are widest. In many cases, believe it or not, they are selling cans of cat and dog food with only a few cents' price markup on each one. But their daycare and hotel businesses, grooming and training operations, and photography asides are moneymakers with no middlemen sharing in the bounty. If you so desire, you can take your pet masseuse talents to these already established businesses and partner with them.

CHAPTER II
Services for Pet Parents

Professional Pooper Scooping

When you add up the increasing numbers of dogs in American households with the increasing numbers of pet owners who lead very hectic lives, the by-product is an increasing demand for **professional pooper-scooping** businesses. Granted, it's not the most glamorous of entrepreneurial roads to venture down, but somebody has to do it. And, strange as this may sound, one person's dog droppings are another person's gold nuggets.

This business opportunity is no laughing matter. Professional pooper-scooping services pick up dog waste from their clients' yards. Clean-up jobs could also include condominium grounds, parklands, and any number of commercial accounts, including kennels.

How Much Does It Cost to Start This Kind of Business?
Here's the good news: Pooper scooping is a labor-intensive business. If you can brave the less than aromatic odors that come with the territory and have some means of suitable transportation to go from job to job, you have the basics to initiate a pooper-scooping business. Additional tools of the trade include something to scoop up the waste products—disposable plastic

gloves, shovels, buckets, and household dustpans do rather nicely. You'll also need some heavy-duty garbage bags to cart it all away, a safe but effective disinfectant, and a good pair of rubber boots.

The pooper-scooping business is taking on a life of its own because there is a genuine demand for the services they provide. Most dog owners adore their four-legged friends, but this doesn't mean that they relish cleaning up after them. Many homeowners are more than happy to pay someone a small fee to do this dirty work for them. And, for pooper-scooping services, these nominal sums can quickly add up to real profits.

Pooper-scooping rates run anywhere from $7.50 to $20.00 per dog, per week. Naturally, these rates are flexible and not set in stone. A lot depends on the job at hand—the size of the cleanup area, frequency of the work, etc. But do the arithmetic. Twenty accounts a day at $10 each equals $200. A five-day workweek would bring in $1,000 in revenue. Fifty-two weeks in a year—$52,000. Sure, these kinds of figures don't materialize overnight, but they are not pie-in-the-sky, either. There are dog-waste management businesses pulling in a whole lot more with multiple employees on their payrolls.

The most successful pooper-scooping businesses are both insured and bonded—as you are often working on private properties. And before you find yourself knee-deep in dog waste, inquire about the requisite licenses and permits needed in your neck of the woods to operate a professional pooper-scooping business. In the big picture, the dog-waste management business is rife with potential, with minimal overhead attached to it.

What Qualifications Do You Need for This Kind of Work?

You need a strong stomach. Seriously, the biggest hurdle for the pooper-scooping man or woman to leap over is where to take the waste products after the finished jobs. This task, of course, depends on the area where you are conducting business, so it behooves you to complete a thorough due diligence on municipal law regarding the disposal of animal feces. In New York City, for example, dog waste products are put in with the household trash. The scooped-up waste could then be left in the garbage cans—neatly secured, of course—outside of clients' homes. In many places, however, the waste materials must be brought to local landfills.

Also, understand that picking up dog droppings often involves coming in contact with those pesky, and on occasion, dangerous canine worms. In the pooper-scooping business, you can't afford to transmit dog diseases from one work site to another. If you are scrupulously clean, careful, and informed, this won't happen.

You'd be surprised how fast you can acclimate to what, on the surface, may seem like rather ghastly work. And when you do, you are uniquely positioned to convert mounds of dung into piles of money.

> Visit the **International Directory of Dog Waste Removal** @ Pooper-Scooper.com for more information on starting and succeeding in a pooper-scooping business of your own. Also, drop by the **Association of Professional Animal Waste Specialists** @ APAWS.org to harvest more of the pooping particulars that come with the territory of this curious entrepreneurial endeavor.

How Do You Find Customers?

As in any service business, you have to let people know that you exist and clue them in on what you do. For a pooper-scooping business, there is no more effective way to advertise than with fliers. Blanket the area that you intend on servicing. Put fliers on car windshields, inside people's screen doors, and on telephone polls. Run advertisements in local newspapers and penny savers. Get a vehicle sign made up with your business name, place it on your car, truck, or SUV, and cruise around town. Print business cards and ask fellow entrepreneurs to pass them out. Most importantly, tell your customers to spread the word that you are open for business. Yapping tongues are the least expensive form of advertising ever invented.

The pet care trade is awash in clever business names. It's almost a prerequisite for joining this fraternity. In the pooper-scooping milieu, there are enterprises with such names as **Doody Calls**, **In the Line of Dooty**, and **Poop Control**. Hey, whatever it takes to get noticed.

Pet Minister

Believe it or not, we live in sacred times—really. More than any other folks on the planet, Americans are members of churches and synagogues. And those who are not affiliated with any particular religion very often consider themselves spiritual beings nonetheless.

Two plus two equals four in every sector of commerce, including the pet care marketplace. So, let's take this simple equation one step further. With increasing numbers of pet owners viewing their companion animals as bona fide members of the family, they are—not surprisingly—welcoming them into the ethereal realm, a place once reserved for those on two legs.

The demographic reality is that there are not very many ordained priests, ministers, and rabbis availing themselves for pet memorial services. This, in turn, opens up jobs for **pet ministers**. That is, for capable persons who can lead pet-specific memorial services, be they on cemetery grounds or at private residences.

Many pet cemeteries extend to their clientele the option of a memorial service before burial, and some outfits have the real thing—men and women of the cloth—presiding over them. But regardless of who is actually conducting the ceremonies, pet cemeteries are quick to underscore that their memorial services are *always* non-denominational—*i.e.*, all are welcome.

How Much Does It Cost to Forge This Kind of Career?

Okay, you are giving serious thought to becoming a pet minister. No, you don't have to attend a pet divinity school, or any other educational institution for that matter. You don't have to serve as an apprentice to a religious elder in a particular religious domination. And, fear not, you don't have to swear allegiance to some kind of pet religious cult—none exists. The bottom line is that you can become a pet minister with minimal monetary investment.

What Qualifications Do You Need for This Kind of Work?

Above all else, what you really need to call yourself a pet minister is a kind and empathetic heart, as well as a measure of sophistication. In other words, you should be able to conduct a bereavement ceremony with both eloquence and substance. It would help if you entered this career with first-hand experience in having lost a beloved pet or pets. Being well read and informed on the natural grieving process, as well as on broad spiritual matters, can also go a long way in ensuring that you are a pet minister in demand.

Of course, while you don't need any special brand of education, sporting a university sheepskin or two—and other pertinent credentials—can only enhance your reputation. For instance, having a degree in anything from psychology to theology will open more doors for you in this unique career province.

23

How Do You Find Customers?

Grieving pet owners are increasingly on the lookout for persons who can say a few words—albeit the right words—at burial ceremonies commemorating the passing of their departed cats, dogs, and other pets. You can fill this niche by offering your services to pet cemetery owners and operators, as well as on an individual basis for private ceremonies.

To showcase your credentials as a pet minister, prepare an attractive-looking brochure, explaining exactly what you can do for your clientele. Make absolutely clear the kinds of things you will say—the quotations you will use, etc.—at memorial services. Also, make it known that you will tailor the service specifically for the deceased. You don't want to offer the equivalent of a pet memorial service in a box—a one-size-fits-all kind of thing. The reality is that pet owners seeking out pet ministers for memorial services are going to want very unique and wholly special services for their very unique and wholly special animal friends.

Pet Grief Counselor

Although it's more acceptable than it once was to outwardly express grief for the loss of a beloved pet, societal blessing has got a long way to go—a very long way. For instance, if your faithful dog companion of many years passed away, more than likely you wouldn't call your job and request several days off to grieve for the loss. If you needed time off because of your heartache, you'd probably come up with an excuse of some kind and not admit the truth. Indeed, many pet owners are compelled to mask their undeniable sorrow, even though it is often as debilitating as the loss of someone close to them on two legs—and even more so, in some cases. This stark reality snapshot reveals why there is a very important place for **pet grief counselors** in today's society.

Individuals regularly seek out grief counseling to help them through rough times when somebody close to them dies. But considering the huge aggregate pet numbers in American households, very few pet parents reach out to pet grief counselors when four-legged members of their family pass away, even though it would be extremely beneficial for them to do so.

How Much Does It Cost to Forge This Kind of Career?

For starters, this career opportunity is rooted in compassion and a thorough appreciation of the magnitude of pet loss for many people. The cost to fashion a career as a pet grief counselor is often the cost of a college education. But, as with so many other pet service occupations, there are no laws that mandate credentials before christening oneself a pet grief counselor.

What Qualifications Do You Need for This Kind of Work?

Many persons who work as pet grief counselors have specialized and advanced degrees—including PhDs—in fields connected to human behavior and emotional betterment. For instance, some are trained in social work and others in psychology. Pet grief counselors quite often have a good handle on veterinary issues, and some are even practicing veterinarians. But when all is said and done this kind of work asks that you empathize—above all else—with those who come to you for comfort.

It obviously helps to have experienced the loss of a cherished pet in your own life, and gone through the grieving process yourself. Indeed, this field of endeavor asks that you have a comprehensive understanding of grief and its many manifestations. Grief is not an emotion that should be swept under the rug, and your role as pet grief counselor is not to say, "Get on with your life and get another pet." To be successful in this role, and make a positive difference in people's lives, you have to know how to listen and connect on a human level with the grief-stricken who seek you out.

The **Association for Pet Loss and Bereavement (APLB)** @ APLB.org (718-382-0690) is a preeminent nonprofit organization in the field. A visit to the association's website is an eye-opener on the subject of pet grief and the individuals who offer counseling. If you are considering pet grief counseling as a vocation, or a supplement to a career, this is an ideal place to gather information and vital counsel on the counseling.

How Do You Find Customers?

If you are serious and committed to pet grief counseling, grieving pet owners will come to you for help. The **Association for Pet Loss and Bereavement (APLB)** lists counselors by state who are members of the organization. It's one place that pet people go to find help in getting over the death of an animal companion. Pet grief counseling is an area where reputation and referrals are critical. Once you've demonstrated you know what you are doing and have made people's lives better, grieving pet owners will find your welcome mat.

Pet Relocation Service

One of the most anxiety-inducing pet care concerns known to keep pet parents awake at night tossing and turning in their beds involves matters of travel and relocation. There comes a time in many pet owners' lives when they choose to—or absolutely must—pack up their tents and move to new addresses in faraway places. And sometimes they take lengthy vacations in locales quite a distance from home sweet home. These scenarios often entail transporting a beloved pet in a jet plane.

The mere thought of placing four-legged and feathery friends in kennel carriers within winged crafts' cargo areas for lengthy flights are—to put it mildly—worrisome affairs for peripatetic pet parents. On top of these very understandable flying qualms, there are also oodles of rules and regulations that must be complied with before ever getting up, up, and away. And, when it's an international flight, there are even more laws to comply with. In other words, relocating somewhere with a pet in tow is a very big deal that frequently involves tons of advance scheduling, mounds of paperwork, and, needless to say, severe angst. This is where a truly professional **pet relocation service** comes to the rescue and saves the day.

To get your due diligence off the ground, call on the **Independent Pet and Animal Transportation Association International (IPATA)** @ IPATA.com (903-769-2267). This association's membership rolls are comprised of pet relocation specialists, as well as animal handlers, kennel owners, veterinarians, and other professionals in the trade. You can search for member pet shippers via the website. Another organization to scope out is the **Animal Transportation Association (AATA)** @ AATA-AnimalTransport.org (713-532-2177). This alliance casts a wide net over all kinds of animal transport issues from cattle farmers and livestock to breeders who ship small and exotic animals. It does include under its enormous bumbershoot pet transport and relocation professionals.

How Much Does It Cost to Start This Kind of Business?

This is an entrepreneurial enterprise that can be initiated with minimal upfront investment, particularly if you already own sufficient vehicular transportation. You don't need a physical location, although you could work out of an office. A home office will suffice. Foremost, this business model is rooted in your knowledge of pet relocation issues both domestically and internationally. As in any start-up enterprise, you need to be properly organized as well as amply insured and bonded. When you are asking pet owners—clients—to leave their animal friends in your care, you had better be prepared for any eventuality. That said, the largest and most successful pet relocation

27

businesses work with associates in numerous locales, including overseas. They arrange for at-home pick-up, but also airport pick-up and transport on the destination side of the journey. There's really no getting around it: To realize this business concept's true possibilities, you must network with reliable pet people and pet service providers the world over.

What Qualifications Do You Need for This Kind of Work?

The qualifications necessary to own and operate a pet relocation service are, principally, a thorough understanding of the many particulars that this business embodies. As a pet relocation specialist, you are in a role that is considerably more than a moving service. This is far from a "When do you leave, we'll send the truck over" entrepreneurial enterprise. You will be dispensing sound advice to pet owners on all that is involved in a big move, apprising them of what choices are at their disposal. You have to know your stuff in this area inside and out. You must be well organized and trustworthy—reliable up to the hilt. And this goes for anybody who works with you in this endeavor. Before starting any type of business, it always helps to get your feet wet in an already established mirror image of what you have in mind—or, at the very least, something akin to it. You'll find, for example, that many pizza shop proprietors first cut their teeth as counterpersons in somebody else's restaurants.

Here are just some of the things that pet relocation services do:

★ Fill customers in on what inoculations and proof of shots are required for their jet-setting pets

★ Arrange for any necessary inoculations and paperwork with a veterinarian (if the pet owners cannot secure them)

★ Make flight arrangements, with an emphasis on locating direct connections wherever possible

★ Procure the requisite sizes and airline-approved kennel carriers for clients' animal companions

★ Deal with all international permits, paperwork, and quarantine issues

★ Pick up customers' pets at their residences and provide transportation to the airports

★ Alert pet owners to destination pick-ups and kenneling alternatives, if required

For a bird's-eye view into the width and breadth of pet relocation service operations, check out a few of them. **Pet Air Carrier (PAC)** @ PetAirCarrier.com (888-293-2210) is a company that underscores its USDA approval. **Happy Tails Travel** @ HappyTailsTravel.com (800-323-1718) and **Airborne Animals** @ AirborneAnimals.com (908-684-1844) offer pet owners in the midst of relocating both an extensive menu of services and copious information on all that it entails.

How Do You Find Customers?

The promotional accent with this kind of business should be placed on your commitment and competence. Your customers will need to be absolutely assured that their companion animals are in good hands. If all goes as planned, you'll accumulate testimonials from satisfied clientele—all-important references to your dependability—that you can freely tout. This business will only take flight (no pun intended) when you assure pet consumers that you are professional to the core.

As for the literal promotional avenues to travel down, it behooves you to erect an attractive-looking and informative website. Alert pet owners that you are open for business. Tell them exactly what you can do for them. In addition, you can advertise in pet-themed magazines and daily newspapers. But for starters, spread the word in pet circles—always a good way to get known and get known fast. Prove yourself in this business and you'll get business because we are at once a nation of pet lovers and people perpetually on the move.

29

Pet-Parenting Tutor

If you've ever had to hire adult tutors for little Johnny or Amber, you know that they charge a pretty penny per hour. And they are well worth the investment if they deliver the goods and Johnny gets into Yale and Amber gets into Harvard.

In the parallel universe of pet parenting, tutors are desperately needed, too. Prospective and inexperienced pet owners are often clueless about what life has in store for them. Keeping up with the rapidly evolving industry is a challenge for even the most seasoned pet parents among us.

There is a genuine market for the **pet-parenting tutor**. That is, for knowledgeable men and women who can supply a service that arms current pet owners, or pet owners-in-waiting, with invaluable counsel and up-to-the-minute information. Just what are we talking about here? Simple: Pet-parenting tutors point pet owners in all the right directions. They educate their clients on everything from critical puppy and kitten care to the differences between canned and dry pet foods to the ABCs of flea and tick control. They are also deep fonts of information ranging from how to locate the best trainers in the business to what to be on the lookout for in pet health insurance policies.

How Much Does It Cost to Start This Kind of Business?

This is a consulting business. That is, a minimal investment is required to get this endeavor up and running. Look upon the process of getting yourself known as the biggest start-up cost.

What Qualifications Do You Need for This Kind of Work?

If you are going to dub yourself a pet-parenting tutor, you have to know your lesson plans. Just as a history tutor has to know that George Washington was our first president, you have to know that cats and dogs have different nutritional needs and things like that. You have to be able to answer your clients' many questions and be up on all of the latest goings-on in the dynamic world of pet care.

The market for pet-parenting tutors is growing with each passing day. This is a reality because the pet care field is so vast and increasingly complicated. With all of the new products and services on the market, how can ordinary pet owners really know what's best for their faithful friends on four legs? In the not-too-distant past, people could get answers to many of their pet-related questions at the pet food and supply stores where they shopped. Nowadays, these answers are hard to come by. More times than not, the aforementioned stores are staffed with poorly trained and unmotivated individuals, many of whom know next to nothing about pet care essentials. When you combine this fact of life with more and more consumers viewing their pets as integral parts of their families, you have a genuine need for folks with answers in this field. And, of course, you have more and more people willing to pay for sage counsel on how best to care for their treasured animal companions.

To further grasp this potential business opportunity and the qualifications that are required of you, what follows is a sample lesson plan straight from the pet-parenting tutor handbook. Our example is an overview of common household items that are also dog poisons. Since young puppies will put anything and everything in their mouths, it is a lesson that could prove very helpful to new dog owners.

The tutoring lesson commences with a discussion on potential canine poisons:

★ Gasoline/motor oil
★ Antifreeze (predominantly *ethylene glycol*, an extremely toxic chemical)

31

★ Insecticides and pesticides

★ Paints

★ Turpentine

★ Detergents/bleaches

★ Chocolate products

★ Many fruit and vegetable seeds

★ Fruit pits (peach, plum, etc.)

★ Onions

★ Raisins

★ Many household plants (poinsettia, Easter lily, etc.)

★ Many outdoors plants, shrubs, and vegetation (acorn, holly, hydrangea leaves, azalea, tomato leaves, wisteria, etc.)

The lesson then underscores the importance of common sense in pet ownership, advocating a *zero tolerance policy* as the best policy to keep dogs from getting accidentally poisoned. That is, *never* permit dogs to chew on plants and vegetation, indoors or outdoors. Don't let them sample wild mushrooms, ivy leaves, or anything sprouting up from Mother Earth. Keep them off lawns, for instance, after they've been treated with weed killers or fertilizers. Keep them away from any chemical spills and any kinds of insecticides or pesticides.

Further, the lesson plan arms pet-parenting clients with knowledge of common poison symptoms: diarrhea, vomiting, staggering, labored breathing, and convulsions. Finally, it wraps up with priceless information on what to do if their pets ever ingest a poisonous substance. Of course, they should contact their veterinarians without delay. Or, if this isn't possible, they should call a national telephone hotline: a service staffed by veterinarians and Board Certified Veterinary Toxicologists @ 888-4ANI-HELP or 888-426-4435.

Following this A to Z approach, further tutoring lessons can be meted out on all sorts of pet-parenting concerns, such as:

★ Finding the perfect companion animal
★ New dog in the house fundamentals
★ New cat in the house fundamentals
★ Training ABCs
★ Grooming concerns
★ Troubleshooting: flea & tick control, pet health insurance issues, etc.
★ Pet death and bereavement counseling

How Do You Find Customers?

Pet-parenting tutors need to go where pet parents go. If you desire to pursue this fertile consulting opportunity, connect with as many of these souls as possible. Foremost, prepare a flier chronicling just what you do. Describe the lesson plans you offer and the sound advice that you are ready to dispense. Just like a law firm, underscore your specialty or specialties. Are you a pet health insurance expert? Is puppy care your forte? Are you highly literate in pet nutrition? Mention your rates and invite a phone call and/or visit to your website. (Depending on your qualifications, charging $50 and up per hour is not unreasonable.)

As you get more known and respected, this is the kind of business that will snowball with time. In the garden-variety tutor business, word of mouth plays a huge role. The same can be said for pet-parenting tutorship. If you do it right, you'll rapidly get known for what you do—and get a lot of business.

Pet Health Insurance Consultant

In stark contrast to the human medical profession, veterinary medicine is not financially supported by an insurance industry. Nevertheless, pet health insurance exists, and has actually been around for more than two decades. Not surprisingly, it is getting more attention and attracting more customers in the fledgling years of the twenty-first century than ever before. Pet health insurance policies are similar to our own health insurance policies in many ways. They have annual premiums and deductibles, and the policies widely vary in what is covered and how much they cost.

Pet health insurance premiums are largely determined by:

★ Pet's age
★ Life circumstances (indoor or outdoor pet)
★ Pre-existing health conditions
★ Breed
★ Location (city, country, etc.)

Where does an opportunity lie here? No, this section isn't going to discourse on starting a pet health insurance business of your own—although real people start these enterprises, too. Rather, it's going to introduce you to a unique moneymaking possibility. There comes a time when occupational roles and business undertakings materialize from the ether to fill important niches in the marketplace. Right now is the supreme moment for qualified persons to step forward and hang out their shingles as **pet health insurance consultants**.

The pet health insurance market is understandably expanding as pet parents encounter more costly veterinarian bills—many of which blow the family budget to smithereens. Most pet consumers do not own pet health insurance policies. In fact, it's never even occurred to the vast majority of cat and dog owners to purchase any kind of pet health insurance. Should pet owners go down this route? That's the question that a pet insurance consultant can answer on an individual basis for his or her clients.

How Much Does It Cost to Start This Kind of Business?

A pet health insurance consultant is a person with vast knowledge of the subject matter. The cost to start this consulting business is the cost of advertising. In other words, this enterprise could jumpstart itself on a shoestring budget.

> If you have any doubt about the escalating demand for pet health insurance, consider the numbers of providers, and who's doing the providing. Recognized as the true original in this field, **VPI Pet Insurance** can be found @ PetInsurance.com (888-899-4VPI). **Pet Care** is yet another popular pet health insurance supplier @ PetCareInsurance.com (866-275-PETS). Pet Care, by the way, is administered via **Met Life**, which also has a site of its own devoted specifically to pet insurance policies @ MetLifePets.com (866-239-PETS). The venerable **ASPCA** also affords interested pet owners with insurance options @ ASPCAPetInsurance.com (866-861-9092). Be sure to check out what these companies—and others in this industry—do and what they charge for their various policies. If you don't find yourself in the pet health insurance consulting business, you might just end up with a job selling pet health insurance for an established and growing company.

What Qualifications Do You Need for This Kind of Work?

As pet health insurance becomes more widely sought out, a profound burden falls on consumers considering this financial protection. Ideally, pet owners should know exactly what they are getting into when they sign their names on the dotted lines and send in premium checks to pet health care providers.

They should be absolutely certain that what they want covered *is* covered in their policies. They should know whether or not a pet health insurance policy is really needed. Pet health insurance consultants can earn their keep—and their fees—by answering these questions.

Foremost, you must be educated on the ABCs of pet health insurance to consider yourself a consultant in good standing. If you have purchased a policy yourself—and experienced pet health insurance in action—you are even better qualified to weigh in on the merits and demerits of this brand of medical coverage. In your role as pet health care consultant, your job is to explain to pet parents who are considering pet health insurance the various options at their disposal. You want to walk your clients through the process. You want to thrash out all of the particulars covered in pet insurance policies, such as:

★ Surgeries
★ Hospitalization
★ Prescribed medication
★ X-rays
★ Ultrasounds
★ MRI/CAT scans
★ Homeopathic treatments, including chemotherapy

In the big picture, your job is to underline that the policy—if any—that your clients ultimately select should be based on their unique circumstances as pet parents. Before your clients consider any pet insurance policy, you should run your clients through all of the important questions that they should have fully answered:

★ **Are all ages of pets covered?** Some insurance policies start and terminate coverage at a prescribed age, and the ages may vary depending on breed and life expectancy.

★ **Are all breeds accepted for coverage?** Some breeds of dogs are precluded from coverage based on common genetic health problems.

★ **What exactly is covered?** Does the insurance cover vaccinations, oral care, acupuncture treatments, etc.?

★ **Does the policy have deductibles or co-payments?** What are they? (The average annual deductible in pet insurance policies is $100.)

★ **Does the insurance cover preexisting conditions?** Many policies define such conditions as anything previously diagnosed.

★ **Does the policy stipulate a maximum payout?** Some policies put a ceiling on their payouts per illness, per year, or per pet.

★ **Does the policy cover prescription medications?**

★ **When does the policy take effect?** Immediately? In thirty days?

★ **Is the policy accepted at all veterinarian practices, or only select locales affiliated with the insurer?**

As a pet insurance consultant, you ensure that your clients read all of the fine print before purchasing a policy. You empower them with the knowledge to determine whether the cost of maintaining one is worth it. With your assistance, your clients can calculate their standard veterinary costs and ascertain whether an insurance policy will save them money or, actually, cost them money over the long haul.

How Do You Find Customers?

In this rather distinctive entrepreneurial venture, you want to get noticed slowly but surely. Start with business cards and a flier campaign. Once you've

37

established yourself, word of mouth will bring you more business. Get the word out in pet-specialty circles that you are open for business and can help pet parents in procuring the right pet health insurance for their companion animals—and save them a lot of money and aggravation along the way.

If one doesn't have pet health insurance, or enough savings to pay for a necessary and costly veterinary procedure, it needn't be the end of the world. A knowledgeable pet health insurance consultant could assist a client by advising him or her to contact a local animal shelter or humane organization and tell them of the dire predicament. A pet health insurance consultant knows the score—*i.e.*, that there are groups affiliated with veterinarians that provide low-cost services for those pets *and their people* in need.

Animal Party Choreographer

An extraordinary phenomenon known as *pet therapy* is working its unique magic in more and more places these days. Pet therapy moments occur in nursing homes, hospitals, schools, and elsewhere. No, this has nothing to do with pets getting psychiatric counseling from licensed and trained therapists. Rather, pet therapy is a form of uplift where the four-legged and the feathered are, in essence, the therapists. The mere presence and handling of these companion animals by the elderly, disadvantaged, and unwell of all ages are known to enhance the most depressing atmospheres and circumstances. The many and diverse coordinators of pet therapy programs simply bring well-behaved and sociable cats, dogs, and other domesticated animals into places in need of a pick-me-up. It's accepted fact now that the serene innocence of pets works wonders in making people feel better about their lot in life—even if only for a brief moment or two at these pet therapy sessions.

What we're leading up to here is not counsel on initiating a pet therapy business. This is not a profit-making snippet of the pet care trade. Generally speaking, pet therapy programs are voluntary programs where pet owners offer to *lend* their personable pets out for occasional visits to nursing homes, hospitals, schools, and such. Pet therapy is all about bringing smiles to the faces of people who otherwise don't have much to smile about. There is, however, a genuine entrepreneurial opportunity that involves sufficiently trained and friendly pets making personal appearances. But this business enterprise links its fortunes with parties and other events for children.

Kids are fascinated with animals. What better way to turn birthday parties, for instance, into very special happenings and memorable affairs than by having a caravan of convivial pets show up to liven up the festivities? You could be an **animal party choreographer** and offer your services to parents seeking to throw one heck of a party for their little ones.

Promote your pet parties as fun experiences, but also educational ones. That is, impart the importance of respect for animals at all of your party appearances. Kids can have a whole lot of fun and learn to appreciate the animal kingdom at the same time. For instance, the best-managed petting zoos often feature reassuring tutorials for the youngsters in attendance.

How Much Does It Cost to Start This Kind of Business?

Assuming that you won't be purchasing any pets for this business undertaking—and because we're not talking about a circus, there's no need for that—you could start choreographing animal parties with a minimal upfront investment. If you don't have the right kinds of pets, or pets with the right temperaments for this entrepreneurial undertaking, then you could partner with others to find the right mix. Keep in mind that in this kind of business, it's imperative that you be both insured and bonded. You can't show up at people's homes, which are teeming with youngsters, and leave both yourself and your clients unprotected from potential mishaps. The safety of one and all who are associated with this business—from the two-legged kids frolicking at these parties to the four-legged and feathery animals who show up to entertain them—must be foremost in your planning and method of operation.

Spell out in detail your party itinerary to interested clients. Leave no stone unturned. Ask if there will be any children in attendance with animal allergies. Fully explain the measures you take to protect your animals and the kids at the party. Run a clean show—literally. That is, make sure that your pets on parade, as it were, are well groomed, properly inoculated, and temperamentally suited for this brand of show business.

What Qualifications Do You Need for This Kind of Work?

There are no specific laws and regulations overseeing animal-themed parties. Nevertheless, it behooves you to be painstakingly thorough in operating as an animal party choreographer. This means that you should accept that this type of work comes attached to certain responsibilities. What we are essentially talking about here is successfully bringing together pets with people. So, it stands to reason that adept trainers and animal behaviorists are the most qualified to choreograph these affairs. In other words, not every pet will do and not any kind of behavior can be tolerated at the parties by the partygoers.

In this business, you not only have to work with adequately trained and good-natured pets, but you also have to determine what you are going to do with your animal troupe when you locate your clientele. Are you going to run your company like a petting zoo, or do you have some kind of show business in mind? That is, are you working with merely cutesy, sociable pets, or pets that can perform a trick or two to entertain children? Whatever route you decide to take for your animal party choreography business, it's incumbent upon you to forbid free-for-alls that could disturb and hurt your animal friends, who could, in turn, disturb and hurt your juvenile party attendees.

Your party appearances should be scrupulously organized from start to finish. That is, you must establish detailed parameters on all that you intend on doing and how you intend on doing it. Likewise, you must establish clear ground rules on what kids at your parties are allowed to do.

How Do You Find Customers?

Once you establish yourself as a reputable business in this field, you could find yourself one busy party animal—or, should we say, animal party chore-ographer. Just like most of the other service businesses in the pet care trade, reputation can take you places that mere advertising dollars can't possibly do. Of course, promoting your unique service business via the traditional channels of newspaper ads and via a flier campaign is also important. But once you have respected professionals in the industry singing your praises, as well as testimonials from satisfied clientele, you and your animal caravan are off and running. Rates to charge for animal party appearances can range anywhere from $200 to $300 or more, depending on what you bring to the table, so to speak, vis-à-vis pets, activities, and the time allotted for the entertainment.

Perfect Dog Locating Service ✖ Perfect Cat Locating Service ✖ Perfect Pet Locating Service

In the era of pet parenting, consulting services in the pet care field are the most untapped business undertakings around. Today, the A to Z process of bringing a new dog into the home assumes a higher meaning than it did in the not-too-distant past. After all, the new dog on the block is now a bona fide family member for many years to come. The nature of this at once intimate and long-term relationship between canine and human family unit has fashioned a genuine need for a **perfect dog locating service**.

Nowadays, many people regard the canine adoption procedure as something akin to child adoption. And this kind of thinking cuts both ways. Pet-adopting outfits carefully vet the two-legged adopters who call upon them to determine if they are up to snuff as pet parents. So, you can clearly appreciate the invaluable roles that perfect dog locating services can play in today's marketplace. This consulting business functions as both the locator of the perfect dog *and* the intermediary between the two parties—adopter and adoptee via the adopting organization or business. In practice, this enterprise performs along the same lines as a dating service by matching the individual or family searching for a dog with *the right dog*. A perfect dog locating service offers its clients a menu of options on numerous fronts ranging from the types of dogs available to places to adopt or purchase them.

How Much Does It Cost to Start This Kind of Business?

You can initiate a perfect dog locating service with nominal investment dollars. To get started, all you really need is a phone. Of course, this business venture has more potential to grow if you have two legs and a means of transportation. That is, going to your clients' homes to properly appraise their living arrangements and fully assess their personalities will make your business shine brighter.

This consulting business opportunity can be tweaked to suit your specialty or specialties in the area of pets and pet care. For instance, if you deem yourself a feline authority, you could commence a **perfect cat locating service**. On the other hand, if your knowledge base runs deep, a **perfect pet locating service** might be in order. This service would assist prospective pet parents in finding the right animal companion for them, but the search would cross species lines. That is, the right pet for their life circumstances might be a cat or it might be a dog, but it could also be a bird, iguana, or ferret.

What Qualifications Do You Need for This Kind of Work?

To commence and build a profitable perfect dog locating service, you need a complete understanding and appreciation of what conscientious dog parenting entails. You should also be learned in the vast and varied world of canines and canine behavior. Again, no college degree or any kind of certification is required in this line of work. Above all else, a perfect dog locating service should knowledgeably assist prospective dog parents in answering the fundamental questions that all persons should ask themselves before bringing a dog into their lives:

★ **How much time and attention can you devote to a canine companion?** Your family and job circumstances are critical. If, for instance, you work very long hours away from home, this is not an optimum environment in which to bring a dog. If you travel extensively, or plan on doing so in the future, this fact alone must be factored into your decision.

43

★ **Are you physically able to care for a dog?** Dogs are high-maintenance pets that require constant care, including daily walking, regular exercising, and grooming.

★ **Can you afford another mouth to feed?** Pet parenting doesn't come cheap these days. It costs money to properly care for a canine housemate. And it's not only the food bills that add up. Veterinary care, for one, comes attached to a hefty price tag.

★ **Are children in the household, or are children expected to be in the household someday?** Very young dogs and very young kids are not always matches made in heaven. Puppies under the tender age of four months tend to frolic with unrestrained abandon. In other words: They play rough. And the same is true for young children. A general rule is that if there is a child under six years of age in your home, a new dog should be *at least* four months old. Of course, you could always adopt an older, more mature dog.

★ **Are there other foreseeable events in your life that could impact your pet-parenting responsibilities?** Ponder this: A dog could be in your family circle for ten years or more. A lot can happen in your life during that period of time. You can't permit your dog to be the odd man out, as it were. You have to offer your canine companion a *lifetime guarantee*. Examples of possible life events include divorce, relocation, children leaving the nest, serious illness, etc.

★ **Are there other pets in the household?** If you are considering bringing a new dog into your domicile—and you already have a feline resident, or even a feathery boarder—you must weigh the possible ramifications of extending your family. Likewise, if you have a dog on the premises and are thinking about adding a second, be prepared for a few bumps in the road. Older, established pets aren't always enamored with the new kid on the block. An adult dog, for example, might not appreciate a young pup's penchant for perpetual play.

★ **What exactly do you want from a companion animal?** No living creature is as loving and loyal as a trusty canine. But what else do you see yourself doing with your slobbering sidekick? Do you desire a jogging partner? Do you want to take your pooch with you on camping and fishing trips? Some breeds of dogs are better outdoor types than others. Some are more suited to sit on your lap or go shopping with you in a carry bag. Some dogs play better with children. Some are more intelligent. Some make better city dogs than others. Think long and hard about exactly what you want out of the relationship.

★ **Do you have enough room to accommodate a dog?** The space issue is rudimentary. That is, space for both you and your dog to comfortably cohabitate. Foremost, remember that little puppies grow up. Animal shelters are chock-full of pets that—lo and behold—grew up, much to the astonishment of their erstwhile owners. Also, it's important to know beyond a scintilla of doubt if you are permitted to have a dog before you go out and get one. If you are renting or in a co-op situation, refer to your lease or contract. Even where pets are allowed, there are often size and other restrictions.

★ **Are you pet-parenting material?** It all boils down to this. Just as not everybody is cut out to be an old-fashioned parent, not everybody is suited to be a dog parent. You have to be prepared to share your physical and emotional space with a needy canine, who will sometimes shed his hair, bark, get sick, etc.

In addition to walking your clients carefully through the aforementioned questions, you need to incorporate into your business model a complete database of information on where interested parties can adopt—or purchase, if

45

necessary—the dog of their dreams. A perfect dog locating service scrupulously combs the most popular places to find canine matches for clients, including such tried and true possibilities as:

★ Animal shelters/rescue groups
★ Breeders
★ Locals (individuals with dogs for adoption)

How Do You Find Customers?

The nature of this business permits you to start slowly. You can comb pet-specialty areas for clients. In other words, distribute business cards and fliers in arenas chock-full of retail shoppers and in other venues populated with pet parents—or, in this case, prospective pet parents. A perfect dog locating service is an enterprise that grows by reputation. With testimonials of satisfied customers in your portfolio, you can then spread your promotional wings—and investment dollars—into newspaper advertisements, penny saver ads, and maybe even the Yellow Pages.

CHAPTER III

Pet Careers: Full-time & Part-time

Veterinary Technician (Vet Tech) ✖ Veterinary Assistant ✖ Veterinary Physical Therapist

In just the past decade alone, the width and breadth of veterinary medicine has transformed itself into a microcosm of our own medical system—well, a reasonably close reflection of it anyway. Startling advances in medicine and related technologies have not bypassed the veterinary hospital. Pet parents cannot help but discern these epic changes when paying calls on their local veterinarians.

Not surprisingly, this mother lode of new technology and know-how comes attached to some pretty hefty price tags. Typically, a pet owner can anticipate plunking down $100 or more for routine visits to the cat and dog doctor. In recent years, consumer veterinary bills have mushroomed at twice the rate of inflation. This increasingly expensive reality is at once fueling the growth of a pet health insurance industry and the palpable demand for highly qualified personnel to assist practicing veterinarians navigate their way around the brave new world of veterinary medicine. Specifically, we are referring to the industry's need for **veterinary technicians**, also known as **vet techs**.

The **American Veterinary Medical Association (AVMA)** @ AVMA.org is a first-rate website to call on. Among the wealth of information on veterinary medicine and all that it entails, the AVMA site also sports a "Veterinary Career Center," with a database of schools that offer vet tech degrees and appropriate accreditation. The AVMA plays a definitive role on what constitutes certification to do the work of a veterinary technician. Another website that is useful for locating colleges and universities with vet tech programs is WhereTechsConnect.com. This informational portal champions itself as the "World's largest online employment site for vet techs and staff." You can not only find educational options here, but where the available jobs are when you earn your degree. Another place to investigate is VeterinarySchools.com (800-940-0080), which has a school directory and various career guidance on its website.

A veterinary technician is an individual who is trained and licensed to work alongside veterinarians. Their jobs are not unlike the roles that nurses play in concert with medical doctors and surgeons. **Veterinary assistants**, on the other hand, are not the same as veterinary technicians. Assistants can be hired to do any number of tasks in the veterinary office, but they are not permitted to perform certain prescribed duties—assisting in surgeries, developing X-rays, running IVs, giving injections, etc.—that are the province of certified and licensed technicians only (and, of course, the veterinary doctors themselves).

There are also jobs for **veterinary physical therapists**—yes, you heard it right. These are professionals educated in animal rehabilitation approaches, including hydrotherapy, massage treatments, and appropriate exercises. What you need in order to call yourself a veterinary physical therapist is certification, which is offered to licensed veterinarians, veterinary technicians, and physical therapists. The certification programs available are varied and include written exams as well as opportunities for independent study.

How Much Does It Cost to Become a Vet Tech?

To become a certified and licensed veterinary technician, you are going to need a two-year degree from a school or other institution that offers a vet tech program. Some colleges and universities have four-year bachelor's degree programs in this discipline. The cost to you is your out-of-pocket tuition expenses. Of course, tuition costs depend largely on what school you choose to attend and whether or not you qualify for some financial assistance. There are many community colleges throughout the country that offer vet tech programs in their curriculums. Do your homework and it'll be a career that can pay real dividends down the road—not only in competitive salaries, but also in genuine satisfaction with the work that you'll be doing.

The cost of veterinary care has become a whole lot more expensive than it used to be. Look around and you'll understand why. Modern, high-tech medicine and procedures have arrived in veterinarian offices, too, which are outfitted with ultrasound, X-ray equipment, and MRI machines. Veterinarians are performing open-heart surgeries and kidney transplants and treating cancers with chemotherapy and radiation. Veterinary dentistry is executing root canals in canine mouths. Increasingly, veterinary doctors are specializing in medical areas, just like their peers in human medicine. This ever-evolving scenario is precisely why veterinarians require trained and accredited veterinary technicians to work alongside them.

What Qualifications Do You Need for This Kind of Work?

Unlike many of the other jobs and careers we've touched upon in the field of pet care, veterinary technicians *require* certification from state government entities before they can ply their trades. A bona fide education—of a minimum of two years—is usually needed to earn an associate's degree (in science, applied science, animal technology, or another related specialty),

49

which confers upon one the rank of qualified veterinary technician. Some schools offer four-year bachelor's degrees. There are other routes to certification in this career field as well.

Where Do You Find Jobs in This Field?

Most veterinary technicians find work in private practices. That is, they work for neighborhood veterinarians. But there is also a growing need for their services in other venues, including at veterinary product suppliers, animal shelters and humane groups, diagnostic laboratories, and other locales with pet and animal matters before them.

Veterinarian

At the top of the totem pole in the field of veterinary medicine is—obviously—the **veterinarian**. The Doctor of Veterinary Medicine (DVM) is an increasingly appreciated and sought-out professional in pet-parenting circles. Courtesy of the advances in modern medicine, including veterinary medicine, veterinarians have more at their disposal than ever before to treat diseases and various conditions.

How Much Does It Cost to Forge This Career?

To reach this career pinnacle, you will have to navigate eight years or more of higher education—four years of college plus four years of veterinary medicine. In other words, it will cost you years of arduous and conscientious study. And, needless to say, you'll simultaneously be socked with recurring tuition bills that could be sizeable. There are available educational loans and other tuition assistance to look into.

What Qualifications Do You Need for This Kind of Work?

Many people don't fully appreciate that veterinary studies are as intensive as comparable schooling in human medicine. Veterinarians are doctors. In fact, they must know an awful lot of scientific and physiological particulars that cut across a variety of species. Veterinarians must also assume multiple roles and responsibilities in their doctoring. They are often surgeons, pharmacists, dentists, diagnosticians—and more—all rolled into one package. It has been rightly said that veterinarians have more difficult jobs than traditional doctors of the two-legged. They cannot ask their patients, "Where does it hurt?"

When all is said and done, you need topnotch marks in college, particularly in the scientific disciplines. There are not a whole lot of veterinary schools in the country, so the competition to get into them is pretty stiff. You are going to have to prove yourself a worthy candidate for veterinary studies with a stellar transcript of grades and references.

If you are contemplating a career as a veterinarian and wonder what precise qualifications you would need to get into a veterinary school, visit the **Association of American Veterinary Medical Colleges** @ AAVMC.org (202-371-9195). This organization represents all of the veterinary colleges in both the United States and Canada. On the website, you'll find links to applicant responsibilities, as well as to the specific requirements necessary to get into individual schools and their veterinary programs. For more veterinary issues and answers, including information on schooling and financial aid avenues, check out VetMedicine.about.com.

How Do You Find Jobs in This Field?

If you achieve the lofty status of a veterinary school graduate—congratulations on a job well done. But you have more to do. You will now have to pass a national veterinary medical board exam, then another exam specific to the state in which you want to hang your "open for business" shingle.

You will also have to take this Veterinarian Oath:

"Being admitted to the profession of veterinary medicine, I solemnly swear to use my scientific knowledge and skills for the benefit of society through the protection of animal health, the relief of animal suffering, the conservation of animal resources, the promotion of public health, and the advancement of medical knowledge. I will practice my profession conscientiously, with dignity, and in keeping with the principles of veterinary medical ethics. I accept as a lifelong obligation the continual improvement of my professional knowledge and competence."

Approximately 75% of veterinarians work in a private practice, but there are many job openings in both the public and private sectors, including work in teaching positions and research. The average starting salary for veterinarians is in the neighborhood of $50,000.

Aquarium Maintenance

When the approximately 150 million freshwater and saltwater fish swimming to and fro in America's tanks and bowls are included in the aggregate pet census, there are more pets than people in the country!

The selling of tropical and marine aquarium fish—in addition to their numerous trappings—is a thriving industry. In fact, fish for aquariums—not consumption—are rapidly becoming big profit makers for retailers and other industrious capitalists. And just why are these fishy sorts and their watery habitats so popular? Gaze into an attractive-looking aquarium and you'll immediately know why. Watching all sorts of colorful and curiously shaped fish completing their rhythmic laps is at once fascinating and relaxing.

Fish and fish upkeep represent not only a sizeable snippet of the pet care trade, but a fast-growing hobby as well. That is, some folks don't consider the inhabitants of their aquariums as "pets," per se, but instead view them as akin to a stamp or coin in an overall collection. Others love their fish to death, and grieve for them when they breathe their last.

A relatively new offshoot business in this lucrative field is known as **aquarium maintenance**. What this commercial endeavor entails is everything from selling the fish themselves to aquarium installation to myriad troubleshooting. The maintenance angle to this entrepreneurial opportunity is key because anybody who has managed a fish tank—big or small—knows that it's not as easy as it looks. Algae grows, parasites wreak havoc on one and all, water temperatures get too hot or too cold. The bottom line is that fish die—sometimes a whole tankful in a New York minute. Thus, experts in fish and aquarium care are indispensable. And, slowly but surely, aquarium aficionados are turning to these men and women to make their experiences in this capricious area as pleasurable and problem-free as possible.

Nevertheless, most aquarium owners with a related problem still rely on the knowledge and help of employees at the retailers they patronize. For years, this was where aquarium maintenance assistance began *and* ended. So, there is a huge untapped market to mine. Nowadays, if you are sufficiently learned in the aquarium hobby, you can own and operate an aquarium maintenance business.

How Much Does It Cost to Start This Kind of Business?

You can inaugurate an aquarium maintenance business from your home. All you really need is a telephone. If the thrust of your business revolves around making house calls and installing and maintaining fish tanks, you can commence your entrepreneurial endeavor on the cheap. If, on the other hand, you want a physical location and an inventory, including fish and aquarium supplies, you are going to need a minimum investment of $10,000 to $15,000+ to get the ball rolling and cover your start-up expenses.

53

Again, as in most entrepreneurial opportunities, it's entirely up to you to forge a business plan and determine how much you can and want to invest, and what you anticipate getting out of the investment in the ensuing months and years. If, for instance, you want to practice aquarium maintenance part-time, you don't need to lease office or warehouse space. On the other hand, if you want to go into the business with guns ablazing—selling the actual fish, tanks, and equipment along with the maintenance services—then you're obviously going to have to plunk down some real dollars. But, of course, the potential to make a quicker and more substantial income is why you'd venture down that road.

What Qualifications Do You Need for This Kind of Work?

Just as in most pet-specific service businesses, you don't need any legal certification or special schooling to work in aquarium maintenance or call yourself an aquarium maintenance engineer. However, just as in the fields of dog training and pet grooming, you have to really know your business to achieve real and sustained success. You have to know the ways of aquarium fish inside and out—*i.e.*, what makes them live long and prosper.

Aquarium maintenance is a business where reputation can take you a very long way. The demand for aquarium expertise far exceeds the supply. Selling fish and aquarium accessories at our Pet Nosh stores meant we had to frequently find knowledgeable employees to staff departments reliant on scrupulous care to keep them up, running, and profitable. This wasn't always easy. We often had to pay top dollar to locate people with the requisite fish experience. And many times we had to hold onto some pretty bad apples because there were no ready replacements around.

How Do You Find Customers?

Aquarium maintenance is the kind of business where referrals and word of mouth are your best advertisements. Of course, you have to establish yourself before any wagging tongues can sing your praises. A flier campaign is a good idea in this kind of work, targeting areas where fish folk are more apt to roam—*i.e.*, parking lots of pet-specialty retailers and such. Ads in local papers and penny savers are other options. Remember, too, that there are many commercial institutions with aquariums in their lobbies and offices. And there are some that might like to bring fish tanks into their business milieus, provided that an expert could set it up and maintain it for them. Target with direct mail the businesses that you think might be interested in aquariums. All you need are a few regular accounts and a budding reputation to make your mark in the aquarium maintenance business.

> If you know your stuff, you can write your own ticket in the aquarium maintenance business. Fish tank installations regularly become maintenance accounts. It's the nature of the business. Do a good job with the installation and you very possibly have a customer for life.

Pet Food Sampler

Fear not. This is not a moneymaking career opportunity that requires you to sample foods manufactured for cats and dogs, although there are several natural and holistic pet diets that are known to appeal to the human palate. Rather, this opportunity involves you dispensing free trial samples of pet foods in retail stores or at pet-related events. You can be a **pet food sampler** and, in practice, not sample anything at all.

When you walk up and down the aisles of pet food and supply superstores, you can't help but notice how stiff the competition is when it comes to canine and feline fare. When we first got into the business more than a quarter of a century ago, premium pet foods were few in number and garnered only a small shard of the overall pet food market. (We stocked only Iams and Hill's Science Diet in our original store.) Today, there are many more self-described premium and all-natural pet foods—and each one is vying for the finite shelf space in stores. The brand names are not only more numerous in total, so too are their ever-expanding lines of products—*i.e.*, special foods for the overweight, lactating, inactive, small breed, overly stressed, etc.

What all this dog-eat-dog, cat-eat-cat competition boils down to is pet food manufacturers scrambling to get their multiple products into pet parents' hands. Beating the competition to the punch is critical in today's market-place. Outside of very expensive print and electronic advertising, the cheapest way to accomplish this is to give away free samples of their foods at retail outlets and elsewhere.

With armloads of free samples to dispense, salespersons from the various pet food companies are often spotted at shops and shows. They push these freebies onto consumers and discourse on why their particular diets are better than all of the rest. But as you can imagine, the regular sales forces for these many pet food companies are few in number when compared to all of the pet food and supply stores, as well as the never-ending stream of pet-themed goings-on throughout the country. Manufacturers are thus on the hunt for men and women who can appear at these myriad places to tout the benefits of their products. The free-lance pet food sampler can earn some decent money and not be run ragged in the process. In most instances, the job merely requires you standing at a table with samples of pet foods. You have to occasionally hurl a query out to passersby: "Would you like to try a free sample of Iams?" "Interested in sampling Nutro Max? It's free!" The free part always gets people's attention.

How Much Does It Cost to Find This Kind of Work?
This is a job opportunity that costs absolutely nothing out of pocket. You might have to expend a little of your time and attend a seminar explaining

why brand A is better than brands B, C, D, E, and F. But, armed with the requisite talking points, you are ready to begin dispensing samples.

One route to becoming a pet food sampler—and field rep, as it were, for a company—is to call on **All-Ways In-Store** @ AWInStore.com. This outfit is continually looking for physical bodies to promote products for companies in all fields, including the pet care trade. Most of the available positions are for weekend gigs. These jobs are ideal routes to earning additional income.

What Qualifications Do You Need for This Kind of Work?

It certainly can't hurt to know a little something about pet nutrition before you begin pet sampling, but the learning curve is not too sharp. The aforementioned seminars are ordinarily sufficient tutelage. In this line of work, it also helps to be both a pet *and* people person. After all, your role as pet sampler will necessitate you standing behind a table and talking with folks about their pets and their pets' nutritional needs. If the thought of being in the midst of the pet-parenting masses causes you to break out in a cold sweat, there are plenty of more suitable opportunities for you in this book.

How Can You Find These Jobs?

If you spot a representative from a pet food company dispensing free samples, ask him or her about the opportunity. On weekends, pet food samplers are regularly seen at pet food and supply superstores and often at the smaller independents, too. You might very well encounter a full-time salesperson who would welcome turning over *to you* these all-day affairs.

In addition, query store managers about pet food sampling jobs. They often have the right contacts that can make things happen. Manufacturers regularly comb the pet food and supply stores—and their employees—for the pet food samplers of tomorrow.

You could also go straight to the top and contact the pet food companies themselves and ask if any pet food sampling opportunities exist. The top three premium pet food makers are Iams, Hill's Science Diet, and Nutro. These manufacturers are not only the marketplace behemoths, they are also renowned for giving away free samples of their products to drum up business.

Premium Pet Food Manufacturers

What follows is a list of the top premium pet food manufacturers, including their company websites and toll-free numbers. The websites provide you with copious information on the companies and their various product lines. Some of the sites—Nutro and Natural Balance, to name a couple—link to job opportunities, including product demonstration hiring programs. You could effortlessly query any one of them via email. Inquire whether or not they do pet food sampling, and if they do offer such opportunities, whether or not jobs exist in your neck of the woods.

Iams	Iams.com	800-675-3849
Hill's Science Diet	HillsPet.com	800-445-5777
Nutro	NutroProducts.com	800-833-5330
Bil-Jac Foods	BilJac.com	800-842-5098
Breeder's Choice	BreedersChoice.com	800-255-4286
Diamond Pet Food	DiamondPet.com	800-442-0402
Eagle Pack	EaglePack.com	800-255-5959
Innova	NaturaPet.com	800-532-7261
Natural Balance	NaturalBalanceInc.com	800-829-4493
Natural Life	NaturalLife.com	800-367-2391
Nature's Recipe	NaturesRecipe.com	800-237-3856
Neura Wellness	OldMotherHubbard.com	800-225-0904

Home Delivery Service

Our pet care business odyssey began in a mom-and-pop shop on Main Street (well, actually, it was on Northern Boulevard in the Little Neck section of Queens). Initially, we supplemented our in-store sales in this petite retail outlet with home deliveries. We delivered pet food and accessory items—including tons of cat litter—to private homes and apartment buildings in every direction on the compass and for many miles from our physical location.

Home deliveries were a critical building block in our company's growth. However, there came a moment when we could no longer do them because of both time and manpower constraints. Fortunately, someone from the outside provided us with a **home delivery service**. In this instance, he was a former employee of ours. He knew both the business of pets and the surrounding neighborhoods. He also owned a van. This chap offered to do home deliveries for us—for a nominal fee. He'd both put together the merchandise orders and deliver them. It was as uncomplicated as that. He received $3 per delivery plus tips in those days of yore. Now, of course, with inflation and high gas prices, the fee is higher.

How Much Does It Cost to Start This Kind of Business?

If you already own a means of transportation—a car, van, or SUV—that you are willing to cram with pet merchandise, some of which may be less than aromatic, you have what it takes to operate a home delivery service. If you have to purchase a vehicle, then it's going to cost you a few bucks, but you could find something used that could do the job and not send you to the poorhouse ($1,000 to $2,000).

What Qualifications Do You Need for This Kind of Work?

Foremost, you have to know how to drive. Doing home deliveries on a bicycle won't cut the mustard (unless you're delivering for a pet pharmacy).

59

It also helps to be good with directions and know a thing or two about the area where you'll be delivering the stuff. Of course, today there are outfits like **MapQuest** @ MapQuest.com, which can solve just about any direction problems. Always keep in mind that time is money in a home delivery business. Getting lost eats up both a lot of precious time and expensive gas.

Delivering pet merchandise to homes and apartments requires a lot of heavy lifting, too. From start to finish, you are hauling around twenty-five and fifty pound bags, along with bulky cans of cat and dog food. It's not work for the 99-pound weaklings among us. In addition, you will come home after a day's work reeking of pet food, not Armani Black Code or Donna Karan Gold Eau De Parfum.

How Do You Find Customers?

Potential customers in a pet-fueled home delivery service are:

★ Small retailers
★ Veterinarians
★ Groomers who sell food and supplies
★ Trainers who sell food and supplies

Approach these businesses and tell them what you can do: home deliveries. Convince them that you are offering a service that will make them money. Underscore that you will do all the heavy lifting, as it were. They take the orders and make all of the profits (minus your delivery fees), and you do all the grunt work. Sounds like a good deal because it is a good deal.

Rip a page out of Don Corleone's playbook and make your prospective clients an offer that they can't refuse. If you can convince retailers and other prospects that they'll make money through your services, with minimal hassles, why wouldn't they jump at the opportunity? Pitch your home delivery as a win-win relationship.

There are people running home delivery services and charging $5 per order. This may sound like peanuts, but it's not unusual for a service to do twenty-five deliveries in one fell swoop. When you do the arithmetic, that's $125 plus gratuities. With several accounts on the books, these numbers can add up fast to a fair living.

Pond Design and Maintenance

There are many pet, animal, and nature lovers who fancy the thought of installing ponds in their very own backyards, and then stocking them with fish and appropriate plant life. But the reality is not everyone is capable of doing this work. The average Joe and Jane cannot purchase a how-to book, or read a magazine article on the subject, and then set to constructing a viable pond or water garden on his or her property. Most folks would rather have a professional person do the job for them. If you have the requisite skills and know-how in this lush entrepreneurial playground, you could start a **pond design and maintenance** company and find yourself a very busy bee in big demand.

How Much Does It Cost to Start This Kind of Business?

No storefront or physical location is required for this brand of work—that's the good news. An investment in a cell phone—if you don't already have one—and some brochures and business cards is really all you need to get started. Of course, if you plan on turning this craft into a genuine business enterprise, you will have to procure the requisite government permits and licenses, as well as the necessary insurance and bonding. This kind of work obviously places you on your clients' properties. And just what are you doing? You're digging holes, running electrical wiring, attaching water pipes, etc. So, you need to protect both yourself and your customers from any mishaps and misunderstandings.

What Qualifications Do You Need for This Kind of Work?

Foremost, this business asks that you know what you are doing in areas ranging far and wide from municipal codes and regulations to the best locations for the ponds to the plants and fish that can best thrive in them. You can't operate a pond design and maintenance business reading step-by-step instructions out of a book and praying that everything turns out as planned. When you charge your customers real money for your services, they are going to expect in return some real guarantees on a job well done. In other words, you can't build a pond, stock it with fish, frogs, and plants, only to witness the whole kit and caboodle die and fall apart in a nanosecond. Pond installation comes attached to critical care issues, including:

★ Not overloading the filtration system
★ Keeping algae growth at bay
★ Maintaining good water quality at all times
★ Properly transferring fish to the pond
★ Keeping nature's predators from poaching from the pond

If you are considering this kind of work, visit **Aquascape** @ AquascapeDesigns.com. This website touts a philosophy of *Ponds Done Right; Customers Served Right*. It's an informational portal with stuff for everyone from hobbyists to contractors to retailers. It is noted here that ponds and water gardens are the "fastest growing market in the green industry."

How Do You Find Customers?

It would certainly aid and abet your business start-up cause if you had an installed, attractive, and well-maintained pond to serve as a model of your proficiency in this field. Maybe you have one in your backyard, or have installed one for a friend or neighbor. There's nothing quite like showcasing your handiwork with the genuine article for all to see. As time goes by and you amass a roster of testimonials from satisfied clientele, this particular show-and-tell wouldn't be necessary, but until you have photographic evidence of multiple creations and choruses of people singing your praises, it'll certainly boost your business prospects to have at least one living and breathing sample of your *savoir faire* as a pond designer and maintainer.

Invisible Fence® Installation

The Invisible Fence® brand system of containment is the most popular pet product of its kind in the entire world. Utilizing a potent one-two punch of advanced electronic technology and old-fashioned hands-on training, the Invisible Fence permits dogs to run as free as their wolf cousins. That is, free to roam in their own backyards and property boundaries without the necessity of erecting unsightly and costly visible fences, as it were.

This electronic containment system has been given the imprimatur from many veterinarians and humane organizations, including the ASPCA. One of the leading reasons for this product's smashing commercial success is that it is not available on the shelves of pet specialty stores, or via any other retail source. Instead, interested consumers must purchase them from exclusive dealers of the product. Only highly trained individuals, who know what they are doing from soup to nuts, set up the Invisible Fences—not the purchasing pet owners. These professional installers put these containment systems in the right and proper ways, but they also assist in training the canine crowd to adapt to them. Are you interested in a career in **Invisible Fence installation**? There are legitimate opportunities for interested and capable men and women in this ever-expanding field.

For more information on **The Invisible Fence®**, visit the company @ InvisibleFence.com (800-578-DOGS). On the website, you'll encounter a zip code search to locate the exclusive dealers of the product nearest you. There are various job possibilities in this training bailiwick from sales to customer service to installation. Check out **Canine Fence** @ CanineFence.com (800-818-DOGS). This exclusive distributor of the product in several northeastern states has a specific link on its website for career opportunities in this business.

Pet Talk Radio Show Host

At some point in the early 1990s, we learned that popular radio talk show host Warren Eckstein availed himself for public appearances in pet venues. We promptly contacted his behind-the-scenes schedulers and struck a deal: Mr. Eckstein would appear on a specified date in our Yonkers, New York, store. We promoted his impending visit for weeks, and when the dust settled, he did in fact attract quite a gaggle of admirers, many of whom had never previously set foot in our place of business. Perhaps you have both the knowledge and charisma to make it as a **pet talk radio show host**, just like Mr. Eckstein. And, even if it's not in the cards that you will achieve his renown—he is a nationally syndicated talk show host—there are many other personalities in this growing field that you can emulate.

Warren Eckstein is the host of **The Pet Show**, a nationally syndicated radio talk program on the subject of—you guessed it—pets. The show's website can be found @ ThePetShow.com. The site describes the host as *America's Most Trusted Pet Expert & Pet Humorist* and is replete with all kinds of testimonials.

How Much Does It Cost to Forge This Kind of Career?

This is obviously a career move that is based more on grit and determination than money down. There are countless ways to break into this expanding, albeit highly competitive sphere. First of all, there are thousands of radio stations all across the country. Many of them are very small and reach a limited demographic. In other words, there are genuine opportunities to get a start in radio, particularly at these places with a lower talent and experience threshold. Let's not forget the role the Internet and satellite radio now play in generating more job possibilities for men and women behind the microphone. So, here's the unadorned reality: When this increasingly wider playing field is coupled with the surging interest in pets and their overall health and wellness, it means you have a better shot than ever before to be heard on the public airwaves.

Tracie Hotchner is the author of *The Dog Bible: Everything Your Dog Wants You to Know* (Gotham Books). She is also the host of a pet talk radio show. Visit DogTalkRadio.com for more information. Her rather comprehensive tome spans a broad spectrum of subject matter from the routine to the more controversial, including the canine nutrition debates and the efficacy of the commonly administered vaccinations.

What Qualifications Do You Need for This Work?

If you are dispensing with pet care wisdom over the radio, the wisdom should more closely resemble erudition than ignorance. Again, to be a pet talk show radio host, you don't need any special qualifications, but your audience is going to want to know your background. They are going to want to know where you get the unmitigated chutzpah to sound off about this and that.

The most renowned radio talk show hosts in the field of pet care are often authors of pet-related books, or are practicing veterinarians, trainers, and

65

such. Whether you have degrees gracing your walls or not, you have to first get known in some distinctive way. If you can make a name for yourself in your community at large as a pet care oracle, this is a sure-fire way to light a fire under a potential career as a talk radio show personality.

How Do You Find Pet Talk Radio Show Jobs?

You really want to establish a portfolio of sorts before considering this line of work. That is, showcase your promising talents as an on-the-air personality. Make demo tape recordings of yourself. Call pet talk radio shows and record yourself going toe-to-toe with the host. If possible, try to get guest spots on the programs or other talk radio shows when pet topics are being discussed. Serve as an intern at radio stations. Learn the business from the ground floor up. Just being at a radio station in some capacity adds to the prospects of you getting on the air at some point in time. It's happened to many others and it can happen to you too.

Pet Party Host

They are the stuff of legend: Tupperware parties. According to the company website, one such party starts every two seconds in homes throughout the world. That is, in living rooms all across the planet, Tupperware products are selling between mouthfuls of cake and bites of hors d'oeuvres. These myriad gatherings furnish guests with the very latest in kitchen gadgetry and up-to-the-minute home innovations. As a business sales tool, the Tupperware party has built a vaunted reputation and a $1 billion multinational company along with it.

Not surprisingly, the concept of at-home parties to peddle products has been duplicated by countless other businesses. The very successful Tupperware model has worked its way into the business of pets in the form of festive pet product parties. Yes, you heard it right—parties revolving around pet-themed merchandise for sale rather than kitchen accoutrements. You could be a **pet party host** and make some serious money in the process.

How Much Does It Cost to Start This Kind of Business?

You could begin hosting these so-called pet product parties with minimal or even no up-front investment (with the exception, of course, of the requisite party spreads). But above and beyond the pretzels and potato chips, what you most need to host one of these parties is merchandise to sell. More to the point, you need the right kind of merchandise. You don't want to host a merchandise party with typical stuff for sale. Find products that will stand out and that your guests will gobble up along with the mixed nuts and corn bugles.

There are many sources for pet merchandise that you can sell for a tidy profit. The most obvious sources are the pet-specialty retailers and whole-salers in the trade. Consider approaching a retailer near you and explaining what you have in mind—pet product parties. That is, ask the owner or manager if he or she would be interested in partnering with you in these parties by furnishing you with the merchandise. (Retailers deal with many suppliers of vast and varied products.) In return, offer the retailer a percentage of everything you sell. This kind of arrangement is a win-win opportunity for both sides. In addition, by following this course, you could take orders and receive payment in advance at the parties, then deliver the merchandise at a later date. This method of operation would enable you to work with minimal cash outlays and no inventory.

On the other hand, if you want to go full throttle from the starting gate, register your pet party business with appropriate government agencies. As an official business with an identification and sales tax number (where applicable), you are then armed with the necessities to purchase through whole-sale sources in the industry.

67

You can sell all kinds of merchandise at pet parties. Pet parents are always on the hunt for new and intriguing products. The merchandise can be utilitarian in nature—grooming tools, shampoos, flea and tick remedies—and/or luxury items, as it were—playthings, bedding products, after-meal delicacies. Just insist that your product line be forever unique and not readily available on grocery store shelves or at Wal-Mart.

What Qualifications Do You Need for This Kind of Work?

If you have a roof over your head, you have the most important qualification for this kind of work. But it also helps to be a social animal. After all, you'll be hosting parties. And you want to make them real happenings. You want these pet-parenting extravaganzas to be at once fun and profitable.

Now, should you invite *both* pet owner and pet to your parties? This is only a good idea if you carefully scrutinize those who will be in attendance. You must be certain that any four-legged folks who come a-calling are both properly vaccinated and well behaved. Otherwise, pets mixing together can augur big problems. Pet product parties are, above all else, entrepreneurial events. You don't want yourself, or any one of your guests, to get scratched or bitten. And you don't want any harm to come to the cats and dogs in attendance. This reality is something to consider when organizing your pet product parties. And, on top of real safety concerns, don't extend invitations to furry friends if you are in any way, shape, or form worried about pet hairs landing on your furniture and possible accidents staining your rugs.

How Do You Find Customers?

You organize pet product parties just as you would Tupperware parties. When hosting parties in your humble abode, it's unwise to place advertisements in newspapers or put up fliers on telephone poles. You don't want just any local yokel to show up at your door. Find prospective guests and customers among:

- ★ Relatives
- ★ Friends (and their friends and relatives)
- ★ Neighbors (and their friends and relatives)
- ★ Coworkers
- ★ Former classmates
- ★ Religious congregations
- ★ Sports teammates
- ★ Club memberships
- ★ Pet-related acquaintances

This is a list with a whole lot of tentacles. Once you get these pet parties up and running, you'll get a better feel on how best to organize them. You'll know everything from whom you want at your parties to what foods to serve them to, most importantly, what products to sell.

If you need a helping hand in organizing pet product parties, check out **Shure Pets** @ ShurePets.com (888-SHURE-PETS). For a fee, this company will ordain you a Pet Consultant and afford you access to merchandise that you can resell at parties and elsewhere. The pet product parties are known here as "Pupperware parties."

Reptile Breeding

Sometimes we forget that the width and breadth of pet parents encompasses mamas and papas, so to speak, to more than felines and canines. Indeed, there are large and growing numbers of bird, reptile, amphibian, and "pocket pet" parents too. Pet owners and animal aficionados of all stripes are contributing to the industry's inexorable makeover.

While mom-and-pop pet shops that sell live animals like parakeets, hamsters, frogs, and snakes have taken their lumps in the sometimes-smothering shadows of big superstores—which also sell these pets—they are still around and have an undeniable niche market that nobody will ever fully snatch from them. Whether independently operated or a sprawling national chain, retailers need these pets to sell. They have to get them from somewhere, such as live-animal suppliers. These vast and varied household pets don't originate from the wilds of the Serengeti Plain or the Amazon rain forest. Retailers acquire them directly from breeders both big and small, or other wholesale sources, which, in turn, get them from individual breeders. Are you a reptile aficionado and herpetology enthusiast? If you are, you might be a prime candidate for **reptile breeding**.

A Breeder's Responsibility

If you are considering breeding any kind of living creature—snake, gecko, gerbil, canary, et al.—it behooves you to be highly knowledgeable of all that it entails. And along with this vast storage house of wisdom on the breeding process itself should come comparable doses of compassion and conscientiousness. Esteemed breeders respect and truly appreciate the animals they work with. The humane treatment of animals is foremost in their minds as they do what they have to do to make one plus one equal two. The business side of breeding—of any kind and on any level—comes with genuine responsibilities.

It's little wonder that the breeding and selling of live animals is perpetually steeped in controversy. There are, in fact, many less than savory characters in this business bailiwick. But the facts remain that pet people desire everything from guinea pigs to ferrets to boa constrictors, and nothing short of the Doomsday Clock running out of ticks is going to squelch this yearning. So, it's best that knowledgeable and caring breeders of these many household pets fill this sizeable marketplace vacuum. And, as for making a fair financial return for your meticulous breeding efforts, there's nothing unscrupulous about that.

How Much Does It Cost to Start This Kind of Business?

You can launch this entrepreneurial endeavor with a small investment in the various trappings of the breeding process, including the mating animals and equipment. In this field, it is sensible to start slowly. Get your feet wet before doing anything in a big way. Prove yourself as both a competent and conscientious breeder and then take the next step.

What Qualifications Do You Need for This Kind of Work?

Breeding any kind of pet necessitates that you know your business inside and out. This field of endeavor is for pet people who are at once extremely informed on their preferred animal species and accountable for their actions. Before breeding reptiles or anything else, you should be the closest thing possible to an expert. A college education, or legal certification, isn't required to breed animals, although it can help to have had a formal and higher education in the appropriate sciences. The bottom line is that you have to know an awful lot about the breeding process. This means understanding the optimal conditions for the matchmaking, as well as the myriad care issues inherent in raising the newborn reptiles of today into the adolescent herps of tomorrow.

Herpetology is a sliver of zoology that incorporates reptiles and amphibians. So, don't be confused when you encounter references to *herps* and *herpetological culture*. Two sources of information on herp issues, including breeding, are **The Reptile Information Network** @ ReptileInfo.com, which also contains a comprehensive list of herpetological societies, and **Reptiles Magazine** @ ReptilesMagazine.com. This magazine can be purchased on newsstands and in bookstores.

How Do You Find Customers?

Breeders of animals should appear at pertinent pet-specialty shows. In this field, it's essential that you make a reputation for yourself in the right circles. For starters, reptile breeders should strut their stuff at reptile shows. If you are good at what you do, the contacts made at these venues—the networking—will light a fire under your entrepreneurial endeavor.

Bird Breeding

Courtesy of the most recent pet census conducted by the **American Pet Products Manufacturers Association** @ APPMA.org, caged birds are the most popular household pets behind cats and dogs (that is, of course, if we don't count aquarium fish—freshwater and saltwater—which total in the neighborhood of 150 million). Our feathered friends, from the hearty parakeet to the highly intelligent macaw, have quite a dedicated following.

America's pet-specialty retailers need all kinds of caged birds to satisfy Americans' obvious passion for them. The mega-stores sell live birds now, as do independent and smaller pet shops. There are also many successful retail stores solely devoted to the sale of caged birds and bird supplies. And, let's not forget all of the transacting that transpires at bird shows and bird-themed affairs. If you fancy birds and are highly educated on their particular needs, you can soar into the **bird breeding** business.

How Much Does It Cost to Start This Kind of Business?
You can commence this entrepreneurial foray with a small start-up investment in the particulars of the breeding process, including the mating birds, cages, food, and equipment.

What Qualifications Do You Need for This Kind of Work?
You have to understand the breeding process inside and out, including a full

appreciation of optimal conditions for the matchmaking and care issues that come with the territory of raising the newborn birds.

If you are seeking a one-stop source of information on birds, including breeding matters, a good place to start is **Birds n Ways** @ <u>BirdsNWays.com</u>. Here you'll unearth an entire library of articles on subject matter running the entire gamut of bird care matters. In addition, check out <u>BirdShows.com</u> (901-878-1307) for the most comprehensive bird event calendars, as well as critical information on existing bird clubs and the current buyer's marketplace. For books and reading matter on bird care, training, and breeding, stop by **Avian Publications** @ <u>AvianPublications.com</u> (800-577-2473).

How Do You Find Customers?

Breeders of any species of animal benefit by appearing at pertinent pet-specialty shows. Make a good reputation for yourself in this bailiwick and you will be sought out.

Small Animal Breeding

Small animal breeding is an area where attentive care and proper breeding protocol is called for. The largest pet food and supply retailers sell small animals, as well as the many old-fashioned pet shops along the highways and byways of America. People appreciate small animals, particularly families with children. Kids love hamsters and guinea pigs, and they are relatively easy to care for (in contrast to the greater responsibilities inherent in looking after the needs of cats and dogs). But there is also a demand for small animals in areas beyond the familiar pocket pets just mentioned—and some are considered downright exotic.

73

Indeed, the pet care trade is selling everything from chinchillas to degus to fancy-colored mice to squirrels to rats (which, believe it or not, make fine pets courtesy of their intelligence, cleanliness, and gentle natures).

How Much Does It Cost to Start This Kind of Business?

A minimal start-up investment will do for the initial mating animals and all the necessary accoutrements for a safe and healthy breeding experience.

What Qualifications Do You Need for This Kind of Work?

You have to appreciate all that breeding entails. It is not simply a matter of placing male and female together. There is no such thing as a baby machine. It's a conscientious endeavor that requires a long-term commitment to the health and well-being of the animals.

How Do You Find Customers?

Traverse the pet-specialty shows in the hunt for business. Make a reputation for yourself in this bailiwick and you will be a sought-after business.

Aquarium Fish Breeding ✖ Tropical Fish ✖ Marine Fish

There is something fishy transpiring in the trade. Yes, tropical and marine aquarium fish are increasingly big business. For a long time, this particular sliver of the industry was largely looked upon as a hobby. That is, fish in fish tanks were considered, first and foremost, collectible pieces for hobbyists. Keeping an aquarium in the house—or even a goldfish bowl—was not to be placed on the same plane as caring for a cat or dog.

We are not here to claim that this mindset has wholly changed. For many people, aquarium building and upkeep is, in fact, a bona fide hobby that they are truly passionate about. Adding particular fish and plant life to a tank is akin to adding special coins to a coin collection or special stamps to a stamp collection. But, let's face it, this is a different time we are living in, and even our finned friends are getting more respect these days. To a lot of people, their aquarium fish are undeniable pets and much-admired members of their households.

There are multiple places to turn to glean the ABCs of what is entailed in breeding aquarium fish. Doggie paddle on over to **Aquatic Community** @ AquaticCommunity.com. Check out, too, the magazines in the field, including **Tropical Fish Hobbyist** @ TFHMagazine.com, which is considered the leading and oldest aquarium magazine around. Another is **Aquarium Fish** @ AquariumFish.com. Both publications are available where magazines are sold. To get a sweeping view of where many retailers purchase their livestock, visit **Fish Mart** @ FishMartInc.com. This company is where we purchased many of our tropical and marine aquarium fish. It's a wholesaler that has been in business for many years and grown quite a lot in scope. They sell birds and small animals now, as well.

Regardless of what consumers' precise motives to purchasing them are, the tropical and marine aquarium fish trade is setting new records with each passing day. Some folks may indeed be fish parents; others may consider their collections of aquarium fish enjoyable pastimes and nothing more. But what this all amounts to is demand and more demand. In other words, there is money to be made in **aquarium fish breeding**, both **tropical fish** as well as **marine fish**.

How Much Does It Cost to Start This Kind of Business?

You can commence this entrepreneurial foray with a small start-up investment in the particulars of the breeding process, including the tanks, foods, and other equipment.

What Qualifications Do You Need for This Kind of Work?

You have to grasp the fish breeding process from soup to nuts. The optimal conditions for fish matchmaking must be fully understood and executed.

How Do You Find Customers?

Breeders of any tropical or marine fish can make waves by attending trade shows. Advertise in appropriate periodicals. Contact retailers and wholesalers in the industry. If you are proficient in this area, there are customers hungry for what you have to offer.

CHAPTER IV
Pet Product Manufacturing & Inventions

Premium Dog Food Maker

The recent titanic recall of oodles of pet food brands for both cats and dogs blew a gaping hole in conventional consumer wisdom. That is, the belief that manufacturers of pet diets—notably the premium kinds—were scrupulous in their quality controls. Needless to say, this conventional wisdom was *and is* a bit off the mark. All the corporate mission statements and press releases in the world can no longer mask the reality that some of the most prominent pet food manufacturers around are subsidiaries of multinational conglomerates—part of mega-companies that also sell things like paper towels, dish detergent, canned string beans, and toothpaste. Should we be surprised that in an industry not rigorously regulated—the pet care trade—many pet food makers cut corners to sweeten their bottom lines? Imagine that!

Like so many products in this day and age, big and bloodless corporations own many of the pet food brands sold in the marketplace, including myriad premium brands. But long before the widespread recall, growing numbers of independent pet food makers were finding niche markets for their diets. There is no doubt that the wave of the pet food future is crashing down on the shorefronts of organic diets and pet foods manufactured from human-grade ingredients. In other words, pet foods for Fido and Fluffy that are fit for your palate as well. The contaminated pet food scare merely grabbed hold of this already rising wave and turned it into a tsunami. The trend was *and is* toward healthier pet foods. Safe, high quality, nutritionally complete and then some are where it's at in the marketplace. And it's a wide opening for pet nutrition authorities with entrepreneurial spirits.

Before the industry at large took flight and soared into today's lofty stratosphere, premium pet food users were an infinitesimal bunch. In the not-too-distant past, pet diets were almost exclusively purchased in supermarkets and general merchandisers. Small, independent pet food and supply stores existed, but most of them were considered *pet shops*. They were known, foremost, for selling pets like parakeets, hamsters, and tropical fish—not specialty foods for cats and dogs.

A Short History of Pet Food

To fully appreciate how far we've come in this field, a little history is in order here. The first commercial pet food dates back to merry old England, circa 1860. Interestingly, American ingenuity was behind this innovation. Peddling lightning conductors on a sales trip in London, an electrician named James Spratt didn't realize he was on the cusp of making commercial history and fathering an industry. Observing that many of the Dickensian city's canines dined on discarded hardtack biscuits, he reasoned that he could concoct a more palatable dog diet. Unlike most others, Mr. Spratt put his money where his mouth was!

Using wheat meals, vegetables, beet root, and beef blood, the pet food pioneer's groundbreaking formula found a hungry audience of English country gentlemen eager to feed it to their stables of sporting dogs. It was christened "Spratt's Patent Meat Fibrine Dog Cakes" and initially advertised with the slogan: "Your Best Pal's Best Pals." ("Fibrin," sans the "e," is an elastic, insoluble protein that forms a fibrous network in the coagulation of blood. Late nineteenth-century and early twentieth-century products—pet-related and otherwise—frequently employed such scientific descriptions in their names.)

To make a long business story short, Spratt's entrepreneurial spirit came back home with him, and a commercial pet food industry was soon launched in the land of the free. Scores of dog food manufacturers debuted in the fledgling years of the twentieth century, many promoting their products as high-quality diets that would simultaneously make life easier for pet owners. Sound familiar? James Spratt, for one, claimed that fresh beef fed to the canine crowd could "overheat the dog's blood." Even nutritious table scraps, he said, "will break down his digestive powers" and "make him prematurely old and fat." In other words, dog owners were advised to feed their pets Spratt's brand of food or risk the unhealthy consequences.

The first commercial dog food in a can surfaced in the immediate aftermath of World War I. It was horsemeat put out by the Chappel Brothers of Rockford, Illinois. *God only knows what parts of those noble beasts went into its manufacturing.* One account of the day calculated that more than 50,000 horses were slaughtered in a year's time to make dog food. A decade later, in the early 1930s, canned cat food appeared on grocery store shelves. It's no stretch to say that a torrent of water has gone under the pet care bridge over the past century. Today's pet owners are more sophisticated and much more discriminating than they were in days gone by. They are more demanding with more disposable income to spend on their pets, too. This entertaining survey of the roots of it all accents the dramatic changes that have occurred in the business of pets over the ensuing century. It also reveals the inherent opportunities that always exist in taking pet foods to the next level.

A Healthy Opportunity

You don't need us to tell you that the consumer market for pet merchandise and pet services has undergone a radical metamorphosis, with more and more people on the prowl for the healthiest possible diets for their companion animals. This is where we stand right now. Pet parents' incredible dedication to their four-legged friends is fueling the modern-day market for all of those *premium*, *natural*, *organic*, *gourmet*, and *holistic* foods, which are now considerable commercial forces to be reckoned with.

Encouragingly for entrepreneurs, as the marketplace for so-called premium pet foods widens, so too does the market for alternatives to them—for even more options to all of the choice diets sold in stores and via the Internet. Indeed, the very formidable pet-parenting mindset of today has spawned a ripening niche market within the broader premium pet food market. There are pet owners who won't settle for anything but the absolute best for their dogs—and this means the closest thing possible to human-quality ingredients in their diets. In other words, they want their dogs to eat foods on par with their own daily repasts. So, if you are willing to do a heap of research—on, for starters, all of the legalities regarding quality and labeling in your particular state—and a lot of work, you could be a successful **premium dog food maker**.

They answer to a higher authority. Martine Lacombe and Marc Michels, that is, founders of **Kosher Pets** @ KosherPets.com, the first dog and cat diets to comply with the letter of Jewish dietary laws and attain the imprimatur of one of the largest orthodox rabbi groups in the country. Lacombe says, "There's no real need for kosher pet food, but there's a real demand." Kosher strictures, where no dairy and meat products are mixed, have historically applied to only human food consumption. But in the new millennium, the lines separating the worlds of people and pets are getting blurred. The Kosher Pets product line is available via the company website and in various pet food and supply stores throughout the country. The footnote to this story is that the company's two founders are *not* Jewish. Never lose sight of the reality that every successful entrepreneurial endeavor begins with a good idea. Turning these good ideas into thriving businesses is what separates the doers from the dreamers.

How Much Does It Cost to Start This Kind of Business?

While this opportunity is understandably layered and somewhat complicated (food preparation and packaging of foods always is), it is rife with grand possibilities for those with a supreme dedication to—and understanding of—first-class canine nutrition. Many authentically *natural* dog diets—with recipes created by real people in their real kitchens—are sold to local retailers and by way of the Internet to the ravenous public at large.

> Most people who opt to manufacture dog foods from the comforts of home are highly erudite on the subject of canine nutrition. It is this mother lode of nutritional sophistication that inspires their kitchen wizardry vis-à-vis serving the canine community both appetizing and healthy meals. There are countless books and websites on dog food and canine nutritional needs. A fine portal of information in this area can be found at Drs. Foster & Smith's @ PetEducation.com.

The cost of manufacturing a dog food from home is minor at the outset. It's time to reach deeply into your pockets *only* when you've completely satisfied yourself that you have a winner on your hands. At this juncture, make the requisite investment in a genuine business start-up, procuring necessary licenses, permits, and proper packaging. Then, of course, you have to take your product to the consumer. And this will entail promotional dollars.

What Qualifications Do You Need for This Kind of Work?

Before you advance another step in the dog food manufacturing sphere, ask yourself if you have the capacity to produce and package dog food in your home. If the answer is yes, then proceed with a scrupulous due diligence on what the law requires from at-home manufacturers of dog foods.

The very best kitchen dog food makers know their way around the kitchen. This may sound strange to the ears, but good cooks often make the best cooks for the canine crowd, too. If you encounter difficulty scrambling a couple of eggs or boiling a pot of water, try your hand at another pet-related business. This venture is for those persons who know the ABCs of canine nutrition and know a great deal about cooking in general.

The Regulatory Minefield

For starters, the U.S. Food and Drug Administration (FDA) governs the federal Food, Drug, and Cosmetic Act. This Act assumes the responsibility of ensuring that both human and animal foods are safe and properly labeled. Technically, the Act requires that pet foods, just like their human counterparts, contain no harmful substances and follow prescribed labeling guidelines. However, it does not amount to sweeping regulation of the pet food trade. *Pet food companies do not require FDA approval to manufacture their products.*

Before manufacturing any dog food or related product that you intend on selling to the purchasing public, visit the FDA and its **Center for Veterinary Medicine** @ FDA.gov/cvm (800-INFO-FDA or 240-276-9300). This is a worthwhile starting point for learning all about fundamental legal requirements, as well as uncovering constructive information on where to turn next. Next, meticulously explore the **Association of American Feed Control Officials** website @ AAFCO.org. Be sure to bone up on "Government Regulation of Pet Food." This organization assumes a critical role in pet food manufacturing and labeling regulations. Another website with practical information in this field is the **Pet Food Institute** @ PetFoodInstitute.org. This organization represents many of the manufacturers of pet food and can supply you with essential minutiae on all that dog food making entails.

In other words: The FDA does not regulate the pet food industry. Individually, the fifty states assume this particular duty. They exact more control over what goes into pet foods and how they are labeled than does the federal government. But the assorted state rules affecting pet food production generally ask for only voluntary compliance on consequential quality concerns. And, state-by-state, these rules vary widely. So, a pet food manufactured in Massachusetts might follow considerably different guidelines than one produced in Ohio, Florida, or California.

In stark contrast with human food manufacturing and distribution, the pet food trade is rather broadly and haphazardly regulated. Nevertheless, each state has specific regulations that pet food manufacturers—big and small—must adhere to. If you are making and selling a dog food—be it a complete diet or a biscuit treat, it doesn't matter—know the pertinent laws and strictures of your state inside and out. Otherwise, you could find yourself slapped with hefty fines and possibly be ordered to cease and desist from conducting further commerce. Also, if you intend on selling your pet foodstuffs across state borders, or nationwide, make certain that your ingredients, labeling, etc., meet the compulsory legal requirements in each one of the locations that you conduct business.

The Association of American Feed Control Officials (AAFCO)

Beyond the aforementioned federal and state governmental regulatory bodies, which do not hold pet food makers to rigorous and consistent standards of quality, there is an organization called the **Association of American Feed Control Officials (AAFCO)**, which plays the principal role in "regulating" the industry. AAFCO includes within its membership rolls federal, state, and local government agencies—*i.e.*, those legally charged with managing the production, labeling, and distribution of pet foods. Every single state has at least one individual from its department of agriculture working with the organization.

While not an official arm of government, AAFCO—in conjunction with bureaucratic agencies—nevertheless oversees pet food ingredients, additives, preservatives, and the ABCs of proper labeling. It also publishes uniform ingredient descriptions and definitions to aid consumers in their understanding of what is literally going into pet foods. AAFCO standards are at once comprehensive and coherent. But, again, pet food producers need only voluntarily adhere to them.

How Do You Find Customers?

Okay, you have a finished dog food product that complies with all of the state edicts regarding ingredients, labeling, and the like. Where on earth do you go to sell it? Retailers? This is certainly an uphill climb.

Let's face it. The competition is fierce in the dog food market, and dog parents aren't necessarily going to jump at the chance to purchase something made on somebody's home stovetop. There are too many variables at play here. *Is the food what it says it is? How do I know if it is safe? Is it nutritionally complete?* These are very reasonable concerns, and you are going to have to address them time and again.

What should the new dog food maker on the block do? Throw in the towel? No, you should test market your product in as many pet venues as are possible. Dispense free samples and more free samples—everywhere and anywhere. What you must do is generate a demand for your fine fare. Query local retailers about the possibility of you and your special food appearing at their places of business with, of course, loads of freebies in hand. Retailers understand that consumers—their customers—relish getting something for nothing. (You might have to sweeten the pot a bit and grease the palm of the retailer for the privilege of appearing. However, should you go down this route, negotiate encore performances where you are eventually permitted to sell your product for a profit.)

No matter where you materialize with your dog food, have a brochure or flier of some kind that details exactly what's in your product, and why it is so exceptional and different from the competition. Mention its great taste appeal and how it'll win over even the most finicky eaters—all of those dogs who turn their noses away from those dime-a-dozen commercial foods. Sing the praises of its super-high nutritional quality. Tell them that your fussy dog just loves it and is the picture of health, too. (Yes, it is always an enormous plus to be a dog food maker with a pooch who is eating your product.)

When Clay Mathile purchased part ownership of the Iams Company in the mid-1970s, the struggling business had few dollars to spend on advertising and marketing. So, in the basement of his home, Mathile and his family hand-packed sample bags of the company's dog foods. They spent many of their weekends driving long and far, meeting and greeting potential customers, all the while dispensing *literally* tons of free samples. Kennels, dog shows, and breeders were favorite stopovers. In lieu of a massive advertising budget, this intimate customer contact grew a small, regional business into the international leader of premium pet foods.

Dog Biscuit and Treat Maker

Manufacturing complete diets for pets is a multi-layered undertaking—there's no getting around it. There are nutritional bars that you must surpass before marketing your foods, even in the haphazardly regulated pet food industry. That is, when you produce pet foods and brand them as nutritionally whole, they are supposed to sustain healthy living all by themselves. To create these *meals*, you must comply with an exacting script in areas governing minimum dietary requirements.

On the other hand, to call yourself a **dog biscuit and treat maker**, you have significantly more leeway as to what goes into your products and what comes out

85

of your oven. You still must abide by governmental and industry edicts ensuring that your goodies are up to snuff regarding quality concerns, and not unsafe to pets in any way, shape, or form. But again, we are talking about between-meal snacks and not complete and balanced diets—and there's a big difference.

This build up to this particular entrepreneurial avenue isn't to suggest that you bake dog biscuits and assorted pet treats with anything but the healthiest of ingredients. On the contrary! The running thread in this slice of the pet food business is *healthy*—producing edibles that are deemed *all-natural*, *organic*, *gourmet*, and the like. In other words, your dog biscuits, cakes, and cookies shouldn't be the four-legged equivalents of cheese doodles, Devil Dogs, and licorice twists. Instead, when you conceive them from the finest ingredients on earth—relatively speaking—you increase your chances of unearthing customers. The current marketplace is exceedingly hospitable to the little guys and gals who make dog biscuits and assorted indulgences. Doggie bakeries, for example, often make their very own pet delicacies on the premises, or they purchase their product lines of biscuits and treats from various independent suppliers—people just like you.

How Much Does It Cost to Start This Kind of Business?

To get started as a dog biscuit and treat maker, you can start with the bare essentials: healthy ingredients, molds, and packaging. This inaugural volley can happen on a shoestring budget—under $500. Once you find clientele, you can invest more and take the business to a higher level.

What Qualifications Do You Need for This Kind of Work?

To make dog biscuits and treats, you need good recipes. There are books on the market and websites that feature recipes, or you can create your very own. Knowledge of canine nutrition and baking ABCs are important. In the end, you want to manufacture quality goods that dogs will not only like, but that are not injurious to their overall health and well-being.

How Do You Find Customers?

As a dog biscuit and treat maker, you have many places in which to peddle your edibles. Take your products to pet-themed shows and flea markets. Sell them to retailers, and not just in the realm of the pet care trade. More and more, gourmet dog biscuits are found in gift shops and elsewhere—even supermarkets. Visit doggie bakeries. Launch a website and promote it. These are all venues where dog biscuit and treat makers are realizing success.

Need some dog biscuit recipes and links to pet bakeries and pertinent book titles? You'll find them all on **Gourmet Sleuth** @ GourmetSleuth.com. Search the sprawling website for dog biscuits and related recipes. Check out, too, **Good Dog Express** @ GoodDogExpress.com (877-682-PETS) for dog bone-shaped cookie cutters and muffin pans, breed molds, as well as all kinds of bakery packaging, including treat bags and boxes.

Premium Cat Food Maker

There are certainly more entrepreneurs selling dog diets prepared in their home kitchens than there are individuals whipping up succulent spreads for picky felines. This reality bite is a matter of economics. While there are more cats than dogs in American households, the feline species—in aggregate—doesn't consume near as much as their canine cousins. And, on top of that fact of life, cats are notorious for thumbing their noses at more of their suppers, too—even when they are prepared from the finest ingredients on Mother Earth.

If you are interested in making money—be it as a full-time business or part-time aside—life as a **premium cat food maker** will require that you leap over a somewhat higher hurdle than life as a dog food maker. Nevertheless, the homemade pet food competition in the cat food market is a less crowded place. You'll distinguish yourself from the pack much more readily—because the pack will be so much smaller.

How Much Does It Cost to Start This Kind of Business?

There is no need to break the bank in getting started as a premium cat food maker. It's only when you see yourself taking the product to a broader market that you'll require a significant investment in the particulars: ingredients, packaging, promotions, and so on.

Evolution has seen to it that the feline species has distinct nutritional needs, and cat foods are formulated with this physiological fact in mind. While dog and cat foods may appear alike to the naked eye and naked nose, they are vastly different in composition. Because the ratio of intestine to body length in a cat is 4:1 versus 6:1 in a dog, foods spend more time in a canine's innards and this allows for more absorption of their nutrients. Cats require more proteins and amino acids than do dogs, and this is reflected in the diets on the market. You should not feed cat foods to dogs. Nor should you ever manufacture a food that claims it is nutritionally complete for *both* the feline and the canine class.

What Qualifications Do You Need for This Kind of Work?

If you are seriously weighing taking a stab at producing a cat food that'll make feline mouths water, remember that there are laws and regulatory concerns to consider. In fact, the very same legal issues that exist for dog food makers also exist for cat food makers. You should therefore do the very same due diligence that is prescribed for dog food manufacturers.

It must also be stressed that this kind of business is for individuals who understand feline nutritional needs from top to bottom. The manufacturing of complete and healthy diets for a pet of any kind is a science. You shouldn't be cooking up cat food in your kitchen unless you know a great deal about feline health and wellness. We knew a few customers in our retail lives who fed both their cats and their dogs the very same thing. When we tried to educate them on the truth about cats and dogs, they opted to remain ignorant and on the path of convenience—to, alas, the detriment of their animal friends.

How Do You Find Customers?

Bring your products to cat shows and pet-related events. Partner with retailers. Sell your quality food via the Internet. If you have a quality diet that passes muster with all the laws regarding pet food safety, you need to go out among the cat people and let them sample your stuff.

Cat Litter Inventor

This business story began rather inconspicuously in the small town of Cassopolis, Michigan, in 1948. The players in this entrepreneurial soap opera were Kay Draper, a woman with a truly stinking problem on her hands, and her neighbors, the Lowe family, who operated a local company that sold industrial absorbents. One bitterly cold January morning, Kay discovered that her outdoor sand pile was frozen solid, courtesy of an extended stretch of extremely harsh winter weather. Without ready access to her mound of sand, she was left with nothing to put into her cat's privy. Compelled to improvise, Kay used ashes from her fireplace as a substitute.

What Ms. Draper got out of her noble experiment was a seemingly infinite series of black paw prints tracked throughout her house coupled with a tenacious malodor that could peel paint. Desperate, she sought out her entrepreneurial

89

neighbors for advice. She wanted to know if they could recommend anything that would solve her feline waste predicament. Twenty-seven-year-old Ed Lowe, just home from a stint in the navy, badly wanted to diversify and expand the family business. He reasoned that their kiln-dried clay product sold to garages, known as Fuller's Earth, might do the trick as a cat litter as well. He gave Kay a bag and suggested she try it in her cat's box. Ed explained to her that garages used the stuff all the time to soak up oil spills. *Why wouldn't it work in absorbing a cat's "spills," too?*

Kay took the clay product home with her and was immediately pleased with the job it did. It was better than plain old sand, she concluded, and recommended it to her friends with house cats. Fuller's Earth eventually caught on as a cat litter, with Ed Lowe himself coining the term *kitty litter*.

Lowe ultimately hit the road and visited hundreds of cat shows and pet shops, promoting his newfangled product. When he retired in 1990, his business net worth topped $200 million, thanks in large part to cats and cat litter. Lowe's pioneering efforts on behalf of cat litter enabled more and more people to bring their feline friends indoors. So many, in fact, that cats now reign supreme as the number one pet in American households, surpassing the long-time canine champions during the 1990s.

Let's just say that you've been given the lowdown on becoming the next **cat litter inventor**, manufacturer, and successful entrepreneur. Since that day more than a half century ago, when Lowe's clay kitty litter became a commercial sensation, all kinds of copycats have appeared on the market, some with fragrances added, some less dusty than others, some bargain-priced, etc. The bottom line, however, is that clay-based litters have continually dominated this ever-growing slice of the pet product market. Only in recent years, with the introduction of a popular *clumping clay* alternative, has the original clay litter concept lost its absolute competitive hegemony, although it still accounts for 55% of all cat litter sales.

How Much Does It Cost to Start This Kind of Business?

Always encourage the business idea stage to be innovative because you never know what kind of inspiration will spring out of it. Inventing a product that becomes the next commercial sensation is admittedly a long shot. Nevertheless, every single day, ordinary people are seeing their handiwork sell on store shelves, in catalogues, and via websites.

Untold items of merchandise on the pet-specialty market have the most intriguing histories behind them. In other words, there are genuine, no-frills folks just like you who invented everything from the Alpo dog food brand to the Four Paws shampoo line to the hooded cat litter box. Indeed, many of the cat litters and cat litter additives in the marketplace are the brainchildren of everyday people. The popular pet products that have originated in one woman's kitchen or one man's garage are legion. So, yes, you can invent the next cat litter, cat litter additive, or cat litter box contraption.

You very likely can invent a product like cat litter on a tight budget. It's when you are absolutely convinced that you have a sellable product on your hands that you'll need some serious investment dollars for particulars like patenting, production, inventory, and promotions.

What Qualifications Do You Need for This Kind of Work?

Through our years in the hustle and bustle of retail, we repeatedly heard from customers of ours who moonlighted as inventors. They weren't shy in telling us about their creations. Most of these inventors used their innovations to better the lives and times of their own cats and dogs. We very often heard the refrain, "I should market it." But, in the final analysis, not many of these amateur inventors took the next fateful step. In the competitive business realm, it's only the doers who go places, not the "I should" crowd.

If you have an idea or have already invented a product that you deem unique and commercially viable, the first thing you should do is contact the federal government's patent office. Find out what the patenting process entails. Acquire a patent for your invention before bringing it to market. The **United States Patent and Trademark Office** can be accessed @ <u>USPTO.gov</u> (800-786-9199).

To invent the next must-have cat litter, you have to know a great deal about cats and what they prefer in their litter boxes. Cat litters on the market run a wide gamut, which includes unscented clays, scented clays, clumping clays, recycled newspaper, and biodegradable brands (the only ones recommended for flushing down toilet bowls). There are also cat litters made from cedar, corncobs, peanut shells, and other shards of nature. Indeed, the cat litter panorama is widening as these words are being written.

As an inventor in this area, you have to carefully consider these questions:

★ What's the cat litter going to be made of?
★ Will it appeal to fastidious cats?
★ Will it be dusty, the bane of many commercial litters?
★ Will it be user-friendly for cat consumers?
★ Will it be scented?
★ Is it environmentally safe?
★ Can the litter be flushed down the toilet?
★ How often will the litter box have to be cleaned out?
★ Is it a safe product all around for both the two-legged and four-legged?

Inventors in any field have to do their homework. You want your product to distinguish itself from others. You want your product to win over the hearts, minds, and pocketbooks of consumers. In the final analysis, the answer to this simple question is everything: Will people buy it?

How Do You Find Customers?

It's a good idea for inventors and manufacturers of anything to test-market their product before rushing into any sort of mass production. Inventors of pet merchandise have found great success at those ubiquitous pet-themed shows we keep mentioning. What better place to dispense with samples of your cat litter creation than at cat shows?

Go forth among the people whom you are targeting as your consumer demographic. Many of the most popular pet products on today's market were discovered at pet shows. New pet foods are regularly seen at these extravaganzas, as are the latest training devices. Every imaginable pet plaything is spotted at these events. And, sure enough, the latest cat litter innovations often debut at these affairs.

There are businesses that assist would-be inventors in navigating the invention process from A to Z. **Invention Home** @ InventionHome.com (866-THINK-12) is one such company that is staffed with experienced inventors. The company mission is to aid fledgling inventors in their travels from raw idea to finished product selling in the marketplace. The stark reality is that most inventors lack the management skills and knowledge to market their products in a big way, such as understanding the often convoluted process of getting things onto the shelves of big retailers. Hiring the right professional assistance in this area often pays rich dividends in the end.

If you are financially and emotionally armed and ready to assume center stage, other areas to explore with your new product are consumer magazines, such as *Cat Fancy* and *Cats*. Place ads and retail your product. You can also run ads in the trade magazines and sell directly to retailers and wholesalers. In the big picture, you want to prove to the world that your product can sell. And, of course, the world includes those omnipresent pet-specialty superstores.

An important aside to keep in mind is that environmentally friendly products are the way to go in the current marketplace. Cat owners are more aware than ever before that there are safety concerns to weigh regarding cat litter purchases. Nevertheless, when all is said and done, it's entirely up to the feline species to say "ay" or "nay" to your product.

> The next cat litter and cat litter box invention is on the horizon. You can go to the bank on that one. A recent addition to this lively genre of products is **CatGenie @ CatGenie.com** (888-SELF-WASH). This more technologically advanced product than most in this field is a genuine cat toilet. CatGenie works with permanent granules rather than any kind of disposable or flushable litter. It liquefies waste products, which then are automatically flushed down the drain. The product also operates with sanitizers and a hot air blower that dries the permanent granules for another go around.

Cat Toy Inventor

Through the years at Pet Nosh, our most reliable seller in the packaged cat toy department was—hands down—the Cat Dancer. For lack of a better description, this "toy" consisted of a coiled steel spring with a few petite strips of rolled-up cardboard attached to its "play" end. The Cat Dancer was designed for humans to wave at felines in their company. That is, this unpretentious product was crafted to encourage cats to do what countless cats relish doing—batting at objects in their inimitable and endearing styles. And, naturally, such swatting and boxing at tiny cardboard pieces attached to a spring causes the spring to ripple to and fro—and to and fro some more—thus instigating further feline flailing.

The Cat Dancer, and its rather rudimentary concept, was the brainchild of a man named Jim Boelke from Neenah, Wisconsin. On the official Cat Dancer website, Boelke's product is described as "a basement inventor's dream come true." Year after year, the Cat Dancer is a multimillion dollar seller. Visit **Cat Dancer** @ CatDancer.com and look upon it as a living and breathing inspiration for the inventor in you. The pet care marketplace is waiting with bated breath for the next Cat Dancer.

You could be the next **cat toy inventor**. Before assuming this vaunted title and getting to work, there are a couple of key questions to chew over. *What do cats enjoy playing with? What truly excites their "inner kitten"?* Granted, the answers to these queries are not clear-cut. Feline aficionados will tell you that their cats are one-of-a-kinds—true originals all. In other words, there is no single cat toy that will win over the hearts and minds of the entire feline species or even the preponderance of these individualistic and hard to please companion animals. So, perish the thought of inventing a product that every cat will endorse—it's not going to happen. Even the ultra-popular catnip doesn't interest and affect every single cat. Feel free to lower your inventor's bar a bit.

How Much Does It Cost to Start This Kind of Business?

To invent a cat toy and successfully market it will require a sizeable investment when you feel you have a product that can sell in the marketplace. Inventing most toys can be done on the cheap—often under $1,000. Mass producing them and marketing them will cost you a fair chunk of change— $5,000, and perhaps way up depending on the piece of merchandise and strategies to get it in stores and such.

What Qualifications Do You Need for This Kind of Work?

Foremost, you have to have a good idea and the capacity to turn that idea into more than that. You have to also be committed to manufacturing a quality and safe product. Essentially, an inventor's charge in this dynamic merchandise arena is to ascertain what an ample portion of the general cat census will take a shine to. The inventor of the Cat Dancer did just that. And, you might have noticed that there are various Cat Dancer epigones on the market. Toy mice of all varieties—from faux-leather to felt to catnip-filled cloth—are also coveted cat playthings. Another toy product worth mentioning here is the Crazy Circle, which appeals to a lot of cats—but hardly all and definitely not most felines—as they bat at an excitable ball cozily tucked inside a rounded track made of plastic. This attention grabbing—but again, rather unsophisticated—product consistently sells well. This is precisely where you want to take your invention—to the market and reliably in demand today, tomorrow, and next year.

Foremost, as a budding cat toy inventor, you would be wise to comb the aisles of pet-specialty retailers and see what's out there and selling on their myriad shelves and pegboards. Check out relevant websites, too. What are cat consumers buying? Where is there room for improvement on already tried and tested products? Is there an opening for a truly new concept in cat toys? Ask and fully answer these questions and you never know what will spring from this exploratory brainstorm. Needless to say, inspiration for cat toy inventors often comes from their feline cohorts. Indeed, many of the cat accessory items of today are the derivatives of owner-inventors solving a problem—creating merchandise to satisfy their exceptional cats. Getting an all-important paw up from a feline in residence is often at the top of the cat toy inventor's checklist.

How Do You Find Customers?

Take your winning creation to cat trade shows, craft fairs, flea markets, and gift shows. Advertise in pet-themed periodicals. Visit retailers with your product. If feasible, work with pet merchandise wholesalers. Get your invention out there among the consuming masses.

Dog Toy Inventor

The pet products that receive the most ink and air time—the feature stories in magazines and newspapers, the segments on TV news shows etc.—are, predictably, the most whimsical and peculiar items: things like edible greeting cards, rhinestone tiaras, doggie sunglasses, pastel and glitter nail polishes, and molasses madness cookies. These unmistakably offbeat selections of dog things do, in fact, underscore the far-reaching arms of the modern-day pet care trade. Dog toys and assorted canine playthings and paraphernalia are certainly among the chief contributors to the abiding industry's well-earned reputation for remarkable innovation, unpredictability, and eccentricity. Consider becoming a **dog toy inventor** or some other kind of dog product inventor and manufacturer. There is plenty of room in this wide-open field to innovate and—yes—profit from a sound idea converted into a sound product.

When Pet Nosh first opened its doors more than a quarter of a century ago, the nature of the business was a far cry from what it is today. If the differences between those days of yore and present reality had to be summed up in one word, it would be *choices*. In the colorless past, there weren't a whole lot of alternatives on a whole lot of fronts in the pet care trade—from foods to every imaginable accessory product.

In our original Pet Nosh store, canine playthings consisted of rawhide products, Nylabones (just the basic bones, by the way), some primitive rubber rings and pulls, and a smattering of vinyl and latex squeak toys. There wasn't too much else to choose from in the area of dog fun and games. No Kong or rope toys. If your life depended on it, you couldn't find a fluorescent Frisbee for the four-legged. And nothing manufactured from plush fabrics was manufactured to fit into a dog's mouth. In other words, there is a dramatically

97

wider market for inventors of extracurricular dog stuff to tap into and, of course, to conquer. When we entered the retail slice of pet care, we were startled that a latex stalk of broccoli and vinyl milkman existed as dog playthings. We showed our family, friends, and, yes, our dogs too. Courtesy of all sorts of inventor-types and far-sighted entrepreneurs, times change. The dog toy inventor has a lot of room in which to roam—in which to create the next coveted big seller.

While romping through the dog product field, it would be prudent to pause and activate the **Bow-Lingual Bark Translator**, a device conceived by Dr. Matsumi Suzuki, Ph.D., president of the renowned Japan Acoustic Laboratory. What the Bow-Lingual Bark Translator does is analyze a dog's bark. It accomplishes this mean feat by taking a voice—or bark, if you will—printing. This scientific print is then scrutinized as to what the bark is trying to convey emotionally: happiness, sadness, anger, assertiveness, frustration, neediness, etc. The key technology behind the Bow-Lingual Bark Translator is the Animal Emotional Analysis System (AEAS). Right now the Bow-Lingual Bark Translator is out on the fringes of the canine merchandise marketplace. It is one of those inconceivable items that has barreled down the pet pike and been received with more hoots and gasps than actual purchases—a much talked about pet-inspired product but hardly mainstream. However, countless pet accessory products have debuted through the years to resounding thuds in sales, but over time turned out to be red-hot, must-have pieces of merchandise. Who knows? The Bow-Lingual Bark Translator might soon find itself in every dog owner's household.

How Much Does It Cost to Start This Kind of Business?

Inventing a dog toy needn't break the bank. Getting it into the hands of dog owners and into the mouths of canines will likely necessitate an investment of $5,000 or more, depending again on exactly where you want to take your invention.

What Qualifications Do You Need for This Kind of Work?

Know your target market and precisely what you need to do to mine the brisk demand for dog toys. Put safety and quality at the top of your agenda. Consumers look for dog playthings in categories (often overlapping) such as:

- ★ Rubber toys   ★ Plush toys
- ★ Ball toys   ★ Durable toys
- ★ Nylon toys   ★ Rope toys

In addition, as an inventor, don't ignore the power of the holidays, especially Christmas. During the season of goodwill, for instance, we sold every imaginable Christmas-themed item. If only you could have witnessed the conditions of our stores after the holiday madness. Decimation! Santa Claus squeak toys were huge sellers, as were rawhide products shaped like Christmas trees and candy canes. It seemed that we could never stock enough canine Christmas stockings with a variety of toys and treats in them. The larger point here is that if you have a unique holiday dog toy in mind, don't fret about the seasonality of sales. The quantities of attention-grabbing items that sell during holiday stretches are often worth their weight in gold, frankincense, and myrrh.

For a wealth of information and insight on marketing inventions from soup to nuts, drop by author and small business guru Don Debelak's website @ DonDebelak.com. Debelak offers inventors heaping helpings of encouragement and guidance. He notes that the marketplace always has the welcome mat out for distinctive products with a real appeal to consumers. Among many slivers of sage advice, Debelak discusses how a newly invented product's manufacturing costs must never surpass 25% to 30% of the approximate retail price. With retailers expecting at least a 50% discount off the retail price, Debelak reveals how exorbitant manufacturing bills can fast obliterate your ability to realize profits.

How Do You Find Customers?

Go to where dog owners go. Countless mega-popular pet products debuted at trade and gift shows. Other big selling dog toys found their first takers via industry trade publications. Sell your invention via an Internet website. Champion its uniqueness and benefits directly to pet parents through dog magazines and other appropriate periodicals.

Bird Toy Inventor

You may think that this section is for the birds—and, you're right, it is. Bird toys are a big business. Bird parents are a large and expanding group of people. Whether they own a canary, parakeet, cockatiel, lovebird, parrot, or any number of other species, there are bird accessory products for them ranging from swings to pacifier beads to bells to rings to every imaginable plaything made of everything imaginable from rawhide to cotton to wood to plastic to wicker. If you have what it takes, you could be a **bird toy inventor** and manufacturer and see your product or products soar like an eagle.

How Much Does It Cost to Start This Kind of Business?

Again, the world of inventing a product and getting it to market is a process. An investment in real dollars—often $5,000 and a whole lot more—is required to manufacture it, market it, and realize real profits.

What Qualifications Do You Need for This Kind of Work?

You need, of course, the inventor's touch and a commitment to providing the feathery among us with both a unique and quality plaything. Being a bird-brain rules you out. However, thinking like a bird is an important attribute for a bird toy inventor to possess.

How Do You Find Customers?

New bird toys find a lot of takers at bird trade shows. Advertise directly to bird lovers in bird-themed magazines. Consider ads in pet industry trade magazines to reach retailers. If you have a genuinely good product, it will take flight only if it's seen and sampled by consumers—and lots of them. Erect a website. Do flea markets and craft shows. Leave no stone unturned.

If you want to get a good handle on what's selling in bird toys, visit pet-specialty retailers or, better yet, bird-specialty retailers, which are increasing in numbers, as caged birds become more and more popular pets. You can also surf the Web and check out Birdalog.com, BirdToyOutlet.com, and SmartBirdToys.com. On the latter's site are such intriguingly named bird toys as Bon Appetite, Parrot Piñata, Dinkie Duckie Mirror, Mardi Gras Ball, Hol-ee Roller, and hundreds more.

Climb Every Hartz Mountain

We'll conclude here with a little inspirational story, albeit not of an inventor per se. What follows is an accounting of a man who took the concept of selling cat, dog, and bird products and ran with it. It's something that you as an inventor and manufacturer of any kind of pet product can do also. And, it's fair to say that you will encounter a more hospitable—albeit more competitive—consumer climate than Max Stern met with in 1926. So, consider yourself ahead of the game.

In that snapshot in time more than three quarters of a century ago, Max Stern left his native Germany for a better life in America. He was virtually penniless when he entered his adopted homeland at the tender age of twenty-six. Stern, however, fast concluded that his faith in America as the *land of opportunity* was justified. His entrepreneurial success story took flight when a childhood friend of his—a seller of pets in the early American trade—borrowed a substantial sum of money from him, and then couldn't afford to pay it back. Without another option, Stern agreed to accept his friend's alternative form of repayment: 5,000 canaries! He reasoned that it was better than nothing at all.

What does one do with a jungle's worth of birds? An entrepreneur like Max Stern takes the canaries—singing their unremitting lullabies to the days and nights—to New York City and sells them to recoup the dollar amount of the loan that he had bequeathed his financially strapped friend. But he does more than that.

Max Stern's sojourn to the city that never sleeps propels him into the bird accessory business and the Hartz Mountain Company is soon born. Beyond bird supplies, the business quickly adds cat and dog merchandise to its product line and for the decades to come, few variety stores or supermarkets in the United States and Canada are without Hartz Mountain pet products ranging from parakeet seed to rawhide bones to kitty litter.

Aquarium Ornament Inventor

With the very latest census taken by the American Pet Product Manufacturers Association (APPMA) putting the numbers of fish in Americans' aquarium tanks and bowls in the neighborhood of 150 million, a not surprisingly strong demand for aquarium paraphernalia exists. What we are leading up to here is you cashing in on this thriving marketplace as an **aquarium ornament inventor**. The most eye-catching aquariums around are chock-full of both interesting fish and alluring ornamentation.

There are countless creative roads to venture down as an inventor of aquarium ornaments. So many varieties of this ornamentation exist, ranging from miniature reflections of things one might literally find 20,000 leagues under the sea, such as sunken ships and treasure chests, as well as scary-looking sea monsters of the kinds that Thor Heyerdahl encountered on his *Kon Tiki* rafting adventure across the Pacific. But there are also aquarium ornaments that have precious little to do with watery ruins and terrifying marine creatures. There are castles, dragons, church replicas, and every imaginable design to dazzle one's eyes with vivid colors and reflections of light. So, the bottom line is that—if you know your stuff, of course—creating a winning aquarium ornament, or a whole line of them, is within your grasp. There are legions of enthusiastic aquarium-owning consumers just chomping at the bit to purchase the next charming and unique ornaments to work their way into the marketplace.

One of the largest manufacturers of aquarium-related products, including ornamentation, is **Penn-Plax** @ PennPlax.com. Perusing the company's aquarium supply line is quite enlightening vis-à-vis what is selling out there. All kinds of painted resin aquarium ornaments are available. There are ornamental castle ruins and deep-sea divers; wizards and dazzle stones; shale mountains and sunken gardens. Yet another area to consider taking your knack for inventing products to is aquarium backgrounds. Many aquarium owners purchase elaborately crafted backdrops—constructed of rock, bark, and such—to enhance the visual appeals of their setups.

How Much Does It Cost to Start This Kind of Business?

Inventing a product such as an aquarium ornament usually doesn't cost much, except in time expended. Finding it in the marketplace and selling in large numbers requires an investment in real dollars.

What Qualifications Do You Need for This Kind of Work?

You have to be capable of inventing a unique and safe product. An aquarium ornament must be durable and—this is key—non-toxic. Not everything meshes well with water and the maintenance of tropical and marine fish.

How Do You Find Customers?

Like Luca Brazzi, you should swim with the fishes in your marketing forays—metaphorically speaking, of course. That is, take your aquarium ornament or ornaments to the fishiest of places: trade shows, retailers, craft fairs, and so on. Sell them in appropriate magazines and via a website.

CHAPTER V

Throwing Your Special Talents to the Dogs, Cats, and Birds

Doggie Fashions Designer ✦ Dog Jacket and Coat Designer ✦ Dog Sweater Designer ✦ Dog Shirt Designer

One of the many things that surprised us in the fledgling years of Pet Nosh in the early 1980s was the consumer demand for dog jackets, coats, and sweaters. It seemed especially odd to us because we had never personally witnessed a single man or woman walking a dog wearing a jacket, coat, or sweater. Times have certainly changed and the streets are now teeming with bundled-up canines in the wintertime and dogs sporting T-shirts and raincoats all year round.

Looking back on the earliest sales of our pet clothing apparel, we'd be less than forthright to suggest that they were on the hefty side of the financial ledger. However, as the years progressed, we sold more and more clothing attire and offered more and more of a fashion selection as well.

In the new millennium, the doggie fashions industry has blossomed beyond recognition. Sure, more dogs are clad in winter-weather outfits. But what's really driving this peculiar sliver of commerce to new heights everyday are canine parents' desire and utter willingness to purchase stylish shirts, cravats, collars, sunglasses, hair bows, and hats. There is money to be made as a **doggie fashions designer**. You could be a **dog jacket and coat designer**, **dog sweater designer**, **dog shirt designer**—or a combination of all three.

If you are in any way a Doubting Thomas that an indisputable consumer demand exists for doggie apparel, look no further than PetFashionWeek.com. **Pet Fashion Week** is now an annual event that transpires in New York City—the world's second home. This extravaganza brings together a colorful array of designers and makers of clothes, jewelry, collars, headwear, etc., for the pet-set. This *happening* is merely one glaring example of the sizeable marketplace out there for pet fashions.

How Much Does It Cost to Start This Kind of Business?

To get jumpstarted as a dog fashion designer, you need the tools of the trade: the materials to make jackets, coats, sweaters, and shirts. This could include a sewing machine in addition to the requisite fabrics. A minimal investment is all that is required to test the waters in this field. You don't need to generate a vast inventory of clothing, only representative samples of your works.

What Qualifications Do You Need for This Kind of Work?

If you are adept with a needle and thread, and know your way around a sewing machine, then you have the requisite qualifications to be a doggie fashions designer. If you know how to knit, then you have the necessary skills to turn a profit in this intriguing and unpredictable sector of commerce. (Dog sweaters are big sellers!) If you are not competent in either of these two disciplines, you could always learn. Hooking up with somebody who can sew or knit with a bit of élan is also something to consider. You can run the doggie fashions business side, while somebody else manufactures the fashion line.

> If you pine for any sort of information on the vastly popular craft of sewing, surf on over to the **Home Sewing Association** @ Sewing.org (412-372-5950). This outfit can assist you in learning how to sew, or improve your already existing skills. The site also features a link on *Sewing for Pets*. The **Craft Yarn Council of America** @ LearnToKnit.com is the best place on the Net to unearth more than a good yarn. Other places to visit while you are out and about in virtual reality: Sewing.about.com and Knitting.about.com. Don't bypass CraftAndFabricLinks.com, which has a wealth of links.

How Do You Find Customers?

As with so many other pet-specific pieces of merchandise, the first places to check out are retail stores in the trade. Unique and otherwise quality dog garments are in demand and have a very definitive market. Sweaters for all breeds and in all sizes are coveted during cold times in cold climes. Winter jackets for all sized dogs are popular sellers, especially if they are both very warm *and* waterproof. These everyday products are the biggest and most consistent sellers in the doggie fashions world. In addition, with the growing popularity of small breed dogs, both utilitarian *and* stylish winter wear are in greater demand.

There is also an ample niche market for unusual pet fashions running the gamut from bowties to headwear to booties. These attention-grabbing items are most often seen in pet boutiques—that is, in places that highlight merchandise beyond mere foodstuffs and conventional accessories. Websites, too, are replete with doggie apparel that ranges from simple one-color sweaters to diamond-studded tiaras.

Keep in mind that before anything takes off as a big seller, doggie apparel has to be seen and touched. So, take your dog jackets, coats, and sweaters to pet trade shows and craft fairs. Show the buying public what you have and harvest orders from retailers and wholesalers. If possible, take custom orders from consumers for whatever piece of clothing they want and in whatever size they want. In today's highly competitive pet care market, catering to pet-passionate individuals puts you on solid business ground. Many dog parents are loath to buy off-the-rack stuff. They want specially tailored items for their very special four-legged friends. Yes, this is the reality, but it's a gaping entrepreneurial opening for anyone who can proficiently and imaginatively manufacture dog apparel.

Pet people spend a lot of money on their companion animals. No kidding. The billions of dollars speak volumes. They even buy silly things that their dogs and cats would rather they hadn't purchased. In the world of animal apparel, there are closets full of stuff bought solely because they strike the fancy of pet owners. Sweatshirts, hats, and hair bows, for instance. The same can be said for all of those pet costumes that sell around Halloween and Christmas time. More than likely, Max doesn't want to wear those reindeer antlers. In other words, you can sell practical jackets, coats, and sweaters for the four-legged, as well as very extraordinary items that appeal, above all else, to the two-legged.

Pet-Themed People Clothes

It isn't just clothing apparel for the four-legged that's finding increasing numbers of takers. There is yet another entrepreneurial street in this fashionable neighborhood that is paved with gold. It involves peddling people attire with pet themes and pet images on them. We're talking about outerwear for the two-legged that celebrates the dynamism of the pet care trade and people's incredible devotion to their feline and canine companions. This is a considerable but still largely untapped market. **Pet-themed people clothes** sell in retailers, at trade shows, flea markets, and fairs, as well as on the Internet.

In addition to this broad marketplace overview, unquestionably one of the fiercer currents running through it is the popularity of breed-specific merchandise. Aficionados of particular cat and dog breeds are renowned for buying everything under the sun that features in some way, shape, or form their preferred kind of pet. In other words, a Golden Retriever parent rides around with an "I Love Golden Retriever" bumper sticker on the car; wears a catchy Golden Retriever t-shirt; drinks coffee from an emblazoned Golden Retriever mug; has a ceramic Golden Retriever magnet on the refrigerator; and hangs a multi-hued Golden Retriever ornament on the Christmas tree.

How Much Does It Cost to Start This Kind of Business?

You can begin designing and marketing pet-themed people clothes with a minimal investment. In this line of work, you can put your designs in front of the consumer without manufacturing assembly-line quantities. See what sells and what doesn't sell. Churn out what you need to fulfill orders when you have money in hand. This is a wise way to go at the onset.

What Qualifications Do You Need for This Kind of Work?

If you have the aptitude for design—or have a winning idea that somebody else could design and manufacture for you—pet-themed people clothes could be your ticket to the land of champagne and caviar. And, as already under-scored, a line of attire and, in fact, other accessory items (carry bags, jewelry, etc.) that showcase individual breeds of pets are always fertile commercial territories in which to plant your entrepreneurial seeds.

How Do You Find Customers?

Sell your pet-themed people clothes to retailers. Bring them to pet trade shows and general gift shows. Sell them at flea markets, as well as on the Internet.

Pet Leash Designer ⚫ Pet Collar Designer

Nowadays, pet fashion is hardly limited to clothing apparel. This reality snapshot means that pet fashion designers can ply their trade in areas well beyond outerwear. In other words, there is more to pet fashion than jackets, coats, sweaters, and T-shirts. The pet fashions designer can also forage in the green fields of pet leashes and pet collars, too.

Indeed, the **pet leash designer** and the **pet collar designer** have a very lush marketplace in which to wander and to set themselves apart from the competition with the latest innovations on two indispensable pet products. Most dogs wear collars—and many cats do, too—and the majority of their owners purchase leads of some kind for them.

Not too long ago, the available leash and collar choices were—like so many other pet accessory items in the trade—very limited and very no-frills in design and appearance. For the most part, dog owners used basic nylon leads to walk their best friends. They were sold in lengths of either four feet or six feet, with not much else to choose from. There were also leather and chain leashes on the market in limited varieties and sizes. And, as for the available collars, they matched in color and appearance of the leash—nylon or leather. For the most part, these two odds and ends of pet merchandise were looked upon as utilitarian in nature. A dog required a collar and a leash to get walked—period and end of story.

As the pet care trade breathlessly tries to catch up with the pet-parenting phenomenon, more fashionable leashes and collars are feverishly working their way into the marketplace. Indeed, more and more pet people now look upon the purchase of a leash and a collar as a fashion choice as well as a practical one. Sure, for most pet parents, leads and collars for their animal companions must be operational above all else, but now they have so many more from which to choose. From the colors to the designs to the sizes, leashes and collars constitute a healthy and diverse market in and of them-selves. And growing numbers of these "ready and willing to spend money" consumers are purchasing things like diamond-studded collars and camou-flage-colored leashes. Rest assured that as a pet leash designer and pet collar designer, you have a substantial consumer class from which to cull—one that is not about to evaporate with the morning dew.

How Much Does It Cost to Start This Kind of Business?

A minimal investment in materials and equipment—if you don't have them already—is all that is necessary to begin designing leashes or collars. When you determine that you have a saleable product, you can pour additional monies, as needed, in growing your business.

What Qualifications Do You Need for This Kind of Work?

You have to know how to how to make quality leashes and collars, which often asks that you know your way around a sewing machine and all that goes into manufacturing safe and appealing merchandise.

If you want a startling glimpse of the variety of pet collars and leashes selling in today's trade, by all means stop by **Glamour Dog** @ GlamourDog.com (877-GLAM-DOG). On this business's website, you'll encounter such merchandise as the Leopard Print Fur Collar, Diva Mink Collar, Pink Plaid Leather Collar, Candystripe Dog Leash, Faux Ostrich Leash, Playboy Glam Lead, and Swarovski Crystal Retractable Lead. This company also sells collars and leashes with a sports theme: NFL, NHL, NBA, and NASCAR. Other sites worthy of calling on are CoolDogToys.com with its designer collars and leashes—tuscan tiles (on deep purple), baubles (on ice blue), jag (on black), etc.—and BarkSlope.com, with such products as the Tropics Collection Dog Collar, Zip-A-Dee-Dog Collar, and Canini Posy Leather Dog Collar.

How Do You Find Customers?

To initially draw attention to your unique leashes and collars, there are no better places to showcase them than at pet trade shows, general gift shows, and craft fairs. Give out lots of business cards with your website address on them, which, of course, you should have in this day and age. Drop in on retailers who sell such merchandise. You can start slow in this field. Once you prove that your merchandise will sell, contact wholesalers in the trade who might be interested in taking in your leash and collar lines.

Pet Bed Designer

There was a time when household pets were expected to sleep beside your bed, not on your bed, or—perish the thought—in a bed of their very own. When we first leaped into the pet care business in the waning months of the 1970s, there were pet beds around and selling in stores, but the styles and sizes were few in number, hard to come by, and not in any great demand.

The first pet beds that we ever stocked were for cats and very small dogs. They were wicker baskets with pillows in them. Soon we added plain pads and some basic foam beds with removable covers to our not very impressive line of pet-bedding choices. Suffice it to say, the bedding genre catered to a tiny clique of pet owners in those days gone by. The consensus opinion of retailers—and the consuming public as well—was that only the most eccentric pet owners purchased beds for their domestic animals. But again—and it's worth repeating over and over—that was then and this is now. You could become a **pet bed designer** and seller of an increasingly popular and very much in-demand product. Pet beds have moved from the commercial category of luxury to one of necessity, and the marketplace is responding in kind with a bevy of choices. The only thing missing is the matching of pets' beds with their sleep numbers, but that kind of thing could well be in the offing.

Nowadays, it's just short of cruelty to animals to expect King or Princess to sleep on a bare floor or room carpet. As for an old blanket—forget about it! Come on already: this is the twenty-first century and we live in a land of plenty. Traditional parents would never permit their two-legged offspring to rough it sans a bed of their own. Pet parents aren't about to allow the four-legged members of the family to sleep through considerable portions of their lives without beds of their very own.

Today, there are all kinds of pet beds that accommodate cats and dogs based on their special life needs and distinct residential circumstances. That is, there are pet beds made of wide ranges of materials. For instance, there are beds manufactured with special foams to cool pets in summertime and warm them in wintertime. There are bedding products made with fabrics that wage battle with assorted bacteria and the foulest of odors. There are pet beds chiropractically crafted with the senior citizen canine—and all

113

those tired and achy joints—in mind. There are comfortable bed pillows chock-full of natural flea and tick busters like eucalyptus and cedar flakes. Some beds have canopies atop them, while others are shaped just like the living room sofa. And we could go on and on in this vein. The bottom line is that there are pet-bedding alternatives for discerning pet owners that cut a wide swath in styles, sizes, and—increasingly important—fillings and special features.

How Much Does It Cost to Start This Kind of Business?

Design samples and test the waters before mass-producing a line of pet beds. This can be accomplished on a shoestring budget with investment in the needed matcrials.

What Qualifications Do You Need for This Kind of Work?

This brand of business is for people who are designer material—no pun intended.

How Do You Find Customers?

Sell your pet beds to retailers, wholesalers, and directly to consumers. Bring your wares to pet-specialty shops. Attend trade shows. Sell your beds via a website.

Pet Carrier Designer

There comes a time in many pet owners' lives when they need to take their animal companions to destinations their furry and feathery friends would prefer not going to, or where they might need a measure of protection or a degree of isolation from less than welcoming surroundings. It is during these pet-parenting moments that a suitable carrying contraption is required. They are simply known as carriers, carrying cases, carry bags, or totes. And there is a sizeable and growing demand for these essential pieces of merchandise and, hence, the innovation of a **pet carrier designer**.

The pet carrier is yet another product in the trade that has sprouted wings, so to speak, and flown to entrepreneurial plateaus previously unimaginable. When we first entered the retail sliver of the industry, the carrier choices were, to put it bluntly, slim. During our first several years in business, in fact, our wholesalers supplied us with only one style of pet carrier. It sported a clear plastic top, which unbuckled on its side to open up. The pet could then be placed into the carrier from the top. As you can imagine, these kinds of top-loading carriers were rather limited in sizes. After all, they were bona fide "carrying" cases with suitcase handles, so they weren't about to support much weight in them. They accommodated cats and small- to medium-sized dogs. Bigger canines were out of luck. The carriers were also expensive for their day—far more so than the plastic, screw together, kennel cabs that subsequently came down the pike in a wide range of sizes for one and all in the diverse pet populace.

What's most intriguing about the pet carrier business today is that it has branched out into areas beyond the mere utilitarian—beyond taking the cat or dog to the veterinarian, to grandma's house in an automobile, or on an airplane flight to distant climes. Nowadays, shoulder and tote bags sold as pet carriers are remarkably popular. Many of these carry bags are, in fact, purchased for the aforementioned utilitarian missions. But others are bought, foremost, because they look hip and sport designer labels and the like. And now it's in vogue to bring along little Princess and Spot to the supermarket and to the beauty parlor.

The very first pliable pet carrier to hit the stores was affectionately known as a *Sherpa bag.* Indeed, **Sherpa** @ SherpaPet.com (800-743-7723) is widely credited with designing and marketing the "original soft-side pet carrier," which has most definitely ushered in a trend. A peep at what Sherpa is currently selling reveals in living color how fast and furious the pet carrier business is growing. In addition, venture down **Pets Alley** @ PetsAlley.com (303-683-2923) and drop by **Arcata Pet Supplies** @ ArcataPet.com (800-822-9085) for further evidence of what's selling in this fertile entrepreneurial field.

How Much Does It Cost to Start This Kind of Business?

Invest a small sum in designing a winning pet carrier or two or three. Test your product's appeal in the marketplace before going big time and mass-producing anything.

What Qualifications Do You Need for This Kind of Work?

If you have the necessities to design a pet carrier, you are a candidate for this business undertaking. If, however, you are contemplating life as a pet carrier designer, it would be in your interest to comb the advertisements in pet-themed magazines and trade periodicals. You'd also benefit from surfing the Internet and further inhaling the width and breadth of pet carriers on the market. Indeed, the marketplace is inundated with pet carriers manufactured with everything from cardboard to faux leather to mesh to micro-fiber. There are carriers that are airline-approved for cabin carry-on and others that are accepted in cargo. The only advice to dispense with here is: Carry on. The pet carrier business is a slice of the pet care trade with no end to its possibilities.

How Do You Find Customers?

You can sell your pet carriers directly to consumers via a website or advertisements in pet-themed periodicals. Visit pet-specialty shops with samples of your merchandise. Trade and gift shows are always great places to get noticed and get business.

> The pet carrier business is reaching for the stars. **Just Pet Strollers** @ JustPetStrollers.com (877-673-7387) sells a comprehensive line of, you guessed it, pet strollers, and Tori Spelling orders from them. The company stocks renowned brand names, too, including the Jeep Wrangler pet stroller. Indeed, the marketplace is chock-full of what some people might deem unusual pet-carrying equipment, such as papoose carriers for cats and small dogs. There are car booster seats specifically designed for the pet on the go. There are carriers with such labels as the *South Beach Carrier* and the *Pink Passion Tote*. In other words, this is an incredibly broad field in which to at once forage for business ideas and showcase your creativity.

Cat Furniture Maker
Cat Scratching Post Maker

There is considerably more shelf space devoted to dog accessory items than their cat counterparts. In fact, it's no contest. This isn't because of any entrepreneurial bias toward the feline species, although some cat parents think so. Rather, it's because the canine crowd is more apt to play with things, chew on things, pull on things, and consume a greater variety of things. Dogs, too, are more amenable to getting shampooed and getting their teeth brushed— and so there are oodles of bath and oral care products for them that dwarf comparable cat items.

Where cats reign supreme on the merchandise frontier is in the furniture business. Yes—furniture business. With the exception of dog bedding products, furniture for man's (and woman's) best friend is limited by comparison. Conversely, there is cat furniture (trees, towers, condos, etc.) made of wood and some manufactured from unadulterated bark straight from the forest. There are countless variations of this furniture, which, because of their ample size, assume permanent spaces in people's homes and apartments, just like sofas, tables, and chairs. The beauty of cat furniture is that each piece is crafted for cats to do one or more of the things that they do best—climb, scratch, and, of course, nap.

For starters, visit pet food and supply stores and investigate what they are selling in this merchandise area. Surf the Net and observe both the variety and the price tags of the cat furniture for sale. (Just google "cat furniture" and you'll be inundated with stuff.) Ask yourself if you could assemble similar pieces of furniture. If the answer is yes, then you are a prospective **cat furniture maker** and/or **cat scratching post maker**.

We found that a certain percentage of cat people—cat consumers—are always on the lookout for interesting and unique selections of feline furniture. The more unusual and the more elaborate, the better. Manufacturing cat furniture for this expanding group of customers can be simultaneously fun and profitable. It affords you a chance to be creative—to build one-of-a-kind pieces of cat furniture—and to make money along the way. This is the ultimate entrepreneurial one-two punch.

How Much Does It Cost to Start This Kind of Business?

A big investment is not required to get this business up and running. Of course, you are going to require a place to make the furniture—your workshop, as it were. A garage is ideal, but a spare room will do nicely. Then you are going to need the tools of the trade:

- ★ Hammer
- ★ Nails
- ★ Power saw
- ★ Staple gun
- ★ Cutting table
- ★ Level
- ★ Materials (wood, bark, carpeting, sisal, etc.)

What Qualifications Do You Need for This Kind of Work?

During the Pet Nosh years, we sold numerous pieces of cat furniture, as it is rather broadly called. Our chief supplier of this particular merchandise was one man, who manufactured everything in his garage. He not only made the stuff, but also personally delivered it in his truck. We purchased specific pieces of cat furniture from him based on their dimensions and a brief, but thorough description of the accoutrements on each one—*e.g.,* carpeting, enclosures, sisal scratches, perches, etc. Retail prices on some of this furniture soared as high as $300 and sometimes higher than that. For sure, the furniture was the work of a talented individual who possessed indisputable skills with a saw, hammer, and nails. But there are a lot of handy people out there who could build and sell cat furniture—*and you might be one of them.*

How Do You Find Customers?

As in other merchandise bailiwicks, your cat furniture can be sold directly to retailers. Prepare a wholesale price list with descriptions of the available items along with accompanying photographs. Mail them to prospective clients. Personally call on retailers with the aforementioned price list and, if possible, samples of your work. Sell them to wholesalers in the trade by utilizing the same formula.

119

If you want to sell a lot of cat furniture in one fell swoop, you could try hooking up with a pet-specialty retailer in your area and pitching the idea of a "Truckload Sale." We often teamed up with companies for such popular events. How did they work? A wholesaler would pull up with a truckload of merchandise, and we would sell the stuff to our customers. Sometimes, we lined the merchandise up in the front of the store. Occasionally, we sold the goods straight off the truck. We advertised these sales in advance and made them happenings. We frequently did this kind of thing with aquarium products, such as fish tanks. We got our usual cut (the retail price) and then paid the participating company theirs (the wholesale price). The bottom line is that we usually sold a ton of merchandise on these days. For us, the beauty of this brand of selling—beyond the profits—was that the suppliers took their unsold merchandise away afterwards. So, we had everything to gain and nothing to lose. Retailers love these win-win scenarios. Unique cat furniture is the ideal product for such an event. Since the furniture is big and bulky, they will appreciate the fact that you'll drive away with anything that doesn't sell. If you don't have a vehicle big enough to cart your cat furniture around, you could rent a truck or van for the day.

Cat shows, other pet-themed events, flea markets, and craft fairs are also places to peddle your wares. These are locales to get noticed—and get noticed fast. This is where you can network with key players in the pet care trade, and of course, make some money in the process. Entrepreneurs who go forth among the people and press the flesh are the very same people who host many of the cat furniture maker websites. They appear at myriad events with their furniture, talk to a lot of folks, sell plenty of stuff, and—most importantly—give out lots of business cards that encourage visits to their websites and ensure future business.

Don't ignore eBay and other virtual reality sale possibilities. Consider advertising on highly trafficked pet and cat-specific websites that link to your cat furniture business. The materials that go into cat furniture making are relatively cheap when purchased in bulk quantities at lumberyards and home centers. It's your labor that is most costly. Therefore you can charge a fair price and get a fair price in return for your efforts and special talents. Let's say that you are looking for a few extra dollars and are in the cat furniture business as a part-time venture. If you can sell one cat tree a week for $300 with the materials costing $25, that's $275 in your pocket. Is that figure worth your time and energy? It all depends on you and how fast you can produce what people want to buy—and, of course, whether you enjoy doing it.

Pet Casket Maker

Like every other service business in the pet care trade, cemetery, crematory, and memorial enterprises are growing in number. Pet parents are increasingly demanding services and products for their deceased animal friends. Granted, the vast majority of pet owners do not bury their departed cats and dogs on cemetery grounds. Nevertheless, more and more of them are cremating their pets and purchasing such things as engraved urns, plaques, and other appropriate memorials.

Pet cemeteries purchase all kinds and all sizes of pet caskets from casket makers. If you have an aptitude for carpentry, life as a **pet casket maker** could be your calling.

121

To appreciate the width and breadth of what pet cemeteries offer consumers in both products and services, call on a couple of them. **Pet Heaven Memorial Park** @ PetHeaven.com (800-427-1669) is located in Miami, Florida. Among many options, it offers customers bronze memorials shaped like a special treat (a dog bone) and another with a generous-sized paw print. **Sugarloaf Pet Gardens** @ SugarloafPetGardens.org (301-972-8882) can be found in Barnesville, Maryland in close proximity to the Sugarloaf Mountains. This strikingly picturesque burial site plants an individual tree for every pet laid to rest there.

How Much Does It Cost to Start This Kind of Business?

By first manufacturing representative samples of your work, you can start this business on the cheap. That is, invest in the necessary materials to produce attractive and quality caskets and take orders. This will enable you to put money in the bank before you crank up the assembly line.

What Qualifications Do You Need for This Kind of Work?

You need to have the requisite tools that make a carpenter a carpenter, beginning with your competence. Once you are satisfied that your most important tool—your aptitude—is sharp enough, you can work with those other tools of the trade to create what consumers want.

How Do You Find Customers?

These *final resting place* pieces of merchandise can be sold to the aforementioned cemetery outfits, as well as to certain pet-specialty retailers interested in walking the last mile. You could also erect a website and market pet caskets directly to consumers. There is a demand for them and there's nothing macabre about it.

A Bit of Heaven @ ABitofHeaven.com (713-690-7449) promotes itself as the "newest and most beautiful pet cemetery in the city of Houston." Founded in 1996, it is a family owned and operated pet cemetery that affords grieving pet owners a whole host of burial possibilities. For instance, A Bit of Heaven's basic burial prices range from $525 (small plot) to $625 (large plot). Plot maintenance costs range from $25 annually to $100 for five years to $350 for twenty years. Casket options run a wide gamut in both sizes and styles from the regular to the deluxe to the "Very Impressive Pet Casket" known as the V.I.P.C. Casket prices range from $165 to $280.

For a bird's eye view into this snippet of the trade, call on pet bereavement and memorial businesses such as **Faithful Friend** pet caskets and urns @ FaithfulFriendPet.com (800-567-PETS) and **T & S Pet Memorials** @ TSPetMemorials.com (910-575-2943). These two companies, which sell vast and varied merchandise from pet caskets to headstones to engraved urns, furnish consumers with options aplenty in appropriately mourning and remembering their late and cherished animal companions.

In the overall picture, pet owners who opt for a burial more often choose a home version rather than interment in an actual pet cemetery. There are, however, town and city ordinances, and deed restrictions, which very often prohibit this practice (typically for health reasons—e.g., wild creatures digging up the remains). And, of course, if a person is renting, or planning on moving anytime soon, such a burial isn't a prudent idea. Still, pet cemeteries will sell consumers caskets for home burials. They can also be purchased in select pet boutiques, on the Internet, and in some mail-order catalogues.

Bird Feeder Maker ✤ Birdhouse Maker ✤ Wild Birds Unlimited Franchise ✤ Wild Bird Centers of America Franchise

As our retail stores grew in both numbers and square feet, we took in more and more pieces of wild bird merchandise, including lines of bird feeders and birdhouses. If you have the imposing one-two punch of artistic and carpentry talents, and can manufacture these popular products, you could be a **bird feeder maker** and/or **birdhouse maker** and make some green along the way.

Bird feeders and birdhouses are products that may be *literally* for the birds, but as moneymaking entrepreneurial fodder they are, most assuredly, not for the birds. We discovered this fact of business life during our retail run in the pet care trade. Sure, we sold many bird feeders and birdhouses through the years, but they weren't what we'd deem colossal sellers. That was because, above all else, we catered to parents of cats, dogs, caged birds, and other household pets. Admittedly, parents and overseers of the wild and free animal kingdom got short shrift from us. Nevertheless, we did indeed peddle tons and tons of wild birdseed, most especially in wintertime when demand went through the birdhouse roof. The natural conclusion we drew from the brisk sales of this perpetually purchased product was that those many bags of seed our customers took home with them ended up in bird feeders—thousands upon thousands of them. One further extrapolation we made was that many—if not most—of these devoted wild birdseed customers also had birdhouses on their properties as well.

How Much Does It Cost to Start This Kind of Business?

To begin the manufacturing of bird feeders and birdhouses, you need the tools of the trade: hammer, nails, saws, etc. And, of course, you require the materials that will go into the overall production process of your business undertaking: woods, glass, paints, etc. There are numerous types of bird feeders. As for birdhouses, they cannot be pigeonholed, so to speak. Many are utilitarian; others are more ornamental than practical. Some are both ornamental and practical. This means that you have a tremendous amount of leeway in this entrepreneurial bailiwick.

Check out **Wild Birds Forever** @ BirdsForever.com to get a grip on the width and breadth of possibilities for entrepreneurs in this fertile field. This company sells a vast and varied range of merchandise for outdoor birds. Among this bird business's popular sellers in the feeder class are: wood-hopper-style feeders, metal bird feeders, recycled plastic feeders, seed and suet bird feeders, platform feeders, decorative copper-topped feeders, decorative redwood songbird feeders, decorative painted feeders, decorative stained glass feeders, large capacity and gazebo bird feeders, tubular bird feeders, triple tube feeders, globe feeders for small clinging birds, window feeders, suet feeders, thistle/finch feeders, fruit feeders, blue bird feeders, seed cake feeders, woodpecker feeders, and squirrel-proof bird feeders and baffles.

It's entirely up to you to ascertain what you are capable of and what you want to do with your talents. Then you have to do it—and this is what separates the business success stories from the mere dreamers. For instance, you can mass-produce simple and functional bird feeders and birdhouses. There is a consistent demand for just these kinds of products that do what they are supposed to do—feed and house outdoor birds. Or, you could customize birdhouses for individuals. Make a birdhouse that looks like the local post office or one that resembles a church replete with an attractive steeple. If your faith in your artistic abilities knows no boundaries, then go to it and produce a diverse line of wild bird merchandise. The bottom line is that this business endeavor can be initiated with minimal initial investment dollars.

What Qualifications Do You Need for This Kind of Work?

You have to be able to pick out a hammer and nails in a lineup. That is, you should know the difference between a kitchen spatula and a screwdriver. The making of bird feeders and birdhouses boils down to you knowing what you are doing and turning out quality products that people will buy. If you produce bird feeders and birdhouses that are durable, you'll have little difficulty finding customers, be they retail storeowners, wholesalers, or consumers in the wild bird-loving public.

How Do You Find Customers?

Depending on the particular style of bird feeders and/or birdhouses that you opt to manufacture, there are multiple and diverse avenues to travel down to sell them. Selling them directly to retailers in the pet care trade is the most obvious place. Keep in mind that many non-pet-specialty shops also stock bird feeders and birdhouses. Garden centers sell a lot of wild bird merchandise. Of course, you would need to charge wholesale prices to these stores, so you have to determine if it's worth your time and effort to do so at what they'd be willing to plunk down for your stuff. You have to make a fair profit and they have to make a fair profit—that's how it works.

If you're very prolific in your production process, you could likewise sell to wholesalers, who would in turn sell them to retail outlets. You'd then need to come up with prices that would make your items attractive to these buyers—sub-wholesale prices. Of course, selling them directly to the buying public—at the full retail price—would be the most profitable. You can sell your bird feeders and birdhouses at craft fairs and flea markets. Inaugurate a website and sell them from cyberspace with no middlemen sharing in the proceeds. As always, the best bet is to pursue all of the above and more.

The proof is in the pudding or, in this instance, in the suet cakes. If you have any lingering doubt that there is indeed a robust market for wild bird merchandise, visit a franchise business exclusively devoted to the sale of—yes—wild bird merchandise. **Wild Birds Unlimited** @ WBU.com (888-730-7108) and **Wild Bird Centers of America** @ WildBird.com (800-WILD-BIRD) are franchise opportunities to weigh if you have investment capital and the yearning to operate a retail business. To open up a Wild Birds Unlimited store, the company estimates start-up investment costs in the neighborhood of $100,000 to $150,000, depending on the size and location of the shop.

Pet Photographer

If you patronize pet food and supply superstores, you've no doubt noticed that these mega-retailers offer a range of specialty services. We're talking about training and grooming, as well as daycare and hotel accommodations for companion animals. Also in this scintillating mixture of pet-themed services is photography—pet portrait taking and such. Do you know the ABCs of photography and how to operate a camera? If you do, you are a candidate for the fruitful entrepreneurial opportunity of **pet photographer**.

How Much Does It Cost to Start This Kind of Business?

If you are interested in renting a location for a photographic studio and purchasing costly equipment, you are going to need an infusion of investment capital ($15,000–$25,000). Conversely, if you want to offer your services as a roving photographer—a photographer-for-hire who goes to his or her customers—you could clearly get a business off the ground with considerably less of an investment. Either way, you are going to have to make yourself a known quantity via promotional efforts of some sort. How much you expend in your advertising labors is entirely up to you. And the nature of your photography business would determine your promotional selections.

Surf on over to one of the Web's most edifying sites on the art of picture taking—Photography.com. This portal of information furnishes articles and advice aplenty on photographic matters that range far and wide, from equipment to color and lighting to techniques. There are also copious materials to peruse on the increasingly popular digital photography.

What Qualifications Do You Need for This Kind of Work?

Quality photograph-taking is an art form. You have to know how to take a good picture. This is the fundamental qualification that you need for this kind of work. You don't have to be the next Ansel Adams. No college degree or special certification is required to call oneself a photographer or to operate a business in this field. Nevertheless, it helps to have taken courses or completed studies in the ways and means of picture taking.

It's also important to keep in mind that you'll be working with pets. This is an additional challenge for the pet photographer. Getting pets to pose for pictures isn't always a piece of cake. And pet photographers are often asked to capture that frolicking dog or cat in the great outdoors. This is yet another considerable challenge for the pet photographer, but a genuine opportunity, too.

Whatever your picture-taking aptitude, you will need a photo portfolio to win over customers. Prospective clients are going to want to check out your work. They won't just take your word for it in this entrepreneurial endeavor. Remember the old saying, "One picture is worth a thousand words." In the photography business, it's worth even more than that. Show—don't tell!

The **New York Institute of Photography** @ NYIP.com (800-445-7279) is the country's most venerable photography school. If you are contemplating a career in pet photography and feel that you lack the critical skills, or need to sharpen your current photographic know-how, NYIP offers a wealth of online courses. Never lose sight of the fact that quality photography encompasses more than just saying, "Smile, say 'cheese,'" and pressing a button on a camera.

How Do You Find Customers?

Many pet photographers are finding work via alliances with pet-specialty retailers. It's a logical marriage. Photographers offer their services on mutually agreed-upon dates that are advertised in advance in the stores' windows, via fliers, and in other promotions. The retailers then get a cut of all the picture-taking business that is generated. If you can partner with a business or multiple businesses in this way, you could do very well without a leased studio or any kind of brick-and-mortar location. Pet consumers materialize in large numbers every single day of every week at these hot spots. These are the ideal places to chum for photography business.

Is there really a broad market for pet photography? You better believe there is. And the proof is in the pudding—or, in this instance, the pictures. In today's technologically driven world, photographic possibilities are many, including the computer/digital imaging process. Contemplate all that you can do with digital photographs. Shall we count the ways? These photographs are placed on everything from T-shirts to beach towels to patches of quilt to throw rugs. The entrepreneurial possibilities in digital imaging alone are staggering.

129

Photographic Evidence

There could be no more apropos time than the present to recount a Pet Nosh occasion of monumental proportions. Of course, it has something to do with the incredible power of the photograph. That is, the lengths that pet parents will go in bringing their animal companions into the world of the two-legged. Let's turn the clock back a few years—to 1985, as a matter of fact. This was the year that we hosted what was—at that snapshot in time—a truly novel event. Appropriately christened "Have Your Pet's Picture Taken with Santa Claus," this affair was scheduled to commence at seven o'clock on a December eve, just minutes after our store officially closed for business. It was a cold night with a mixture of rain and sleet pellets falling from the skies. We surmised that this unwelcome present from Mother Nature did not augur well for us.

Nevertheless, we had advertised the occasion for weeks. An enormous sign was posted in the shop's front window. We ran ads in local newspapers. And, we must have plopped a couple thousand fliers into our customers' shopping bags. The extravaganza was billed as our way of saying "thank you" to our loyal patrons. The picture was free and no reservations were required. Still, we were clueless as to what to expect from a happening of this kind. To our knowledge, it had never been tried before. We considered ourselves the Lewis and Clark of this unique pet promotion of inviting the furry and four-legged to visit with Ol' Saint Nick, long the sole prerogative of little boys and girls.

As the bewitching hour approached, we wondered if the night would be a total washout, and not merely because of the inclement weather. It was, after all, a rather peculiar concept. Asking people to venture out into the darkness and chill of a winter eve, just days before Christmas, was one thing. But asking them to bring their pets along for the ride—well, that was something else entirely. Would only a handful of pet-owning eccentrics show up? Would there be a cacophony of barking, brawls (two-legged and four-legged!), and nervous pets relieving themselves in every nook and cranny of the store? Time would soon answer all of our questions.

As anticipated, the clock spoke volumes. Hours before Santa dropped down our chimney, customers and their dogs began congregating in the store. A hearty band of pet owners wanted to make history, with their pets counted among the very first furry creatures to pose on Santa's lap for a photograph. To quell the growing and restless minions, we hastily scribbled "reservation numbers" on shreds of scrap paper and passed them out.

As the scheduled kick-off time drew nearer, it became apparent to the Pet Nosh team that "Have Your Pet's Picture Taken with Santa Claus" was going to be big...*really big*. We found ourselves surrounded by more than our regular clientele and their canine companions. Men and women who had never set foot in Pet Nosh before were also materializing in large numbers. Their dogs accompanied them, but so did their cats, birds, ferrets, hamsters, snakes, iguanas, and even turtles.

We felt as if we were deck hands on Noah's Ark, ushering one and all into some semblance of an organized line—a line that soon was out the front door, into the parking lot, and winding around a block leading into a residential neighborhood. It was an amazing spectacle to behold.

Despite the persisting precipitation turning increasingly icy, people and their diverse menagerie of pets just kept on coming. Drivers on the heavily trafficked Central Avenue in Yonkers, where this Pet Nosh store called home, were honking their horns and staring in astonishment at the hundreds of pet owners and their animal mates standing in a twisting row in the frosty darkness.

By today's retail yardsticks, this Pet Nosh store of ours was microscopic in size. Pet food and supply superstores didn't yet blanket the highways and byways of America. Thus, our very modest parking lot was predictably jam-packed. If they desired having their pets' pictures snapped in the presence of the man with the white beard and red suit, many folks were compelled to park on faraway back streets and walk long distances.

Mr. Claus was indeed run ragged in his two-hour layover at Pet Nosh that night, as one pet after another was plopped onto his busy lap. His celebrated patience was sorely tested. In fact, in the midst of the proceedings, we were duty-bound to send out for more film. Fortunately, a Waldbaum's supermarket across the street had a photo department, which stocked the instant film we needed, or we might have had a full-blown riot on our hands.

When the last pet's picture was taken, the Pet Nosh staff was a weary bunch. We were left to reflect on what had just transpired. For sure, the promotion was a smashing success. The hundreds of men and women who braved the elements and patiently waited on a lengthy line—in some instances, for hours—couldn't stop talking about it. And we were likewise awestruck. The night was at once festive and downright bizarre, but positively indicative of what was around the corner for the business of pets.

This curious event in one small store was a microcosm of an entire industry and a societal mind-set. It illustrated in living color what was occurring within the confines of the pet care trade at large, as well as in the hearts and minds of the pet-owning populace. The longtime lifeless and grubby world of pet commerce was a thing of the past.

If pet owners were perfectly willing to stand outside in the darkness of night, with a cold rain and sleet falling on them, to have their pets' pictures taken with Santa Claus, what else would they do for their animal brethren? As this entire book demonstrates in edifying detail: *a whole lot more*. Today, Santa Claus picture taking at pet-specialty retailers is commonplace. But the bottom line is that pet photography has assumed a life of its own. There are numerous profitable avenues to venture down in this field.

Pet Artist

The width and breadth of today's pet care trade is a genuine boon to artists with a broad range of talents and specialties. Courtesy of our tremendous devotion to the four-legged in our households, a legitimate and conspicuous market has burst open for the **pet artists** among us. If you are gifted artist, there are many lucrative pathways to venture down in the green fields known as pet commerce.

How Much Does It Cost to Start This Kind of Business?

Selling customized works of pet art—be they oil paintings, watercolors, woodcarvings, pencil sketches, etc.—is not the kind of work where a physical presence on Main Street is required to make money. Of course, if you have the appropriate artistic aptitude, a portfolio full of works, and testimonials that'll garner you both attention and business, you could lease a brick-and-mortar location. But for the preponderance of struggling artists, this route isn't very practical. And, really, it's wholly unnecessary when most of these artistic services can be accomplished from the comforts of home.

What Qualifications Do You Need for This Kind of Work?

You make the call. You ascertain whether or not you have what it takes to be an in-demand pet artist. To call yourself an artist, a university degree from an art school isn't a must. Nevertheless, a formal education in your field of endeavor can only help in enhancing your credibility as the genuine article. But, when all is said and done, if you are going to catch both the eyes and pocketbooks of pet-parenting consumers, you have to be good at what you do, whether you call yourself a painter, sculptor, or digital artist turning out pop-art portraits. What can be classified art is a very subjective business, and, yes, art is in the eye of the beholder. But it ordinarily takes a fair share

133

of artistic flair to achieve recognition and generate sustained business as an artist—and, more specifically, a pet artist.

The diversity of the artistically endowed strutting their stuff in the business of pets can be nicely gleaned on the Net. Several websites worth looking over are **Pets In Pastel** @ PetsInPastel.com, with lifelike portraits by artist Sarah Theophilus; **Pet Portraits** @ PortraitsOfAnimals.com from artist Cherie Vergos; **Hands of Caesar** @ DogSculptures.com, with animal sculptures, oil on canvas paintings, and more by artist Caesar Yanez; and **Art Paw** @ ArtPaw.com (888-225-4278), which does pop-art portraits inspired by the unique and colorful style of the late Andy Warhol. Finally, surf on over to the **League of Animal Artists** @ AnimalArtists.org. Here you'll encounter information on pet artists in general, including listings and biographies of many talented folks in this exhilarating and emergent creative field.

How Do You Find Customers?

The life of a pet artist often requires a jumpstart. And there's no better way for an artist to prove his or her mettle than by going out among the people. Artists who strut their stuff in the public square get noticed and, if they are good at what they do, business too. If you are supremely confident in your capacity as a bona fide artist, approach pet-specialty retailers and ask if you can set up a table in their stores to display your special talents. Offer them a percentage of the generated sales. Appear at as many pet-themed shows and arts and crafts fairs as possible. Make yourself visible in pet-parenting circles. Put up a website and pass out business cards pointing people to it.

Let the masses see what you've done and don't be shy about letting others sing your praises. Testimonials from satisfied clients will bring you more and more business.

Pet Writer

As the business of pets charts new territory with each tick of the clock, a concurrent demand exists for information and the men and women who can furnish it by way of the pen—the written word. There is a genuine need for the **pet writer**.

If there is any doubt about the opportunities that exist for pet writers, just look around. Peruse the pet sections of bookstores. Comb the magazine racks in the same stores and on newsstands for pet-themed periodicals. Surf the Internet for pet-inspired websites. There are more pet books, pet magazines, and pet websites than ever before. The common thread that binds them all is the pet writer.

What Qualifications Do You Need for This Kind of Work?

If you have the ability to string together several literate sentences, you may have what it takes to be a pet writer. You may be able to make some bucks by getting a magazine article published. You may see your words careening through virtual reality. You may even get a book deal. Who knows?

The writing business is completely subjective. Granted, in the real world, most people are not cut from the writer's cloth. Writing, after all, is a craft. But this doesn't stop many folks from writing and writing some more, valiantly trying to get published somewhere and by somebody.

It's entirely up to you to make the determination whether or not you can parlay your abilities into an article or a full-length book. If you truly believe you have the capacity to convert your knowledge of pets—cat, dog, bird, or whatever is your specialty—into words that people will appreciate reading, then go for it. Don't sell yourself short.

135

If you have a pet book idea, visit **Bow Tie Press** @ BowTiePress.com. On the company website, this publisher of pet books and magazines includes a link for "Manuscript Guidelines." Another publisher of solely pet books is **T.H.F.** @ THFPublications.com. Check out the kinds of books these companies publish and ascertain if your manuscript idea is in sync with them. If your book is not the right fit, don't waste your time and money printing and mailing materials to them. Look elsewhere.

How Do You Find Writing Jobs?

If you are interested in writing pet articles for compensation, first check out the popular consumer magazines: *Cat Fancy*, *Dog Fancy*, *Dog World*, *Bird Talk*, *Aquarium Fish*, etc. Get a feel for the kinds of articles and stories they publish. Most of the general interest pet-parenting magazines want informational pieces that address care issues. In other words, you have a better chance getting an article published on subjects like training, grooming, and nutritional concerns than on what a unique and colorful pet you have. In addition, cat and dog magazines often feature breed-specific articles.

Another fertile area to explore for writing opportunities is the industry's trade publications, such as **Pet Product News** @ PetProductNews.com, **Pet Age** @ PetAge.com, and **Pet Business** @ PetBusiness.com. These industry bibles are chock-full of feature articles written for the trade's movers and shakers: manufacturers, wholesalers, retailers, and service providers. Trade publications consistently need competent writers with knowledge of the products and trends in the industry.

If you have what you deem a viable pet book idea, you could try to get a literary agent to represent you to the publishing trade. The fact is that most of the biggest book publishers around will only consider material submitted to their editors via literary agents. This is important: If your idea is solid, you could very possibly pitch it with a book proposal instead of a fully completed manuscript. There are many routes to attaining the services of legitimate literary agents, including books with lists of names and contact information, what they represent, and what they've sold. The **Association of Authors' Representatives** @ AAR-Online.org lists members in good standing of their organization. **Publishers Marketplace** @ PublishersMarketplace.com has many literary agents as members. **Writers Net** @ WritersNet.com is another website chock-full of information, including materials on literary agents. It's critical that you always keep in mind that no legitimate literary agent will ever ask you for money. If you are asked to pay for representation or editing fees, head for the tall grass. There are many fish in this sea.

Pet Reference Book Author

Some of the most successful book titles in the area of pet care are reference works. A compelling example of a popular reference title addresses the topic of pet-friendly travel. In fact, there are several pet-friendly travel books in print. The reason for the growing and enduring popularity of this particular brand of reference book—and the competing titles are frequently revised and updated—is that more pet parents than ever before desire taking their animal companions with them when they travel and when they vacation. Thus, these various books fill an important and not insubstantial informational niche for thousands of pet owners. Perhaps you have an idea for a reference work and want to be the next **pet reference book author**. There are multiple pet-parenting niches out there that would welcome a book into their cubbyholes.

How Much Does It Cost to Start This Kind of Project?

The research and writing of a pet reference book doesn't have to cost you much beyond your time and effort—assuming you already have the tools of the trade, which most definitely include a computer and access to the Internet in this day and age. Remember too that a well-researched book may require some traveling on your part, as well as a lot of phone calls. But any travel expenses and such would largely depend on the nature of the work under consideration.

Where you would need an initial investment of real dollars is at publishing time. Of course, you could endeavor to have your manuscript published by a mainstream publisher in the book trade. This wouldn't cost you a cent outside of, perhaps, printing costs and postage to mail the project to interested literary agents and publishers. But there are no guarantees of success here. However, there are other routes to take to get your book into print, including self-publishing. That is, you could independently print the book and procure a book distributor to get it into stores and other consumer markets. If you categorically believe in the quality of the book and want to get it into the hands of the purchasing public, this is definitely an avenue worth exploring, as many others have realized success in circumventing traditional publishing channels.

That said, self-publishing is not a sure thing and should not be approached as a vanity effort. You might be expending $5,000 to $10,000 just to realize a small first printing. Independent publishing involves a whole range of start-up costs, including book cover design, interior typesetting, printing, distribution, promotions, etc. However, if you have a solid product that consumers want, you can realize a profit—maybe not immediately, but over time—and you might also attract the attention of a big-time publisher interested in purchasing the rights to your book.

By attaining the services of an established and respected independent press distributor to the book trade, such as **Midpoint Trade Books** @ MidpointTrade.com (212-727-0190), a scrupulously researched and written book, combined with attractive packaging and price, can find readerships in bookstores and other profitable markets. A fledgling book business can simultaneously pursue opportunities outside of traditional book channels: gift shops, independent booksellers, libraries via **Quality Books** @ Quality-Books.com (800-323-4241), the largest small press library book distributor, as well as via the Internet.

What Qualifications Do You Need for This Kind of Work?

Writing a book is not for everybody. It's a laborious undertaking from start to finish—certainly not for the faint of heart or those with negligible attention spans. And when the book in question is research-intensive, this is even more the case. Of course, the craft of writing is a talent but what we are talking about here is generating a book that is more about quality reference than quality writing. In other words, you could compensate for a shortage of writing skills with a solid research effort. And no matter what plateau you are on vis-à-vis the art of writing, there are always editors-for-hire who could assist you. Sometimes all you need is a winning book idea, as there are many qualified people out there who could aid you in the process of converting a sellable notion into the genuine article—publishable material.

A rather thorough website with a bounty of free information on book publishing can be found @ BookMarket.com. It is run by author and self-publishing guru John Kremer. Several free databases are available on his site that cut a wide swath in both the self-publishing and conventional publishing bailiwicks. There are lists with contact information of book printers, book cover artists, book distributors, mainstream publishing editors, and much more to aid you in your journey of transforming a good idea into a published book selling in the marketplace.

How Do You Find Customers?

If you produce a finished book and sign on with a distributor to the trade, you can do many things to generate sales for your title. Complementing any sales work done via the actual distributor, your book business can simultaneously promote its title (or titles) by at once innovating and utilizing such tried and true methods as:

- ★ Mailing review copies to appropriate newspaper and magazine editors
- ★ Distributing press releases to various media announcing author availability for television, radio, or print interviews
- ★ Website and Internet promotion
- ★ Advertising in relevant periodicals

In addition, as a fundamental part of your book business's short-term and long-term strategies, you can pursue rights offerings of your work to the bigger publishers, and, if and when it is deemed a profitable route to take, sell a title's rights. Opportunities to sell said rights can be sought independently (e.g., @ publishersmarketplace.com), through literary agents, or by way of a book distributor's cooperative advertising at industry trade shows.

Birth of a Notion

What kinds of information and reference materials could work for a full-length pet-themed book? What follows are some ideas that we will throw out onto the stoop and see if the cat licks them up, so to speak. You could research a reference book called *A Pet-pourri of Products and Services*, documenting the incredible diversity of what's available to consumers in today's trade. How about a reference work entitled *The Right Relationship Is Everything: Choosing Your Best Friend*, with important information on locating the most compatible animal companion possible.

Pet Parenting 101: Dog Ownership ABCs or *Pet Parenting 101: Cat Ownership ABCs*, books chock-full of information and resources for wet-behind-the-ears pet owners, would have a market. *Surviving Basic Training: Training Your Dog...and Yourself*—a self-explanatory concept. Another very fertile reference area is the field of pet nutrition, which is at once wide and contentious, so why not *They Are What They Eat, Too: Dog Diet ABCs* or *They Are What They Eat, Too: Cat Diet ABCs.*

Maybe a reference book about veterinary choices could work called *Is There a Doctor in the Doghouse? Canine Health and Wellness* or *Is There a Doctor in the Cathouse? Feline Health and Wellness.* Proper hygiene and appearance issues in a book entitled *Looking and Feeling Like a Million Bucks (Before Taxes): Dogs and Grooming* might just have attractive legs.

With more and more pet hotels and new-look kennels sprouting up across the fruited plane, *Your Vacationing Dog: Boarding Your Pet in the Twenty-first Century* would find a hungry readership. Yet another interesting idea with real reference possibilities is *It Isn't Your Grandmother's Pet Care Trade Anymore: The Most Unusual Canine Products on the Planet.*

You want a few more pet reference book ideas to weigh and debate their merits? Well, how about *A Twenty-first Century Pet's Prerogative: People Services Go to the Dogs, Sharing Your Pet with the Wider World: Breeding, Clubs, Shows, and Internet Chats,* and *Final Thoughts: Pet Cemeteries, Memorials, and Pet Loss Grief Counseling.* This brainstorming could go on and on. Many of these reference book suggestions could also be combined. The sky's the limit.

CHAPTER VI

Merchandise for Pet People

Pet Button Maker

People love expressing their undying devotion to their one-of-a-kind pets: cats, dogs, birds, and even lizards, snakes, and hamsters. They also love sporting pin-back buttons. The simplest and least expensive method of melding these two hearts together is by arming pet parents with pet-themed buttons—by getting this dedicated brigade of consumers to wear buttons on their jackets and shirts with such slogans as "I Love My Dog" and "I Love My Cat."

We sold a variety of buttons during our retail run. Many of the pin backs were breed-specific: "I Love My Lhasa Apso," "I Love My Persian," "I Love My Cocker Spaniel," "I Love My Maine Coon," etc. We placed the buttons for sale near the store checkouts. In other words, many of our button sales were impulse purchases. Countless customers thought nothing of adding a $1.00 or $2.00 pin-back button to their bags of dog food and cans of cat food. Are you ready to enter the pressing business of **pet button maker**?

How Much Does It Cost to Start This Kind of Business?

Becoming a manufacturer of pet buttons is as straightforward as buying a machine. There are basic, hand-held apparatuses that can be had for under $50 and, of course, more elaborate equipment that cost hundreds and even thousands of dollars. *How far do you want to take this entrepreneurial venture?* That's the $64,000 question for you to answer.

For sure, you can make a few extra dollars as a part-time button entrepreneur. In fact, this is one of the most popular businesses for kids to launch. Purchase a machine you can afford. Acquire the requisite button parts. Get going. You can likewise take this business concept to a higher level with more expensive paraphernalia and a marketing plan to make things happen in a big way.

If you are considering making the pet button business your own, look no further than **Badge-A-Minit** @ BadgeAMinit.com (800-223-4103). This venerable button and badge business has been around for more than thirty years and is considered the industry leader. Purchase a hand-held button machine here for under $50. Depending on your business plan, they offer many more expensive varieties, too. Other button machine companies to explore include **American Button Machines** @ AmericanButtonMachines.com (972-985-5074) and **Dr. Don's Buttons, Badges & More** @ ButtonsOnline.com (800-243-8293). These two outfits sell button design CDs, which can help you conceive the coveted pet buttons of the future. If you have big button business in your mind from the get-go, you would do well to visit **Badge Parts** @ BadgeParts.com (800-776-3633).

What Qualifications Do You Need for This Kind of Work?

Manufacturing and selling buttons is not rocket science. With all kinds of computer artwork programs available—even some CDs that are button specific—you can design your own buttons with pet-related themes and slogans. With minimal effort in this uber-technological age of ours, the designs can be quite colorful and snappy. If this isn't feasible, you can have a button company's art department, or a local print shop, do this job for you. Button machines from the simplest to more complex are transitory, too, so you can bring them along with you to all kinds of places, including community events and flea markets.

How Do You Find Customers?

Depending on where you want to take your button business, there are numerous selling avenues to traverse. The aforementioned flea markets are ideal events to peddle pet-themed buttons, even the simplest ones—like the "I Love" series. The bottom line is that you can manufacture buttons for 30¢, 40¢, and 50¢ and retail them for $1.50, $2.00, and more.

If you're thinking big, design a flier with your merchandise line and mail them to as many retailers as possible. As part of the sales package, send a sample or two of representative pins in your merchandise line. As harried retailers, we were always more impressed by this brand of show-and-tell, particularly when we received unsolicited materials in the mail.

That said, it is not to imply that dropping off your flier and sample buttons in person is a bad idea. Where geographically feasible, this route could prove very fruitful. But avoid the hard sell sales approach with full-length presentations of your merchandise. Surprise visits from aggressive salespeople—or anybody trying to sell something—are not appreciated by retailers, who are often very busy and in the middle of something. The hectic reality is that people are trying to sell businesses things all day long—everything from telephone service plans to a wide range of can't-miss, must-have merchandise lines.

Nevertheless, just popping in and asking a store manager or an owner if you could leave your stuff for interested parties to take a look at in a spare moment is perfectly acceptable. It's not rude or pushy in any way and often produces results. You might even be given some on-the-spot time and, better yet, an on-the-spot order. If not, you'll more than likely have your product considered at a later time, and you'll be remembered as a good-mannered guy or gal. These are the kinds of people we preferred dealing with in the business realm. Be aggressive in your selling objectives, but always courteous. Never lose sight of the fact that it always takes two to tango in business.

If you want to kick your button-making business up a notch, consider peddling your merchandise at pet trade shows, where you can lock in orders with retailers and wholesalers all across the country. You just might make a business friend for life and find yourself on the receiving end of repeat orders for years to come. And, above all else, that's what businesspersons want—repeat business.

> When selling buttons to businesses and organizations, it will certainly aid sales if you offer them something to display the pins on, too. Cardboard displays are available through many button machine and parts companies. You can also create your own displays with a little ingenuity. All these displays need to do is hold pins and stand on countertops.

Pet Bumper Sticker Seller

While toiling on the retail frontlines, we discovered that a fair portion of our customers couldn't wait to unburden themselves and reveal the intimate details of their lives and times. Being in a pet-specialty business, we naturally heard every conceivable pet and pet parenting tale. Regularly lending open *and sympathetic* ears to our clientele, we deduced that working in retail is not unlike the bartending profession. We listened to countless customer boasts—as well as every imaginable trial and tribulation—concerning their beloved animal companions. It went with the territory.

What does all of this have to do with you making a buck in the pet care trade? Well, mining this peculiar quirk of human nature—*to reveal*—has made many entrepreneurs a pretty piece of change through the years. You, too, can make money in a sliver of this very deep mine—as a **pet bumper sticker seller**. Yes, people want to expose parts of themselves to others—it's as simple as that. No, this has nothing to do with a guy wearing a raincoat—it's about interior revelations. They want to tell you that their son or daughter is an honor student. They want to tell you whom they're supporting for president as well as selectman. And, where we're most concerned here: They want to alert the world about their incredible devotion to the particular members of their family on four legs or covered in feathers.

> Although the old-fashioned bumper sticker is still the market leader, it has some serious competition with its magnetized cousin. That is, many people are loath to put adhesive bumper stickers on their vehicles because they are hard to get off. The alternative for them is either no bumper sticker at all or a magnetized version that can be effortlessly removed when the time is right. These magnetized bumper stickers can, of course, be placed anywhere on a vehicle with no sticky residue to fret over. Contemporary bumper sticker makers carry these increasingly popular substitutes for expressing an opinion or revealing a feeling.

What better place to express our opinions and reveal our innermost feelings than on the backs of our cars. Sporting bumper stickers on our automobiles is a noble and longstanding American tradition. As you negotiate the highways and byways, take note of all the bumper stickers on the rear ends of vehicular traffic. Then contemplate the originators and sellers of them. Entrepreneurs are the sticky glue behind these bumper stickers.

How Much Does It Cost to Start This Kind of Business?

You could start a bumper sticker business on the cheap—for under $100 in some cases—by placing a small order from a bumper sticker manufacturer. In fact, there are some bumper sticker companies that have a vast selection of in-stock slogans to choose from. This means that you do not have to submit original artwork and all the particulars that go into designing customized items. Rather, you can readily find "I Love" bumper stickers for any particular breed of cat or dog. You could likewise find pet-themed bumper stickers with slogans for a more general audience of pet consumers—*e.g.,* "The More I Know Man, The More I Love My Dog," etc.

To experience the width and breadth of the bumper sticker business, visit **Customized Stickers** @ CustomizedStickers.com (800-STICKERS), **Absorbent, Ink** @ AbsorbentPrinting.com (866-618-3471), and **Make Stickers** @ MakeStickers.com (800-3-GRAPHIC). These companies can furnish you with copious information on customizing bumper stickers, including pricing details. They will enlighten you, too, on the many possibilities in the bumper sticker business. In your own travels, you very likely have noticed that bumper stickers are all over the place. Marrying the perennially popular and ubiquitous bumper sticker with today's pet merchandise bonanza is an obvious moneymaker for those with the right avenues to sell them.

How Do You Find Customers?

There are millions of cat and dog owners. They are everywhere—in every city and in every town. Sell your bumper stickers to local retailers. Don't confine your selling labors to pet-themed shops. Bumper stickers sell in places like gift, stationary, and convenience stores. If, for instance, you have an in with your veterinarian, groomer, or trainer, you could sell your pet bumper stickers via their offices. If you know of local clubs dedicated to individual pet breeds, you could sell them bumper stickers that tout their fondness for their preferred felines and canines. You could sell bumper stickers at flea markets and pet-related shows of all kinds. Unique bumper stickers can be placed on eBay.

Sell your bumper stickers to businesses with an option to purchase a bumper sticker rack. We sold our "I Love" breed series of bumper stickers via racks on the front counters of our stores. Customers regularly thumbed through them to find their favorites. The bumper stickers were placed in alphabetical order in the racks. Had they been plopped in boxes somewhere, we would not have sold near as many as we did—and we would not have easily known which breeds of bumper stickers needed reordering.

Pet T-Shirt Peddler

What are screen printers for anyway? Everyday, these industrious entrepreneurs crank out thousands upon thousands of imprinted t-shirts, sweatshirts, hats, carry bags—you name it. Who do you think prints the script and logos on all of those little league uniforms and the hampers full of school athletic wear? Screen printers.

When you peruse the popular pet magazines of the day, you encounter advertisements for every imaginable pet product and pet service. In living color, you experience the width and breadth of the pet care trade. It truly knows no bounds. Spotted very often in the merchandise for sale mix are t-shirts and related stuff—all with catchy designs or slogans, such as "If YOU don't talk to your CAT about catnip, who will?" and, a timeless favorite, "Pets Are People Too." These are pet-themed products for the two-legged, which represent an important and expanding subset in the thriving trade. Be it something to wear or to hang on the wall—it doesn't matter—people want pet-inspired items for themselves.

A life as a **pet t-shirt peddler** has its perks. Emblazoning pet themes and designs on t-shirts is really a simple business enterprise to get off the ground. You see, selling pet-themed t-shirts has got nothing to do with fashion designing, because all that is required of you is originating appealing and unusual sayings about cats and about dogs (and, if you like, about other family pets). In addition, if you require artwork, you can more than likely generate it on your computer (or, if you are artistically inclined, sketch it out by hand). If none of that is feasible, bring your concept to a screen printer. A qualified screen printer will then run with the idea, including generating artwork for you.

How Much Does It Cost to Start This Kind of Business?

With as little as a few hundred dollars investment, you could be selling t-shirts and other imprinted items in a variety of places to a variety of individuals and business entities. Here's how it works. You will have to pay a screen printer an initial setup charge for each t-shirt design you want printed. Then you will select the kind of t-shirts you want—100% cotton, 50/50, etc. You pick a t-shirt color or colors. You choose sizes. You get a price quote. Naturally, shop around for a screen printer that is right for you. There are many screen printers to choose from, including online screen-printing businesses. When you feel you have found someone that you can work with and who offers a price that you can live with—a price that will enable you to earn a fair profit—you are up and running.

It's important to keep in mind that when you have t-shirts and other materials printed on, you needn't operate with a giant inventory. You can always return to the screen printer and order more of what you need and when you need it. Many people make the big mistake of placing huge t-shirt orders from the get-go, and then find very few takers for their stuff. Others have seen certain shirt sizes languish forever in cardboard boxes. Ditto certain colors. Remember that once you've set up a design, you will never have to pay that particular cost again. You'll just be paying for the printing job, as the already imprinted screen will be at the ready.

There are many screen printers that do a healthy business via their presence on the World Wide Web. Surf on over to **Custom Ink** @ CustomInk.com (800-293-4232) and **Shirt Magic** @ ShirtMagic.com (888-260-4268). These sites will give you a good idea of the many possibilities in the business of t-shirts, etc. You can imprint your slogan and/or design on a variety of things that people want—from t-shirts to headwear to winter wear. You'll also get a clearer picture of how the screen-printing process works and what costs are involved.

What Qualifications Do You Need for This Kind of Work?

In this entrepreneurial undertaking, you don't have to sew anything together or get out the knitting needles. You can have a ready line of clothing (or a single item—whatever you choose) in a very short period of time. Sure, it certainly helps to be artistically inclined. This would enable you to create your very own designs. But it's not necessary. An aggressive entrepreneur can make money in this line of business regardless of his or her creative aptitude.

How Do You Find Customers?

Approach retailers in the trade. Just like so many other pieces of pet-themed merchandise, t-shirts, hats, and carry bags sell in pet-specialty shops. If you think you are really onto something, consider the wholesale markets in the business, too. Attend trade shows to locate both retail and wholesale customers. If you have sufficient confidence in your product line—and some working capital—consider advertising in *Pet Age, Pet Product News,* or *Pet Business.*

In addition, the various pet-related shows are great places to sell t-shirts, sweatshirts, hats, and bags. Peddle your stuff at flea markets. Some things do better than other things at these "everything and anything" extravaganzas—and t-shirts and baseball caps for the human animal are at the top of the list.

Some years ago, a fad swept through the country in the form of diamond-shaped car window signs. They were all the rage for one brief shining moment with motorists showcasing their diverse passions for everything from pizza to the Boston Red Sox to the German shepherd breed of dog. Remember them? They were small in size and simple in design. They were made of plastic and had suction cups on their reverse sides. Most of these signs read "I ♥" something—and that's all there was to them.

At the pinnacle of this furious fad, we maintained racks of these car window signs in our stores. Naturally, our particular signs featured cat and dog breeds—and they sold like hotcakes for a spell. Then, as all fads do, the fad faded (otherwise they wouldn't be fads). Sure, these signs are still around and can be spotted suctioned to car windows now and again, but—no doubt—they had their day. More than any other sector of commerce, the pet care trade is especially ripe for a fad. In fact, pet-parenting consumers are waiting with bated breath for the next thing that they absolutely must have. Keep an eye peeled for the next **pet fad** and get in on it.

In fact, why not usher in a pet fad? Nowadays, ordinary people with ordinary talents can take an embryonic idea and transform it into a real moneymaker. You don't have be an inventor locked away in a workshop or fiddling around with test tubes in a laboratory to make this happen. The aforementioned car window signs, for instance, can be ordered from various companies that specialize in printing or engraving on all kinds of items ranging from buttons to bumper stickers to key chains to coffee mugs. All you need to do is conceive a catchy slogan or conceptualize a winning design that will get noticed and take flight.

Pet License Plates and License Plate Frames

Vanity license plates and license plate frames were an almost-fad at one point in time. And they've remained popular sellers, even after their fifteen minutes of fad fame. Yes, you could sell vanity **pet license plates and license plate frames**.

How Much Does It Cost to Start This Kind of Business?

You have many choices in this commercial area. You could purchase blank license plates and license plate frames—along with the machinery to perform the physical printing on them. The machinery would be costly. Or you could take a good idea and have somebody else do the printing or engraving for you. By going down this path, you could do it all on the cheap—under $1,000—with small initial orders.

What Qualifications Do You Need for This Kind of Work?

If you purchase printing machinery to do the work, you'll have to learn how to operate it. You know the deal. If you can follow directions, you can print on license plates and license plate frames. If you farm out the business to enterprises that do the printing and engraving for you, following directions and worrying about the mercurial personalities of machines is not an issue.

How Do You Find Customers?

Sell your merchandise at flea markets. Attend pet trade shows. Peddle them to retail shops and directly to consumers via a website presence.

There are many businesses that specialize in printing and engraving on a wide range of products, including license plates, license plate frames, mugs, glassware, commemorative plates, ash trays—you name it. Here are a couple of outfits to check out. For a vast selection of license plates and frames, as well as engraving machines if you are interested, visit **Auto Plates**, a division of Custom Engraving, @ AutoPlates.com (888-605-2572). For everything from mugs to porcelain plates, **Discount Mugs** @ DiscountMugs.com (800-569-1980) is certainly a site for sore entrepreneurial eyes. Plenty of pet-themed merchandise possibilities can be hatched there.

Pet Coffee Mugs

During our many years in business, we gave away—from time to time—promotional freebies to our legions of loyal customers. Pet Nosh T-shirts were popular giveaways through the years, as were coffee mugs that commemorated our tenth-year anniversary in business and another heralding our newly acquired 1-800 number. The reason for this particular stroll down memory lane revolves around the actual costs of these items to us. Imprinted coffee mugs with our logo and such printed on them didn't break the bank. This is our circuitous way of introducing you to the entrepreneurial possibilities of selling **pet coffee mugs**.

Besides our promotional coffee mugs, customers of ours also purchased coffee mugs from us featuring sketches of the most popular cat and dog breeds. People buy coffee mugs for themselves. Sometimes they sip java from them—other times they place them on the mantle or curio shelf. They buy them as gifts. In other words, pet-themed mugs, drink ware, and glassware have a market. Again, it's up to you to determine what you want to put on the coffee mugs, beer mugs, travel mugs, etc. The right design or pet-themed verbiage could easily locate an audience of thirsty buyers.

How Much Does It Cost to Start This Kind of Business?
You could inaugurate your pet coffee mug business with a small, upfront investment of $500 or even less than that.

What Qualifications Do You Need for This Kind of Work?
You need a good idea or design to put on the pet coffee mug. You also must possess the capacity to convert this winning idea into an attractive piece of merchandise. If you meet these two criteria, you can sell pet coffee mugs in the marketplace.

How Do You Find Customers?
Mugs and their many drinking buddies are the perfect pieces of merchandise to sell at pet-specialty shows, to retailers, and in cyberspace.

Pet Collector Plates

There was a time when plates were manufactured, foremost, to place food atop them. Nowadays, many plates are made to hold fare—as in the past—but others are produced with the collector in mind. These decorative plates are displayed in cabinets and on shelves. Indeed, the collector plate has found a niche in the twenty-first century, and with the pet care trade a bona fide commercial juggernaut, **pet collector plates** have real moneymaking potential.

How Much Does It Cost to Start This Kind of Business?

You could start this business with a minimal investment of $1,000 or less. You have ample opportunities in this particular business bailiwick to test-market your product in a small way before taking it to the big time and increasing your line of collector plates.

What Qualifications Do You Need for This Kind of Work?

You need an idea and a vision. That is, you have to take your idea to the people in the form of a product that they will want to buy. You don't need to be an artist or especially creative. If you need help in this area, there are art departments in various businesses that can assist you in converting a mere notion into a tangible and coveted piece of merchandise selling in the marketplace.

How Do You Find Customers?

Even if you don't initiate a nationwide fad that makes you millions of dollars, you could still sell your merchandise at pet-related shows and flea markets. You could sell your stuff to retail shops and via a website. The favorable reality of the pet care marketplace permits you to test-market your idea—the next pet fad, perhaps—with a small initial order and not too many upfront dollars.

Pet Greeting Card Maker ✛ Hand-painted Pet Greeting Cards ✛ Pet Postcard Maker

Greeting cards are a big business. There are many holidays in which people exchange them. There are, of course, greeting cards for birthdays—and everybody's got one of those! Greeting cards are purchased for special occasions ranging from weddings to bar mitzvahs to school graduations. The greeting card business goes through the roof on Mother's Day! There is, too, an unceasing demand for greeting cards and those *thinking about you* moments—from *get well soon* to *my condolences*. Interestingly, in every one of the aforementioned classifications, pet and animal images and themes are increasingly spotted on greeting cards.

In addition to all of the traditional greeting card categories, there are further moments and happenings that call for sending someone you know a greeting card. Welcoming a new four-legged addition to the family is now greeting card fodder. Offering sympathy for the loss of close animal friend is also the stuff of a greeting card. There are also birthday cards crafted specifically for the cat or dog in the family. So what if they don't know how to read.

We sold greeting cards in our stores. We carried lines of cards that were pitched, by and large, for people to give to people. There were *Happy Birthday* and *Thinking About You* cards aplenty. But the threads that stitched together all of the cards we sold were pets. The cards featured cats, dogs, and birds in a variety of poses and doing a variety of things. An adorable puppy or kitten on a card always finds an audience. In other words, they were simply irresistible. And, yes, some of the cards we carried were to be presented to Fluffy and Fido on their birthdays and upon achieving various milestones (graduating from training school, new mother, etc.).

157

In the greeting card business, both eye appeal and a degree of originality have large and sustainable markets. People are always buying cards because there are always occasions. And this consumer reality isn't about to change, so why not be a **pet greeting card maker**.

The demand for greeting cards is fail-safe. Even though e-greetings are all the rage, there is still no substitute for a card you can hold in your hand and set atop the mantle. The greeting card business is a never-ending story. What you want to do is knot the enduring popularity of the greeting card with the modern day pet-parenting phenomenon. If you can devise catchy birthday cards, appropriate condolence cards, and colorful holiday cards, you can make a greeting card business come alive. Use the pet care trade to jumpstart your greeting card business and turn it into a real profit maker.

Popular greeting card software includes **PrintMaster Platinum**, **The Print Shop Deluxe**, **Greeting Card Factory**, and **Hallmark Card Studio**. Foremost, you want to find a software program that's easy to use. Naturally, some are more complicated and less user-friendly than others. Then, of course, you want plenty of features: fonts, photo editing, special effects, etc. Ease of use is hunky dory, but you have to have the necessities to make nice looking cards. Finally, you want a software program that comes attached to good help and support. Check out the Internet reviews on any software product you are considering. For one, **Amazon** @ Amazon.com sells software and features many beneficial customer reviews alongside them.

How Much Does It Cost to Start This Kind of Business?

Courtesy of the many technological advances of late, you can manufacture appealing greeting cards for any and all occasions and never leave the comforts of home. That is, you can purchase greeting card software and then design cards for resale on your home computer. By utilizing your computer along with the right software, you can crank out attractive and coveted greeting cards that you can sell in pet-related venues and elsewhere. Greeting card software can be had for under $50. More expensive versions exist. Card stock paper and the cost of printing is what you'll have to contend with when you price your creations.

What you want to do is generate a product that people want and get it in front of as many prospective customers as possible. The bottom line is that people will buy appealing pet-themed greeting cards. They'll buy them at Christmastime. They'll purchase them for birthdays. They'll send them to sick friends. They'll commemorate all kinds of occasions with them.

What Qualifications Do You Need for This Kind of Work?

If you are going to make greeting cards on your computer, you have to know your way around the machine. The reality is that most of these *make your own* software programs are pretty straightforward. That is, there are step-by-step instructions that unfold before your eyes. If you are anywhere near computer literate, you can make greeting cards. If you are not especially computer erudite, you can readily make yourself so. All you have to do is get over the fear of computers and all that they represent. People of all ages sit in front of them. They surf the Internet with ease. They make many things with computer software programs—including greeting cards. Of course, it never hurts to be artistically inclined when taking on this kind of job. If artistry runs through your veins, you have a better chance of getting something out of the pet greeting card business. But, you don't have to be a Picasso.

In fact, if you are artistically gifted, **hand-painted pet greeting cards** are something else to consider. They are always big sellers at craft fairs and in specialty gift shops. Again, keep in mind that pet-themed cards are huge right now—and will be so tomorrow and the tomorrow after that. If you can come up with one-of-a-kind designs coupled with the appropriate sentiments—or just leave them blank for individuals to pen their own greetings—you can take your finished product to a printer and reproduce them in large quantities. In other words, you can get your very specially designed greeting cards out there in great numbers, without having to hand-paint every single one of them. This would also make them more affordable and available to a wider audience.

How Do You Find Customers?

For starters, test out your greeting cards with family and friends. If their reactions are overwhelmingly positive, bring your card line to pet-specialty retailers. Don't ignore the many general gift shops that sell cards. Pet-themed cards sell outside of the pet care trade. If you're hand-painting greeting cards, bring them to arts and crafts shows. Put up a website that showcases your designs and point as many people as possible to it.

> The big greeting card companies are always on the lookout for new designs. Contact them if you think your greeting card creations are right for them, and, of course, if you want to go down this route; that is, if would prefer someone else selling the cards for you.

One last offshoot worth mentioning are postcards, which are increasingly used in lieu of traditional greeting cards. In other words, they are not only purchased during vacations to send to family and friends. Nowadays, postcards are more than *Wish You Were Here* items. Pet-specialty retailers, gift shops, and bookstores—to name just a few—sell postcards festooned with images of cats, dogs, birds, and other animals both wild and domestic. These outlets sell cuddly cute postcards of the aforementioned animal kingdom. They sell animated pet and animal postcards with humorous sayings on them. They sell countless varieties of pet-themed and general animal-themed postcards. Consumers gobble them up. Consider the entrepreneurial potential of being a **pet postcard maker**.

Pet Candle Making

It's a fact of life: Millions of cats and dogs bestow on millions of pet parents a mother lode of unconditional love. However, lurking amidst all of this slobbering affection are those notorious and par for the course pet odors, proving the old adage that everything good in life comes attached to some kind of price.

Fortunately, where there are foul-smelling problems, there are also industrious capitalists hard at work in solving them. Through the years of Pet Nosh, we sold rivers of odor-busting products, including liquid stain removers, aerosol sprays, pop-top air fresheners, and—yes—candles. We had notable success with candles that were specifically marketed as pet-odor eaters, even though they were no different from ordinary candles. And, the *pièce de résistance* is that this commercial triumph occurred long before the colossal popularity of candles as cure-alls for everything from repugnant stinks to the bluest of blues. The bottom line is that you can now marry the popularity of both pets and candles with **pet candle making**. By seeing through this match made in heaven, you can earn some serious bucks, too.

Pets and candles are both big businesses. Thus, marketing candles specifically to the pet care trade makes sound entrepreneurial sense. There are even opportunities in this commercial sphere for a little cross-marketing to snare consumers of aromatherapy products. Candles sold as aromatherapy represent a substantial and expanding market. Not surprisingly, aromatherapy has woven its way into the world of pet merchandise. So, your pet candles can be promoted as more than mere odor busters, but as aromatherapy for your four-legged friends, too.

How Much Does It Cost to Start This Kind of Business?

Pet odor control is a multimillion dollar business. While you learn the ropes and master the process of candle making, you can join this fraternity with a minimal investment in candle supplies. You can literally commence a full-fledged business or moneymaking aside from the stovetop of your kitchen. All that is required to be a candle maker and entrepreneur are several basic staples:

★ Bulk wax (which can be inexpensively purchased)
★ Pot to melt the wax
★ Fragrance oils
★ Wicks
★ Thermometer
★ Containers or molds

Light a fire under yourself and head on over to **Candle and Supplies** @ CandleandSupplies.com. This large wholesaler of candles and candle supplies not only has everything you need to make candles, but scrupulous instructions on how to make them. The website is replete with information on all that candle making entails, including critical safety concerns and legal requirements, and it will open your eyes wide to the entrepreneurial possibilities in this area. **Candle and Supplies** operates from a sprawling physical location that is open to the public in Quakertown, Pennsylvania (215-538-8552). The **Candlewic Company** @ CandleWic.com is another candle-making supply outlet worth exploring. You'll find oodles of material here detailing the ABCs of candle making.

Each one of the aforementioned candle-making supplies is readily available online and in craft stores. Your candle-making options are numerous, too, starting with candle types ranging from votives to tapers to pillars. You can even produce designer candles. There are molds available in the shape of cats and dogs. You can make candles in apothecary, mason, and aluminum tin jars.

You can employ waxes ranging from the venerable beeswax to soy wax, which, by the way, is growing in popularity because of its clean burning and environmentally friendly composition. You can create a variety of candle products based on your vision, your capacity to produce them, and where you intend on selling them.

What Qualifications Do You Need for This Kind of Work?

If you are not living in a refrigerator box and have access to a stove and pot, you are definitely a candidate for the pet candle business. While most of us aren't competent chemists capable of concocting pet-odor control formulae, devices, and potions, we can make candles. Indeed, the beauty of candle making is that it can be initiated from the comforts of home. The A to Z process of making attractively packaged candles with equally appealing scents is not brain surgery. It's very doable.

How Do You Find Customers?

Once you've mastered the art of candle making, you need to design a label and market the fruits of your labor as *pet candles—i.e.*, odor-busting pet products. The key here is packaging them as pet-specific merchandise and peddling them through pet venues.

Send your sample products, along with a price list, to retailers and whole-salers in the pet care trade. You can sell your candles to gift shops, too. Pet-related merchandise is sold everywhere these days. Sell your candles online, at craft fairs, and at flea markets. There are countless selling avenues to travel down with this kind of product.

As an example of profit possibilities: a small votive candle might cost you 50¢ to manufacture and a 16oz. candle in a glass jar, approximately $4.00. You could turn around and wholesale the votive candles for 75¢ and retail them for $1.00 or more. The candles in glass containers could wholesale for $6.00 and retail for $10.00 or more. Once you have your assembly line

163

operating and the candle making down pat, you can produce your products as needed—that is, on demand with orders placed and money in the bank.

You may have noticed that many pet-odor cleaners and air fresheners are citrus based. In the candle bailiwick, the two most popular scents for vanquishing unpleasant odors are variations of citrus and vanilla.

Pet Memorial Markers

The pet memorial business is alive and well. This shouldn't come as any big surprise. Since more and more people view their pets as family members in good standing, they are increasingly commemorating their animal companions' passing with memorial markers of some kind. If you have a talent for engraving, you could create both appropriate and impressive-looking **pet memorial markers**.

Many pets are interred in the very backyards where they frolicked in life. Sure, there are often municipal ordinances and deed restrictions that prohibit this practice. Nevertheless, pet parents are increasingly on the hunt for fitting and attractive memorial markers to commemorate the final resting places of their pets.

Some of the more popular pet memorial items are engraved urns, which contain the deceased pets' ashes. Other desirable pet memorials are engraved stones, slate, marble, and various metals and plastics. Pet memorial markers are frequently placed in memorable locations that simultaneously underscore and celebrate the life lived of a beloved pet. Some of these memorial markers are employed as headstones at the site of burial.

How Much Does It Cost to Start This Kind of Business?

If you want to engrave pet memorial markers, you are going to need engraving tools that suit your purposes and overall ambitions. Engraving drills greatly range in price and, naturally, in what they can and cannot do. (Some are suitable for engraving in stone, while others are used on metals such as pewter urns.) Do your homework on the various tools available. Then, based on what you can afford, and where you see your engraving business venture headed, choose an appropriate drill. Go to the bank on this market fact: Pet memorials of all varieties are in demand.

What Qualifications Do You Need for This Kind of Work?

Engraving is an art form. Some of us are more gifted in the arts than others. Nevertheless, engraving is a skill that can be learned and improved upon. You need a steady hand and a lot of patience. You also need a place to do the engraving and a worktable of some sort. If you are just starting out in this business, commandeering a little household space is all that is required. When you grow your pet memorial business, a move into the garage, or even leased space, might be in order.

Visit **Dremel** @ Dremel.com (800-437-3635) for information on the available engraving tools and where you can purchase them. Dremel is an international company renowned for its high-quality drills and accompanying parts. The website also features a search button to locate stores near you that stock Dremel products. Just type in your zip code. If you are looking for urns to engrave for customers, you might want to investigate **Discount Urns** @ DiscountUrns.com (888-URNS-888), which offers a wide selection at competitive prices.

How Do You Find Customers?

If you have any doubt that there is a consumer demand for pet memorial markers, google "pet memorials" or some related search. You'll encounter multiple Internet businesses that focus their engraving flair on pets and every imaginable memorial for them. In this day and age, website presences for these kinds of businesses are a major boon. They don't cost all that much to design and maintain—and they can give you instant credibility as an entrepreneur. If you are promoting your talents and product line, a business card with a company website address on it is a powerful sales tool.

To get yourself up and running in this business sphere, commingle with the pet people masses. Take your engraving skills to craft shows and pet-related events. Bring samples of your works. Perform engravings on the spot. And, of course, dispense with a lot of your business cards.

Pet memorial marker makers also benefit from partnering with retailers and service businesses in the trade, including groomers, trainers, kennel operators, and veterinarians. That is, leave samples of your work and a description of the many things that you can do. Take customized orders via these businesses and give them a percentage of the sales. While the pet memorial business stands on a solid foundation of customized orders, you could also do one-size-fits-all items with general and appropriate sentiments.

Pet Memorial Plaques

They are oft-purchased memorial items. For many disconsolate pet owners, they represent both fitting and affordable remembrances for their deceased animal companions. They are **pet memorial plaques** and they come in many sizes and shapes. They are made of many different things too.

We live in an increasingly advanced technological age, so it stands to reason that engraving equipment, along with just about everything else, has crossed the bridge into the twenty-first century. If you are serious about a business involving the process of engraving—and have some ready capital to invest—you might want to cast your eyes on laser technology. For starters, check out **Engravers Warehouse** @ SignWarehouse.com (800-799-5282) and **Engravers Network** @ EngraversNetwork.com (866-727-7256). Take a look at all that engraving machinery can do, and determine if you want to make an investment in it.

How Much Does It Cost to Start This Kind of Business?

The start-up costs involve the necessary equipment and initial advertising volleys. The literal amount of capital necessary for the pet memorial plaque business depends on precisely what you want to do and how fast you want to do it.

What Qualifications Do You Need for This Kind of Work?

In some instances, engraving plaques requires that you have a steady hand and an artistic aptitude. However, engraving machines regularly supplant the necessity for that firm hand and artistic flair.

How Do You Find Customers?

With the right kinds of engraving equipment, you could enter the pet memorial marketplace with guns ablazing. You could also tap into other fertile nooks of the pet care trade. For instance, you could generate wall plaques for the general pet-parenting consumer—*e.g.*, particular breed plaques. You could also offer your plaque-making services for customized jobs.

CHAPTER VII

Brick-and-Mortar Pet Retailing & Franchises

Pet Food and Supply Retailer ✺ Pet Shop ✺ Bird Shop ✺ Aquarium Fish Retailer

When our original Pet Nosh store opened in November of 1979, there were rival mom-and-pop pet food and supply shops scattered all over the place. Still, when both our business and the industry at large blossomed beyond recognition, we frequently heard a comment all too familiar to successful entrepreneurs' ears. It goes something like this: "You guys were sure in the right place at the right time." When certain people witnessed the pet care trade and our company simultaneously romping through green fields, they concluded that we were merely along for the ride—simply caught up in a commercial and popular culture phenomenon. But nothing could be further from the truth.

Of all the existing small pet food and supply retailers—and there were thousands throughout the country when Pet Nosh first opened its doors—very few of them progressed to the next level. In our neck of the woods, there were a fair number of stores identical to Pet Nosh in both size and concept. But why did Pet Nosh survive, thrive, and grow, while most of these others remained stagnant or breathed their last? After all, weren't they, too, in the "right place at the right time"?

What separated us from our mom-and-pop competitors was Pet Nosh's mission. It went something like this: "Pet Nosh aims to provide its customers with what they want at the lowest possible prices." Granted, this sounds incredibly unoriginal and clichéd, but that doesn't mean we truly didn't mean it. We stayed on the cusp of the countless product innovations and trends that were gradually revolutionizing the trade. And we valiantly endeavored to keep prices in line with or below our competitors' prices by maintaining an attentive eye on what they were doing at all times.

Of course, the times have changed—and rather dramatically at that. In the new century, pet food and supply superstores—largely dominated by the national chains—have cast a smothering pall over many independent retailers in the field. The question before us is: Can you reasonably expect to make it as a David going up against all of these Goliaths? Can you succeed in this day and age as a **pet food and supply retailer**? Can you turn a profit in a **pet shop** or **bird shop** of your own? Can you survive as an **aquarium fish retailer** when the aforementioned big retail fish all have aquarium departments? The answer is a resounding and unequivocal: It all depends. It depends on a variety of factors from, of course, your location to what you can offer your customers. Sure, superstores are located in many parts of the country, but they are not everywhere—not by a long shot. There are geographic slices of the country where independent pet food and supply retailers still rule the roost, because, other than grocery stores, there are very few alternatives to them.

How Much Does It Cost to Start This Kind of Business?

After you complete a thorough due diligence and gain an absolute under-standing of what you will be up against, you are ready to address the partic-ulars of opening and operating a pet food and supply retail business—or another variety of pet retailer specializing in things like birds or aquarium fish. Foremost, investment in any brick-and-mortar business is guaranteed to be substantial, particularly if it's a retail business requiring a considerable inventory. You not only have to lease space, but convert its interior into a user-friendly walk-in business. For starters, this means rental bills and carpentry and fixture costs. Anticipate an up-front investment of $75,000 to $150,000 to do a pet food and supply retail business right in a very competitive marketplace. Depending on your shop's size, location, and overall business plan, you may require a whole lot more than that.

Keep in mind that in the highly spirited pet care trade of today, you are going to have to distinguish yourself from the competition. This will necessitate purchasing an ample and diverse inventory—ah, more outlays of cash. Also, you can never rest on your laurels in this type of business. You are going to have to promote yourself and promote yourself some more—and this requires dollars.

Still, when all is said and done, the pet care trade is big and getting bigger. Naturally, this means that there is room for the right kind of pet food and supply retailer in the right kind of place and selling the right kind of things. But this also means that there is very likely a mother lode of competition on a variety of frontiers—from Main Street to the Information Superhighway. Website businesses now sell just about everything that pet food and supply retailers peddle from their physical locations. Make no mistake about it: There are genuine and serious profits to be made in pet food and supply retail stores, but also immense capital outlays can be frittered away if they are not well-researched and well-planned entrepreneurial ventures.

What Qualifications Do You Need for This Kind of Work?

The truth is that not everybody is cut out for the hustle and bustle and ups and downs of life on the retail frontlines. As there are genuine risks inherent in founding and growing any kind of business, many people prefer laboring for others—*for the risk takers*. Think about it: As your own boss, there are no guarantees of a set weekly paycheck, or even a paycheck at all. You have to go out and acquire your own medical coverage, which is quite costly for the small businessperson. When you are in business for yourself, your fortunes can change from one day to the next—sometimes for the better and often for the worse. You live *always* in an uncertain world. You work long and hard and it occasionally leads to nowhere. When you are feeling poorly, you usually can't call in sick. In many instances, when you don't show up for work, your business ceases to function.

So, really, it's no big surprise that the majority of the population chooses to work in nine to five jobs, or nine to six jobs, as is more often the case in the twenty-first century. They prefer to know exactly when they are supposed to be on the job, when they are going to receive their paychecks, what's going to be in their paychecks, when they can take their vacations, what kind of health insurance they can count on when they get sick, etc. And who can blame people for wanting all of these things, particularly in this financially uncertain epoch? However, as many of these same men and women come to know the hard way, job security and all of those guarantees aren't exactly ironclad.

Life as an entrepreneur—and realizing success as your own boss—is the utmost. It's why so many people enter the business fray, even with all the potential pitfalls and uncertainties that come with the territory. Nevertheless, entrepreneurial success in retail environments calls for genuine leadership and a ready ability to make decisions and more decisions. *Are you leadership timber?* Satisfactorily ask and answer these questions before joining the brick-and-mortar retail ranks:

★ Do you derive pleasure in making decisions?
★ Are you a naturally competitive individual?
★ Are you disciplined?
★ Do you relish the company of others?
★ Do you plan for the future?

Chew over your answers to these queries because, as an active retailer, you will be confronted with critical decision-making on a continual basis. You will always be competing with others in this line of work. You will also be dealing with all kinds of people all of the time—your customers, employees, suppliers, advertisers, etc. Are you primed and ready to take on all of this? Do you really want the fuller than full life as a pet food and supply retailer? Can your personal life harmoniously coexist with this wide-ranging and long-term commitment?

How Can You Distinguish Yourself From the Competition?

Since you've made it this far, we will assume that you are indeed armed and ready to be a pet food and supply retailer—and a successful one at that. So, it's time to figure out how you can distinguish yourself from both the current and future competition. Aside from finding the best location possible for your pet food and supply retail store, there are numerous other things you can do to set apart your business from all the rest—from the superstores to the Internet peddlers and everybody in between.

For starters, providing an intimate and informed customer service will make you stand out from the pack. Conscientious customer service *used to be* at the foundation of retail and service businesses. Once upon a time, employees were actually taught the "Customer Is Always Right" mantra before they ever came into contact with a living and breathing shopper or client. Nowadays, all too many retailers are more concerned about filling jobs with physical bodies than they are with the subsequent conduct of these men and women after they are hired. In the present-day pet care trade, knowledgeable and caring customer service is in increasing demand and decreasing supply.

Uncommon Courtesy

To succeed as pet food and supply retailer, you should first set yourself apart from the off-putting ways that so many others conduct business. Know your stuff and connect with your customers—it's as easy as that. For instance, when customers pulled into Texaco gas stations during the 1940s and 1950s, several uniformed *Merry Texaco Men* would emerge to service them. Believe it or not, a quartet of men filled up gas tanks upon request and checked oils and cleaned windshields as regular courtesies. This was the Texaco corporate policy that filtered all the way down to its gas station franchisees and their employees.

Imagine anything like that occurring today. First of all, self-service is unquestionably the wave of the future. Still, full-service gas stations have hardly gone the way of the dinosaur. But what do most of these full-service gas stations offer us? They put gas in our tanks—end of story. This is now the accepted definition of *full-service*. The longstanding courtesies of oil checks and windshield cleanings have gone the way of leisure suits and manual typewriters.

> When you put on your entrepreneurial armor, you are simultaneously slipping on the apron of a bartender, as it were. That is, on the retail business frontlines you will be expected to lend your ears to your customers now and again. Throughout our Pet Nosh years, we often found ourselves listening to our clientele's pet-related yarns. It's what you have to do in business. If the thought of interacting with shoppers on a human level scares the dickens out of you, then maybe you're not cut from the retail cloth. There's a never-ending stream of personal contact in pet-specialty retailing, and the most successful businesspersons are sociable and understand the value in being so.

Paradoxically, the general demise of yesterday's common courtesies and all those little extras is a prudent businessperson's golden opportunity. It's true. The reality is that businesses that are dependable and enthusiastic in the customer service department stand out like Republicans in Hollywood. At Pet Nosh, we built a reputation for being customer-friendly—and just plain friendly, too. We valued our customers as our business's lifeblood. We chatted with them about their myriad pets, as well as their life and times. We carried out merchandise to their cars. We always said, "Thank you."

The good news is that businesses can insist on treating their customers like the Merry Texaco Men treated theirs more than half a century ago. If you put basic customer courtesies on the top of your pet food and supply retail store agenda—even if you, and you alone, are the company—you will automatically go to the head of the class.

A Little Knowledge Goes a Long Way on the Customer Service Frontier

Is it too much for pet-parenting consumers to ask that employees in the businesses they patronize actually know a little something about the products and services being offered? No, of course it's not—such rudimentary knowledge is fundamental to first-class customer assistance. We knew absolutely nothing about pet care and the products on the market when we entered the trade. We made it a point, however, to hastily and thoroughly learn the business inside and out. This informed approach was particularly important because of the snowballing trends in our industry—*e.g.*, the stirrings of the premium pet food revolution and the countless product innovations coming down the pike at warp speed.

In other words, we furnished our customers with something that many of our competitors weren't giving them. We felt that if Pet Nosh was going to break away from the pack of mom-and-pop stores and move to the next level, we had to convey knowledgeable explanations of the differences between Product A and Product B to our clientele. We had to be able to coherently explain why they should plunk down $16.99 for a twenty-pound bag of premium dog food when they could get an equal size bag for only $5.99.

Presently, poorly trained, or absolutely untrained, employees are the rule in an awful lot of businesses. In the contemporary pet care trade, many, if not most, of the workers in the mammoth superstores are devoid of the education they should have to suitably service customers. Try finding an employee on the floor of one of these mega-stores who can answer your product-specific questions (beyond where is this or where is that). If, for example, you had a question on the differences between the Eukanuba brand of dog food and Purina Dog Chow, you would be hard-pressed to find someone who could tell you.

By genuinely informing customers of the products and services available to them, and explaining how they work, a consumer demand is generated that wouldn't otherwise be there. It's an irony that is lost on many businesspersons in this day and age. At Pet Nosh, we witnessed a dramatic increase in the demand for premium pet foods. We understood that the more that our customers knew about the many diet alternatives at their disposal, the more likely they were to buy them.

In today's indifferent retail climate, an educated workforce is a customer service pearl. The pet food and supply retailers that are genuinely informed shine like beacons in a sea of apathy and ignorance. So, foremost, plant your business flag in the garden of knowledge. You can win over customers—and ensure that they come back again and again—by just knowing your business. Frequently, many of our patrons came to Pet Nosh stores armed with questions about the products we carried, as well as more general questions about pet care. They expected the staff at Pet Nosh to know about these things. And, really, they weren't expecting very much.

Don't Let Special Orders Upset You

Superstores operate with strict formulae—by the book. As an independent retail businessperson, you would be wise to employ another book to your advantage. From day one at Pet Nosh, we made it clear to our customers that we would attempt to get them what they wanted, even if we didn't stock the merchandise. We worked with a *special order book* that was routinely filled with all kinds of requests for special brands of foods, vitamin supplements, collars and leashes—you name it. Sure, it was sometimes impossible to fill a particular request, but quite often we tracked the items down.

Our customers came to appreciate that Pet Nosh was more than just a conventional retailer peddling cat and dog supplies. Instead, they saw it as a business that, metaphorically speaking, would travel to the ends of the earth for them.

We complemented our early retail business with home deliveries. Think about all the things that are delivered these days, as well as the many services that are provided in people's homes. Some dog trainers make house calls, and many groomers have specially-equipped vehicles that can come to pet owners and their pets at their homes. Of course, an entire service industry (within an industry) has sprung up called pet sitting, in which individuals visit their clientele's residences to tend to their pets while they're away. In pet food and supply retailing, consider home deliveries as business that you wouldn't otherwise get *without going to the customer.* The superstores in the trade are not doing home deliveries.

Location, Location, Location

Let's return once more to the matter of location and how vital it is to the success of your pet food and supply retail business. "Location, location, location" is every real estate agent's mantra. But, really, it is every businessperson's rallying cry, too. When we hunted for the prospective properties for our stores, location topped the list, not price (which was a close second!). Could our customers reach the stores without having to travel long distances or through labyrinthine mazes of side streets? In retail business, location is clearly one of the keys that unlock success, and it's part and parcel of good customer service.

Our Pet Nosh store in Yonkers, New York, was an incredible moneymaker through the years. It was a small place that could never be classified a super-store, but per square foot, the place rocked. However, this particular locale had very limited parking facilities. You see, the store was ideally situated. It attracted business from nearby New York City, as well as clientele from its Yonkers' home and the neighboring towns of Southern Westchester County. On weekends, pandemonium reigned in the store's parking lot, with tempers often flaring and some of our customers affixing blame (rightly so) on us for not doing a better job at resolving this quagmire.

But what could we really do? For starters, we purchased the property outright. But, logistically, we couldn't put rooftop parking above our small business, although we looked into it. And we were bordered on one side by a two-story medical office building and on the other side by a chic shoe store called the Shoe Chalet.

So, as we grew the business there, we simultaneously strained our infrastructure. We eventually reached a point where—without additional parking—we couldn't realistically expect to grow the business much more. Fortunately, opportunity knocked, as it often does in business if you are listening for it. The Shoe Chalet building was put up for sale. As you might imagine, it wasn't a cheap piece of property. But we opted to purchase it and tear down the physical building to create more parking spaces for our store. The combined real estate and the demolition costs were a significant investment in the business. However, the added parking spots enabled the Yonkers' Pet Nosh to continue to grow after it had reached a genuine crossroads of too many customers in too tiny a space.

This forward move provided our customers with what they long wanted—a Pet Nosh parking lot with plenty of parking spaces. Remember that from customers' perspectives, there are few things worse than making a trip to a business establishment and having to fret about parking—wondering if there will be a spot available when they get there, or worse still, whether somebody will crash into their vehicles in an overcrowded lot. Ample and accessible parking is part of first-rate customer service.

Quality customer service embodies a great deal more than employing a courteous, knowledgeable staff. It means making sure that your customers don't wait in long lines. It means that your place of business is clean and your shelves are well stocked with the merchandise your customers want. A properly lit store is also part of good customer service. And don't ignore suitable temperatures. During our first few years in business, we often kept the air conditioner off when it should have been on. We were trying to save money on our electric bills, which as many businesspersons know can be quite considerable. But what did this parsimony get us? In the heat of the summer, we heard many cries from our customers to "Turn the air conditioner on!" Shopping in ninety-degree heat or forty-degree cold hurts the shopping experience all around. You don't want your customers to want out of your place of business the moment they walk through your doors. So, always consider what, if anything, you're saving when you switch off the air conditioner in summertime or lower the thermostat in wintertime. Always put yourself in the place of your clientele. Do you enjoy waiting on long lines? Do you like shopping in dark and poorly stocked stores? Do you think getting frostbite or heat stroke is an acceptable part of the shopping experience? Ill-mannered and ill-informed employees drive customers away, but so do long lines, messy aisles, habitual out-of-stocks, and uncomfortable climes.

Real Selection

Since Pet Nosh competed with supermarkets for an important slice of its pet care business, we had to make certain that our stores offered consumers a selection of merchandise that stood apart from them in demonstrable ways. When we first opened the doors of Pet Nosh more than a quarter of a century ago, approximately 95% of pet-owning consumers purchased all or most of their pet foods and supplies from supermarkets and other general merchandisers. As already noted, mom-and-pop pet-specialty shops existed in significant numbers, but they still reaped only a sliver of the overall pet care business.

Nowadays, you are competing with a pantheon of retailers: pet food and supply superstores, supermarkets, general merchandisers, and—don't forget—Internet entrepreneurs, too. We supplied our customers with a selection of products and services that were unique on various planes. And when we speak of selection, we're not referring to more merchandise than the other guy or gal. Having more choices than your competition is critical, but more stuff in your place of business doesn't always cut the mustard—it's got to be the right stuff.

We wanted pet consumers to shop at Pet Nosh for all their pets' needs. It was our objective to supply our customers with everything they desired in a single location—one-stop shopping for all of their companion animals. But we were also banking on them discovering products that they didn't know existed. That is, merchandise that the supermarkets—where they formerly did their pet-related shopping—didn't stock.

We operated a pet-specialty retail store, with the emphasis on the word *specialty*. In other words, we understood that Pet Nosh wasn't going to profit by winning over hordes of supermarket customers and then selling them *only* supermarket products. Instead, cat owners bought their cat food at Pet Nosh, but also cat litter, litter boxes, play toys, vitamin supplements, scratching posts, and even expensive pieces of feline furniture. Likewise, dog owners purchased their canine fare at Pet Nosh, but also rawhide chews, playthings, tasty treats, collars, leashes, and the latest fashions for the four-legged, too.

All that said, we still stocked the popular commercial brands found in supermarkets, because that's what a considerable portion of our customers asked for. We ran sales on some of these known brands, too—such as 9 Lives and Alpo—because they tapped into a well-established and substantial buying audience. They brought people into our stores.

More than ever before, the selection that you provide your customers is vital in distinguishing your pet food and supply retail business from the competition. But before determining what selection of products or services you are going to offer them, you must first settle upon exactly what you want to accomplish in business and whom you are targeting as your clientele. For example, a 99¢ store should sell everything from toilet paper to plate hangers to shower curtain liners—*i.e.*, hundreds of cheap household products. That's the kind of selection consumers expect from them. On the other hand, a specialty grocery shop does not need the same quantity of items as found in traditional grocery stores, but it should have a varied selection of high-quality specialty items that its competitors don't sell.

As a pet food and supply retailer, you have to repeatedly ask yourself what it is that will inspire consumers to make a special trip to your place of business. What are you offering your customers—vis-à-vis selection—that your competitors are not providing them? And these questions will elicit different answers as time marches on, and both consumer tastes and the nature of your competition changes.

Be There or Be Square

When you physically commingle with your customers, you discover what they want from the proverbial horses' mouths. You come to appreciate how they like being treated. This intimate contact influences your business decision-making all across the board including your promotional choices, your store design, the products you carry, and the prices you set for these same products.

Impersonal shopping experiences are the rule in the new millennium, making visible management all but invisible in all too many places. But herein lies that entrepreneurial opportunity we touched upon earlier. As a hands-on business owner or manager, you are ipso facto visible in an increasingly invisible retail world. You stand out like a gold tooth in a pair of dentures.

If you are shopping in your local chain drugstore, for example, there will not be an owner around for you to speak with when a problem arises—you can go to the bank on that one. If you are fortunate, you might locate a sympathetic manager to address your concern. But, you've probably suffered through one too many shopping experiences where the inmates were, in essence, running the asylum. You know how the scenario plays: Loud music blaring over the store's sound system; workers meandering about, but paying little heed to customers. The not very subliminal message is clear: We can't help you in any way, with the sole exception of taking your money.

In a blatant contrast to this frosty business scenario, we made it clear to our customers that they could go right to the top at Pet Nosh with their concerns, and that the top wasn't a very long climb. In fact, the top was often the guy at the cash register, or the fellow stacking up bags of dog food in the middle of the store.

Without our consistent physical presence in our stores, we'd have become grossly out of touch with the workings of the business. Seeing is so often believing in business. We saw with our own eyes that our store counters in the Yonkers' location were patently inefficient, because we were literally stuck in a square-shaped pen with three cash registers cohabitating with one too many counter displays. On busy weekends, with three people punching up sales with their backs practically touching one another, and customers fanning out into the store aisles in every direction on the compass, it was a sorry spectacle. To make a long story short: This dreadful counter setup— in the center of the store no less—went by the boards and we built more efficient and more sensible checkouts in the front of the store. Soon after, we discovered that although they worked smoothly in getting people in and out, the midday sun caused both cashier and customer blindness. Tinted glass was in order.

Being there and experiencing the same travails as working employees and shopping customers made palpable differences in the direction that Pet Nosh took and the rapidity with which positive changes were implemented. Would our numerous store issues have gotten addressed sooner or later? Yes, they probably would have been dealt with eventually, but the sense of urgency wouldn't have been there without on-the-scene management.

Keeping a Vigilant Eye on Price

"Discount Pet Food and Supplies." That's what our very first Pet Nosh store sign read. From the start, our main attraction was as a *discount* place. Each one of the critical business particulars that we've enumerated thus far—the things we did that got us noticed and distinguished us from our competition—were, in the final analysis, built atop a rock-solid foundation of good prices.

In order for customers to fully value our *happening* retail environment, attentive customer service, and wide selection of merchandise, we had to simultaneously have competitive prices on everything we sold. Santa Claus could come to Pet Nosh every day of the year, but if we were overpriced on our stuff, the promotional multiplier effect would be nonexistent. We could run all the Midnight Madness sales in the world, but if there weren't big bargains out there along with our spotlights, they'd amount to nothing in the dark.

Dog-Eat-Dog

Building a reputation and establishing lasting customer loyalty is fundamental to the long-term success of any retail business. But in most business enterprises, a good reputation, and the repeat customers that come with it, is tied together with pricing. Had we strayed from our commitment to keeping our prices at or below our competitors' prices, we'd have tarnished our reputation, despite being the nicest guys in town. The cold hard facts are that customer loyalty is not the same as the loyalty of a faithful dog. Price will drive even your most steadfast customers away in a heartbeat.

And, really, can you blame the average consumer for basing so much on the best prices? You can't. Many people exist on very tight budgets and seek out savings where they can and when they can. We were sometimes taken aback when we discovered that a longtime customer of ours was buying certain items elsewhere, because they were cheaper. At first, we took these matters a little too personally, until we realized that price is the underpinning for most businesses—*i.e.*, for businesses selling products available elsewhere.

The Retail Business Model

This model that follows—a *user-friendly battle plan*—supplies you with tested business strategies that are effortlessly transferable to your own entrepreneurial undertakings within the confines of the pet care trade. The model embraces ten key points that should be satisfactorily addressed by you. By utilizing this scrupulous approach, you vastly increase your chances of realizing both short-term and long-term business success. The ten key points are:

1. Define what you want to accomplish by enunciating a clear mission statement (and, if you are in a partnership, speaking in one voice).
2. Make certain that you are sufficiently financed by preparing an honest business plan.
3. Scrutinize a successful business in your field and pattern yourself after it.
4. Set high, consistent, and hands-on standards for every aspect of your business from appearance, to what products you carry (or services you provide), to how your employees comport themselves.

5. Know exactly who your customers are and aggressively market to reach them.

6. Avoid complacency and stagnancy by constantly changing and evolving (products, store design, etc.), while simultaneously promoting what the competition doesn't sell *or do*.

7. Reinvest profits to grow your company.

8. Buy right by taking advantage of quantity discounts, dealer specials, etc.

9. Utilize technology to your best advantage. That is, meticulously tracking your inventory (to see what sells and doesn't sell) and fully understanding your terms of sales (*i.e.*, knowing what you are paying for everything).

10. Be a good corporate citizen by positively connecting with the community in which you do business.

Pet Hotel Proprietor

For pet owners who require more than home visitations from a pet sitter or daily daycare, but instead require places to board their dogs and cats overnight, there are reliable old kennel outfits. Kennels have a long history of servicing vacationing pet owners and pet owners leaving town for business and personal reasons. For decades, the prototypical pet-boarding facility, the kennel, consisted of cramped quarters and impersonal service. More times than not, the animal patrons staying the night were accorded minimal exercising and even less tender loving care. As this book demonstrates beyond a scintilla of doubt, this laissez-faire approach to pet care doesn't cut it anymore.

In this era of pet parenting, countless kennels are thus reinventing themselves as hotels, motels, lodges, resorts, inns, and spas. Whether it's a kennel business that's been around for decades, or one with its "Grand Opening" bunting flapping in the wind, their marketing strategies are no longer pitched to mundane pet owners, but instead to enlightened pet parents. The names alone of these businesses speak volumes: Sea Breeze Kennels, Cozy Cats Cattery, Paws & Claws Animal Lodge, Best Friends Pet Resort, Four Paws Motel, America Dog & Cat Hotel, and Paradise Pet Resort. Are you thinking about getting into the hospitality business as a **pet hotel proprietor**?

How Much Does It Cost to Start This Kind of Business?

If you intend on leasing out space and not operating from your own home and property, this kind of business will necessitate a sizeable investment. You will have to rent a considerable piece of property and tailor it to the pet hotel business. You will have to purchase necessary insurance. You will have to acquire equipment—such as pens and cages—and various accoutrements, including playthings. The startup costs alone would be a minimum of $50,000 to $75,000 and up, depending on myriad factors including location, initial advertising efforts, employees, government licenses and permits, and so on. This is a multilayered business that demands serious up-front investment to do it right and make it happen over the long-term.

If you are considering starting a pet hotel from the comforts of your own home, be sure to do your preliminary homework concerning the zoning laws in your area. Not every community and neighborhood has the welcome mat out for pet-boarding enterprises. The nature of this business requires that you know what is legal and what is not before you invest any of your time and money.

What Qualifications Do You Need for This Kind of Work?

There are no laws that require you to have any special qualifications to open up a pet hotel or kennel business. You don't have to go to pet hotel management school. But, let's face it, the most successful pet hotels are owned and operated by persons with in-depth knowledge of pet care matters who sport credentials as pet professionals. That is, many of these outfits are run and staffed by veterinarians, trainers, groomers, and other experienced pet people.

If you are entrepreneurial-minded, but not especially pet sophisticated, be sure to surround yourself with the aforementioned pet authorities. The largest and most successful pet hotels sell themselves to potential customers as capably and compassionately run, as well as prepared for any eventuality, such as a medical emergency.

How Do You Find Customers?

The pet hotel business has untapped potential, but it's not something that you can effortlessly establish, maintain, and grow. On the contrary, it's a business that's rooted in investment, industriousness, and profound responsibility. You are asking that pet parents leave their beloved companion animals in your care for extended periods of time. So, you have to show your clientele that you have what it takes to look out for their pets. Also, you have to distinguish yourself from the growing competition. This means that you have to offer a bill of fare that'll get you both attention and customers.

The Halo House Animal Resort in Gloucester County, New Jersey, for instance, extends to its canine guests limousine pick-up service, if desired, and "large suites with comfortable raised beds." Feline guests are provided "separate quarters away from canine visitors." If they are so inclined, cat owners "can request a condo with an outside view."

The Halo House Animal Resort, like many other businesses in the pet-boarding field, has a full menu of options for its customers. Dog owners can sign their pets up for a hydrosurge bath, which involves a deep-pore massage and thorough cleansing. Also available are supervised pool privileges. Doggie Daycare & Motel in Gallatin Gateway, Montana, which bills itself as "The Kennel Alternative," accents that it has "DAP diffusers throughout its

187

facility." These are *dog-appeasing pheromones* "that a mother dog puts out for her puppies to soothe and comfort them." The folks running Doggie Daycare & Motel say, "This really helps calm the new guy and helps him adjust to his new surroundings." Pet hotel operators are going that extra mile and leaving traditional kennels in the dust.

The Holiday Barn Pet Resorts, located in Richmond and Glen Allen, Virginia, provides *deluxe accommodation suites* for both cats and dogs. This business describes the experience of staying in one of its facilities as follows: "Just imagine walking down a peaceful corridor with fluffy cloud wallpaper and baroque music. You enter a suite that is beautifully appointed with decorator wallpaper, chandelier, fine art and a bed. Dog Suites have color television and Cat Suites have fish aquariums. A cool drink is waiting. Amenities available include hair styling, pedicures, snacks, swimming and aerobics. And then you remember that you are at Holiday Barn Pet Resorts." Now that's a mouthful that Club Med can't top.

Holiday Barn Pet Resorts' prices for overnight stays in regular suites are $24 to $26 for single occupancy; $42 to $46 for double occupancy; and $60 to $66 for triple occupancy. The Grand Suites are a bit more expensive: $45 to $52 for single occupancy and $75 to $88 for double occupancy. Cat Condo Suites are $16 to $18 for single occupancy and $29 to $32 for double occupancy. And this pet-hospitality business does not discriminate either: "*All pets*, from country hound dawgs to cosmopolitan cats, agree that Holiday Barn is a unique mix of traditional southern hospitality and playfulness!"

Are there enough customers out there to warrant founding a pet hotel business? Consider that the country's largest pet food and supply retailer, PetSmart, is in the pet hotel business. In 1997, the company purchased an already established business called PetsHotel Plus in Tempe, Arizona. PetSmart now manages the new PetsHotel (sans the Plus) from its original freestanding location. Since the acquisition, the national chain has inaugurated additional PetsHotels, with most of them in the confines of already established PetSmart retail stores. David Lenhardt, senior vice-president of services for PetSmart, describes the company's PetsHotel boarding businesses as generating a *halo effect*. He notes that wherever a PetsHotel has opened within a PetSmart location, sales in the other services available in that store, such as grooming and training, have increased.

So, yes, even staid corporate types are getting with the pet program. PetSmart and its PetsHotels have hosted what's been called the "Yappy Hour." During this allotted time period, four-legged guests were offered lactose-free frozen vanilla yogurt treats and mashed potato and cheese-filled rubber Kong toys, guaranteed to keep canines contentedly gnawing for hours. Also on the grounds of PetsHotels are "Bone Booths," which enable vacationing pets to receive calls from their owners. PetsHotels also permit their lodgers to have Scent Boxes by their sides, in which something from home sweet home can be kept. And, as far as air quality goes, PetsHotels recirculate the air three times every hour, ensuring that those infamous lingering doggie (and feline) odors linger no more.

Rooted in everything doggie daycares champion—fun, exercise, and fraternization—pet hotels sell themselves as places for pets to holiday, while pet parents are on vacation, out of town on business, or otherwise occupied. As a critical footnote here, it should be underscored that most pet hotel businesses also welcome daycare business.

Advertise your business in all of the usual spots and in the usual ways—local newspapers, a flier campaign. If feasible, make use of co-op mailings that target the area where you are operating. This kind of pet-specialty business is ripe for mailings of this nature.

Don't pass up the many avenues of free publicity. Newspapers and television stations are always on the lookout for intriguing feature stories. The reality is that the pet hotel business makes for just that. Don't be shy about sending out press releases to news outlets.

189

Doggie Daycare ❧ Central Bark Franchise

Doggie daycare is the appellation applied to businesses that take in canines for the day, while their owners are at work or away from home for some other reason. In essence, doggie daycare is the four-legged equivalent of children's daycare. It is an entrepreneurial opportunity that is rapidly expanding to meet increasing demand. Every day, more and more pet parents are opting for *daycare* in lieu of leaving their canine companions home alone for prolonged stretches of time.

The philosophy of doggie daycare rests on three fundamental pillars: *fun, exercise*, and *fraternization*. How individual doggie daycares apply these three principles is what distinguishes one from the other. Rates for doggie daycare services typically range between $20 and $40 per day, or $100 to $200 for the standard workweek. Rates are sometimes tied to pets' sizes, with larger breeds costing a bit more. Often amenities and perks such as personal television sets in pets' living quarters, massages, swimming privileges, or special bakery treats for dessert are offered for additional fees.

There are doggie daycares that provide their clientele with door-to-door pickup and drop-off, piped-in Mozart music during mealtimes, and around-the-clock videos of *The Animal Planet* and other forms of visual stimulation. These curious extras are somewhat atypical, but they are options for pet owners with both deeper pockets and symbiotic relationships with their furry family members. Are you up to catering to dog parents and their best friends? Are you interested in spending your working hours in the company of canines? If the answers are yes and yes, you might consider initiating a **doggie daycare**.

How Much Does It Cost to Start This Kind of Business?

The majority of doggie daycares are operated out of their proprietors' homes. Assuming you have a suitable dwelling and property sufficient to sustain this sort of business, you could get a doggie daycare off the ground with a minimal investment ($10,000 and up). For obvious reasons—no additional rental costs, smaller staffs—home outfits can ordinarily charge clients $20 to $30 per day and still realize a tidy profit.

But prosperity never comes easy. You have to carefully consider how many dogs you can comfortably care for on any given day. Home-based daycares generally have fewer dogs on the premises than do commercial facilities. Aside from the cost-conscious rates that you can offer prospective clients, your homey doggie daycare can also sell itself as a place where human-dog interaction is both intimate and persistent—which is what slobbering and social canines crave above all else. Now crunch the numbers.

If you have more investment capital to work with, you could lease property for your doggie daycare business. Leasing property and equipping it for doggie daycare would be a significantly more costly venture ($75,000 and up). In the marketplace, the larger doggie daycares often sport bigger staffs and more roomy quarters. These outfits habitually impart to their canine clientele a day replete with action, including a heaping helping of socializing with their own kind. This commonly entails a planned regiment of outdoor fun and games (weather permitting). Bigger doggie daycares are also more likely to have staff members trained to deal with any and all problems that might arise, including aggressive dog behaviors.

In any business venture where hosting pets on the premises is part of the package, it behooves you to complete a thorough due diligence along these lines. Query your state's Department of Business and its Occupational Licensing and find out what kinds of operating permits are required. If you plan on conducting this business out of your home, make sure that your local zoning laws permit doggie daycares in private residences. Also, don't forget that you are going to need insurance with this kind of business. So, before you take in even one dog, be a completely legitimate business in the eyes of the law, with all of the compulsory legal safeguards firmly in place.

What exactly will you have to do to compete with fellow doggie daycares? Foremost, doggie daycares of all sizes and in all places work with itineraries that include moments devoted to such things as playtime, snack breaks, and napping. As in children's daycare, playtime is normally a group affair. It is not uncommon to see dogs frolicking with balls, Frisbees, and other toys, just as you would see youngsters doing in their daycares. And, yes, this is a technological age that we live in. The more sophisticated—and, of course, more pricey—doggie daycares have what are called Pet Cams (or Doggie Cams or whatever they choose to call them) on the premises, which enable hardworking pet parents, via the Internet, to observe all that's going on. Dog owners can keep one eye peeled on their bond trading, lawyering, or computer programming, and the other on Fido at play with his peers in daycare.

Pet entrepreneur Chris Gaba labored for many years in the genuinely dog-eat-dog field of advertising. Compelled to put in very long hours as an ad executive, he said that it broke his heart to leave his two Weimaraners, Sophie and Taz, when he went off to work each day. Using his own personal life circumstances as his inspiration, Gaba quit his job and founded Central Bark, a doggie daycare in Fort Lauderdale, Florida. Through the years, the business has grown along with the demand for doggie daycare services. **Central Bark** @ <u>CentralBarkUSA.com</u> (866-799-BARK) now offers franchise opportunities to interested and qualified parties.

What Qualifications Do You Need for This Kind of Work?

Opening a doggie daycare is not as simple as firing your boss, running an ad in the local paper, and concocting a clever name. In order to ensure that your doggie daycare survives and prospers over the long haul, you must scrupulously vet prospective customers—just as customers must scrupulously vet you. Competently run doggie daycares *require* dog owners interested in their services to complete detailed questionnaires about their pets' history, training, and temperament. This procedure amounts to *interviewing the dog*. Possible clients must also furnish proof that their animals have been properly inoculated from such diseases as rabies, DDP (distemper, parvovirus, and parainfluenza), Lyme disease, and bordetella.

Barbra Waldare is the founder of Doggie View Daycare in Studio City, California. Her **Doggie View** website is replete with information on this increasingly popular business. Waldare is "your dog daycare consultant." Visit <u>DoggieView.com</u> (866-DOG-VIEW).

There is nothing more critical to the long-term success of your doggie daycare than maintaining safe and happy environments free from contagious diseases and anti-social and poorly trained pets. One rotten apple can spoil this barrel in a hurry. And safety, for both the human handlers and fellow dogs, is at the top of every doggie daycare's agenda. So, what all of this boils down to is knowledge. You have to be learned in canine behavior and fully prepared to deal swiftly and effectively with any problems that might arise.

How Do You Find Customers?

Notwithstanding the fast and furious rise of doggie daycare businesses, the vast majority of working pet owners still leave their four-legged housemates alone for extended periods of time, and never entertain the thought of hiring a pet sitter or signing on with a doggie daycare. Only 3% to 4% of the very ample pet-owning population currently employs these services, which signifies that there is an enormous untapped market out there.

Successful doggie daycare operations are, in the end, built atop a solid foundation known as *reputation*. Sure, clever and concerted advertising efforts are important in getting your business noticed. But, ultimately, it's testimonials from satisfied customers that'll make or break your doggie daycare. Pet parents want to leave their dogs in good hands. Above all else, the doggie daycare business is rooted in trust.

Pet Bakery

When the NBC primetime drama *Providence* debuted in 1999, the program featured one of its main characters running a bakery for pets. It was rather cleverly called *The Barkery*. And *Providence* was not some kind of fantasy show. The viewing public accepted a doggie bakery, as they are sometimes called, as a very legitimate entrepreneurial pursuit.

And why not? Launched in 1989, in Kansas City, Missouri, Three Dog Bakery, the country's oldest pet bakery, now sports shops from West Des Moines, Iowa, to West Hartford, Connecticut; Houston, Texas, to Boca Raton, Florida. Its wholesale operation ships its pet eats to every state in the union. National retailers and many smaller pet-specialty shops carry Three Dog Bakery products, as well as the company's own all-natural line of pet foods. Three Dog Bakery's retail franchises are an international phenomenon, too, and can be found in such unlikely places as Japan and South Korea. Perhaps you are ready to light the ovens of your very own **pet bakery**.

How Much Does It Cost to Start This Kind of Business?

This is a tough one to calculate. It all depends on what you have in mind vis-à-vis the pet bakery business. If you intend on opening up a brick-and-mortar shop, it's going to cost you a fair sum of money ($50,000 to $75,000 and up) to get things cooking. On the other hand, if you want to sell your goods at pet shows, fairs, via the Internet, and to established retailers, you could bake from the comforts of home what you need when you need it. This would entail a minimal startup investment.

Dan Dye and Mark Beckloff are the founding fathers of the pioneering pet-specialty business called Three Dog Bakery. The two men initially set out to whip up treats that dogs would not only love, but that were also good for them and free from the additives found in most commercial pet treats. With their three dogs—Dottie, Gracie, and Sarah—acting as official tasters, they experimented for months. Once they got the *paws up* from their three canine employees, entrepreneurial history was about to be made.

A pet-specialty bakery business can be a very lucrative entrepreneurial endeavor. Its moneymaking tentacles are many. Pet bakeries—be they on

Main Street or in the virtual ether of cyberspace—can both retail and whole-sale their products. That said, before delving into a business of this kind, you should prepare a thorough business plan and make absolutely sure that you have the gumption and the know-how to succeed.

Foremost, contact your state's Department of Business and Department of Agriculture. Also, check out Occupational Licensing, too. Gather all the necessary legal information regarding operating a pet bakery. Then take this preliminary research process down a notch to the local level. **KNOW BEFORE YOU GO** is essential in all businesses, but most especially in enterprises with a mother lode of rules and regulations. State and local guidelines overseeing the physical process of baking, ingredients, and labeling vary considerably. So, to avoid being shut down or fined, do all of your homework first. You'll be happy that you did.

You must have fire in the belly—as well as the oven—to bake hundreds of lip-smacking treats every single day. You have to know where you are going to do all of this baking. You have to know if it's legal to do so. And, finally, you have to know who will buy your products. Is it going to be retail customers in your own store? Are you going to peddle your delicacies via a website? Do you want to sell to retailers and establish a series of wholesale accounts? Maybe you want to tap into all of these selling possibilities?

What Qualifications Do You Need for This Kind of Work?

If you are going to do all the baking yourself, you obviously have to know how to bake. Take a gander at what pet bakeries are selling. The myriad goodies they offer appear mouth-watering—to the human palate. Remember that it's not dogs and cats that you are trying to win over with these all-important visuals; it's the pet people with the purchasing power. Nevertheless, all of these alluring bakery products must simultaneously have taste appeal to the pet populace. What's the point of preparing gorgeous-looking pet pastries if the furry and four-legged crowd is going to sniff their noses at them? You won't get much repeat business this way.

Another essential qualification in this kind of work is a thorough understanding of pet nutrition. After all, what may look like a scrumptious brownie to our sore eyes cannot, in fact, be manufactured like a traditional bakery's brownie. Above all else, you have to know what constitutes healthy and safe edibles for the pet-set.

How Do You Find Customers?

Let's return for a moment to the acknowledged fathers of the pet bakery business. The notion of a bakery for pets was considered pretty far-out when the first Three Dog Bakery opened its doors in the Show Me State. But oddball ideas very often catch on, particularly when the news media give you free publicity, and most especially in the realm of today's pet commerce. When reporter Richard Gibson from the *Wall Street Journal* did a feature story on the five entrepreneurs—two men and three dogs—Three Dog Bakery had arrived. The notoriety heated the ovens and set the stage for the business to become a national concern, and not just a curious niche lost in America's heartland.

Owners Dan Dye and Mark Beckloff, who refer to themselves as *entre-dogneurs*, were soon getting written up in *People* magazine, *The New York Times*, *The Boston Globe*, *Forbes* magazine, and countless other publications both big and small. The Three Dog Bakery brain trust appeared on *Oprah*, *Conan O'Brien*, *Late Night*, and *The Today Show*, which ran a promo proclaiming, "At last, the place that dogs have been praying for!"

Visit ThreeDog.com for all kinds of information on this trailblazing pet bakery business. The company's history and current menu will clue you in on what the pet bakery business is all about and where you can go with your own venture in this tasty slice of pet commerce.

Okay, so it's highly unlikely that you'll get on *Oprah*. Nevertheless, this is the type of business where a combination of traditional and untraditional promoting can pay off big dividends. Make your bakery a place that not only peddles interesting and desirable merchandise, but is a happening joint, too. A considerable portion of the pet-consumer demographic is drawn to pet-themed events. And the media loves to cover them, too. Free publicity! Advertise in local newspapers. Send out press releases. Put fliers on car windshields and in mailboxes. Make it known that you are in business—and a very interesting one at that.

Pet Boutique

The two most powerfully charged words in the pet care trade are *pet boutique*, for they encompass everything from the most fascinating of products to the most surprising of services. Pet boutiques are legion in the cities and towns of America, and along the Information Superhighway, too: Bow Wow Boutique, Coats and Tails, My Pet's Dream, Posh Pet Boutique, Uptown Hound, Oh My Dog! Cat!, Downtown Doghouse, Bone Du Jour, Pampered Pups, LeDoggie Devine, Diva Paws, etc., etc. Every single day, pet boutiques like these are boldly venturing into unexplored and often very profitable spheres. Can you see yourself in the fraternity of **pet boutique** proprietors?

How Much Does It Cost to Start This Kind of Business?

If you are contemplating inaugurating a brick-and-mortar pet boutique, you are going to need a hearty amount of investment capital ($50,000 and up). You don't want to crash into the wall that all too many businesses hit. It's the entrepreneurial funeral dirge known as under-capitalization.

Absolutely, you could open up a storefront and stock it with merchandise for considerably less than $50,000 (in most locations in the country). But, at the outset of any sizeable business venture, the bills are usually coming through your mail slot at a much faster clip than the customers are coming through your door. It generally takes time—sometimes years—to establish a regular and loyal clientele and to start seeing profits. Don't expect monetary miracles from the get-go, and have enough capital at your disposal to get you over the inevitable bumps on the road to success. This sliver of advice goes for any business endeavor with a retail storefront or leased office space—*i.e.*, any business with overhead: rent, phone and utility bills, taxes, insurance, advertising, inventory, and so on.

What Qualifications Do You Need for This Kind of Work?

To be successful in this retail sliver of the pet care trade, you have to be wholly immersed in the latest trends. As a pet boutique owner, you should be on the cusp of all that is transpiring in the industry—cognizant of the most current products and services on the market.

How Do You Find Customers?

First of all, many doggie bakeries are also full-line pet boutiques. The bakery concept and the boutique concept is a match made in entrepreneurial heaven. When venturing down the various traditional and nontraditional avenues of promotion mentioned repeatedly throughout this book, highlight your boutique's most remarkable and unique products and services. This is the sort of business that craves attention.

Just what are pet boutiques all about? What do they sell? Fetch, a dog and cat bakery-boutique in Alexandria, Virginia, retails fresh-baked goods in the store— one of its big sellers is a line of crème-filled cookies—but also designer leashes and toys for the canine crowd, including a chewable White House. Fetch, like so many of its competitors in this pet-specialty field, accents interaction with its clientele, both those on two legs and those on four legs. The business invites its customers to sign up for things like the Birthday Club, in which pets get a pound of specially baked treats in celebration of their natal anniversaries.

Pawticularly Fine Boutique & Bakery in Menifee, California, offers the pet-consuming public bottles of Oh My Dog! perfume and Oh My Cat! perfume. This pet-specialty shop describes its chic perfumes as "designed in France by an outstanding perfume maker." It further categorizes them as "the first unisex, up-scale perfumes for dogs and cats that combine all of the tenderness of the first hesitant steps taken by a puppy or kitten toward the family. An unforgettable olfactory memory." Customers at Pawticularly Fine Boutique & Bakery can also purchase tubes of Oh My Dog! Shampoo "formulated like a bath product for babies."

Pet boutiques sell such incomparable products as Anxiety Wrap. This stretchable, vest-like body wrap, the brainchild of dog trainer Susan Sharpe, is designed to give dogs the sensation of being hugged. Sharpe describes the product as "a wonderful tool that helps animals to cope and overcome their past and present issues." Further, she adds, "It aids an animal's ability to focus and remain calm and complements the use of gentle training methods."

Palmetto Paws, a pet-specialty boutique in the state of South Carolina, offers its clientele special services, too, like in-store washing stations. Customers can utilize this self-service bath for their dogs. Beth Thomas, owner of Palmetto Paws, says that when the weather turns cold "people don't want to wash their dog out in the yard, so it's a good solution for them."

Commence an Internet search on "pet bakery," "doggie bakery," "pet boutique," or some similar combination of words and you will chance upon a roster of businesses in this intriguing field. Visit their websites to see what they are selling and how they are selling their vast and varied product lines. Get ideas for your own pet bakery or pet boutique. This is also a good way to locate wholesale sources of goods for your business. There are some pet bakeries that purchase all of their merchandise from other sources. So, if you can't see yourself baking them yourself—or cannot legally get the requisite permits—you can get the necessary goodies from wholesalers.

Dog Wash ✦ The Pooch Mobile Franchise

How many times do we have to say it? Yes, the present business of pets is leaving no entrepreneurial stone unturned or, in this particular instance, no entrepreneurial dog unwashed. For countless dog owners, the mere notion of bathing their four-legged friends in their homes sends shivers up and down their spines. Simply put, it's not an aspect of dog parenting that they particularly relish. If they had their druthers, the preponderance of the pooch populace would prefer not hitting the bathtub waters.

The bathing of most dogs is not an uncomplicated undertaking, most especially if the canine in question weighs more than a few pounds. The bathing experience often comes attached to a great deal of writhing to and fro, and, worst of all, a perpetual shaking off of water in every imaginable direction. In other words, after dog baths, there are big messes in a whole host of bathrooms across the fruited plane. Also, since many pet persons with backyards prefer bathing their canine companions in the great outdoors, what happens when the seasons change and the thermometer heads south?

There are also many particulars that you need in order to pull off a successful dog bath, wherever it comes to pass. For starters, you have to purchase the right kinds of shampoos and conditioners. You need grooming brushes, towels for drying, and sometimes even an electric hair dryer. (Wet dogs are very susceptible to catching colds from drafts after bathing.) And, on top of all that, if the bathing affair transpires in your personal bathroom, there is a lot of cleaning up to do afterwards. The dirty little secret in today's pet care trade is that not everybody—even those who love their dogs like they do their own children—appreciates sharing bathtub privileges with the canine species and their bands of shedding hair and distinctive grime accumulated in their various travels. Thus, there is a genuine demand for a **dog wash** enterprise— businesses that importune pet parents to bring their dogs to them for the purpose of a right and proper bath. With each passing day and newly dirtied dog, dog washes are attracting both more notice and more customers.

How Much Does It Cost to Start This Kind of Business?

As with so many other pet-specialty endeavors, dog-washing services are very often affiliated with other businesses in the trade. For instance, dog washes can be found in some pet boutiques and doggie bakeries, and they are frequently associated with grooming outfits, which bathe four-legged clients on a regular basis anyway. Kennels and pet hotels are also adding dog-washing options to their service menus. But this isn't to imply that businesses solely devoted to dog washing can't turn a real profit. There are, in fact, sole dog-wash enterprises that offer self-service and full-service bathing options, and that welcome walk-in business with no appointments required.

Again, and this bears repeating over and over, if you need to lease a physical location—a storefront of some kind—you will have to pay the piper with a sizeable dollar investment. Initial investment requirements could easily range between $25,000 and $50,000, and possibly a whole lot more. There are expensive equipment needs in this type of business (such as raised tubs and the plumbing extras that come with the territory). There are also issues of insurance, which any business inviting dogs onto the premises will have to procure. Don't expect a dog wash business to come cheap—and to attempt to do it on the cheap will more than likely augur poor results. Nevertheless, it is the ideal entrepreneurial road to travel down in concert with, as already mentioned, other service businesses in the trade. For instance, if your dog wash is part of a retail store that sells pet food and accessory products, it would enhance that slice of the business and vice versa. If feasible, why not add the walk-in dog wash concept to an already established grooming business. They really do go hand-in-grooming glove.

There is an authentic demand for dog washes, and it's not some artificial kind created by Madison Avenue advertising mavens. It's a service that people will freely utilize because it fills a real need in their lives as pet parents. More often than not, dog owners are unaware that these types of pet service businesses even exist. Those who do know about them are not always in close proximity of an operating dog wash.

To get an idea of what the dog wash business entails, visit a couple of them. Drop by the aptly named **Dog Wash** @ DogWash.net. This wash is located in Arlington, Texas. Another place worth checking out is **U-Wash Doggie** @ PetWash.com (800-PET-WASH). This business can be found in Burbank, California. If you are interested in a mobile pet wash—yes, they exist too—there are franchise opportunities in this field. Visit **The Pooch Mobile** @ ThePoochMobile.us (866-933-5111) and discover what it's all about. This business provides customers with, among many things, the *hydrobath* and *aromacare*. Begun as the **Aussie Pooch Mobile**, it is an international phenomenon. They can be found @ AussiePM.com.

What Qualifications Do You Need for This Kind of Work?

If you are offering your clientele self-service dog washing only—where the customers wash their own pets in your facilities—you don't need any special skills beyond the entrepreneurial. That is, you should have an extensive knowledge of what is required to establish and run a dog wash properly and profitably—the right equipment, necessary particulars (from shampoos to towels), insurances, government permits, etc. Self-service dog washes are charging in the neighborhood of $10 to $20 and more, while furnishing their clientele access to all that they need to complete the bathing job from the tubs to the flowing warm water to the shampoos to the dryers and towels. Just like a car wash.

On the other hand, if you plan on offering full-service dog washing, with you as the bather-in-chief, you should be sufficiently schooled in handling dogs and know a thing or two about grooming. After all, bathing is an important part of overall grooming. This is precisely why professional groomers are increasingly adding basic dog washing to their other services. As already noted, the canine contingent doesn't ordinarily sit compliantly for these moments. But, as with so many other pet-specialty professionals, you don't need a degree or certification to get your feet wet in this kind of business.

How Do You Find Customers?

The usual methods, including a flier campaign and advertisements in local papers, are good places to start. The dog wash as a business entity is also something that can get you a media mention or two in print or on television. Send out press releases detailing what your dog wash business is all about. This is a surefire way of attracting attention and getting free publicity.

Pet Franchisee

If you have some investment dollars to play with—in some instances, a real heap of change—there are pet-themed franchise opportunities to look into. You could possibly be the next **pet franchisee**. Understandably, many entrepreneurial-minded individuals are attracted to these veritable businesses in a box—tried and tested outfits that want to sell their winning concepts to you. What you are required to do in return is run the chosen business in a prescribed manner—*e.g.*, train in their methods, buy equipment and merchandise from their sources, maintain a certain store brand image, wear particular clothes, and so on.

While purchasing a franchise business has a downside—often a sizeable investment is at risk and you operate from a rather unyielding playbook—it nevertheless has a potentially significant upside. Consider, for example, all that would be involved in starting a fast-food hamburger restaurant. It would be at once costly and complicated on countless levels. *Where do you get the food and supplies? What government regulations do you need to comply with? What machinery do you need? Who do you call when something breaks down?* Of course, once you got the place opened, you would have to lure customers to your door and hope that they come back again and again.

On the other hand, if it was a McDonald's hamburger franchise, you would be supplied with all of the set-up rules. You would be trained and handed the McDonald's blueprint for success. You'd be told what to do if this happened or that happened. In other words, you would know what is expected of you and your business from soup to nuts—or, more appropriately, from burgers to fries. You'd also be given the names of all of your suppliers. There would be no guesswork involved. And customers wouldn't need much coaxing to go to your McDonald's franchise. People know what McDonald's sells and what their foods taste like. The bottom line for McDonald's franchisees is

205

that many of them can and do make a lot of money by faithfully adhering to a longstanding and proven formula.

Now, granted, there are no McDonald's-caliber franchises in the field of pet care. Not yet anyway. But there are many operations that have established formulas for success. There are now franchise opportunities in a variety of fields in the trade, including:

- ★ Pet food and supply retailing
- ★ Pooper scooping
- ★ Dog training
- ★ Dog grooming
- ★ Pet daycare
- ★ And many others

Again, to purchase most franchise businesses, you have to have some green ($25,000 and up) to put down at the onset. But these franchises are all about turning green into greener pastures. Across the board, a franchise's strongest selling point is that you have a greater chance of succeeding in an already proven business model than in starting an enterprise of your own from scratch. Franchisers offer potential franchisees their knowledge and, ordinarily, a lifetime's worth of trouble-shooting assistance. Again, in the rough and tumble business world, this kind of handholding surely has an appeal.

How Much Does It Cost to Start This Kind of Business?

To own and operate a pet franchise, you are going to have to make an investment—and more than likely a sizeable one. Most brick-and-mortar franchise businesses require $100,000 or more in up-front capital. (There are some cheaper ways to go.) Naturally, retail franchise operations necessitate significant investment outlays. The reasons for this are quite apparent. For starters, these kinds of stores must be setup—fixtures, signage, etc.—and stocked with inventory. The final dollar investment is often impacted by location as well. In other words, a franchise operation in New York City will more than likely cost you more than one in a smaller metropolis or suburbia. Franchise businesses on the service side—where you purchase a proven concept—can be found that are more affordable.

What Qualifications Do You Need for This Kind of Work?

If you have the requisite dollars to purchase a franchise business, you are at first base. But in order to make it all around the bases as a franchise owner and successful operator, you have to be fully committed to managing it in a prescribed manner. Franchisers do not sell their concepts to any Tom, Dick, and Harriet who comes their way brandishing a sack full of money. Showing up with the loot won't guarantee you a franchise. In the final analysis, you have to be open to an education—from soup to nuts—on the way the business operates. If you can traverse the sharp learning curve without flipping over, you are ready to roll. In a nutshell, good business smarts and a rock-solid work ethic are the most vital qualities that you must possess to make a franchise business both happen and thrive.

How Do You Find Customers?

You find customers via the traditional routes of advertising: fliers, newspaper ads, etc. But more often than not franchisees are assisted from up above with their marketing strategies. In many instances, franchisees are compelled to advertise in certain places and in prescribed ways.

Pet Business Franchises

Where there is business success, franchises are sure to follow. So it should come as no surprise to you that many of the opportunities chronicled in this book now count franchise possibilities in the scintillating mix. When a businessperson does something right, he or she has a winning recipe that is, naturally, of great interest to others. Logistically, it's not always possible for entrepreneurs to spread their business concepts as far and wide as they would like. This is where franchising comes into play and saves the day. Expect to see many more pet-themed franchise businesses over the coming years.

Here is a sampling of some of the more popular franchise businesses in the pet care trade:

★ **Bark Busters** @ BarkBusters.com (877-300-BARK). This is an in-home dog training company founded in 1989, by Sylvia and Danny Wilson in Wollongong, Australia. This international business teaches franchisees its holistic and humane training system.

★ **Doody Calls** @ DoodyCalls.com (800-DOODY-CALLS). This is a very successful and growing pet-waste removal company with many franchise operations throughout the entire country.

★ **Happy Tails Dog Spa** @ HappyTailsDogSpa.com. The dog hotel business is big and getting bigger. This particular company sports a vast and varied menu that includes daycare, overnight accommodations, spa privileges, training, and a boutique. Franchisees learn how to provide all of the above to their clientele.

★ **Pets Are Inn** @ PetsAreInn.com. This is another popular pet-boarding business that sells itself as an alternative to cold, impersonal kennels. "Host families"—caregivers—are selected for each and every pet that stays in the expanding numbers of these inns, which are independently owned franchises. Potential franchisees should also know that Pets Are Inn is an approved AAA company.

★ **Pet Butler** @ PetButler.com (800-PET-BUTLER). This is yet another pet-waste cleanup and removal company that offers franchise opportunities. The scoop on the poop, as it were, is that it's increasingly big business.

★ **Pet Depot** @ PetDepot.net (626-335-0469). Interested in operating a pet food and supply superstore? This is one successful company that offers franchise opportunities for old-fashioned, brick-and-mortar retail stores.

★ **Pet Supplies "Plus"** @ PetSuppliesPlus.com. With superstores all the rage in the field of pet care, this business is spotted all across the country. The outlets are owned and operated by independent franchisees.

CHAPTER VIII

The Truth is Stranger than Fiction: More Unusual Pet Care Business Ideas

Catnip Farmer ⚬ Catnip Merchandise Maker

How would you like to grow an aphrodisiac and profit from your harvesting efforts? We're talking about a feline aphrodisiac of sorts called catnip, and you being a **catnip farmer** and **catnip merchandise maker**.

When in the proximity of this titillating herb in the mint family, most members of the feline species go bananas. This euphoria is usually brief, and is not known to have any deleterious health effects on the frenzied felines. The bottom line is that catnip is an exceedingly popular pet product in the trade. Catnip is sold loose in plastic tubs and packages. All kinds of feline playthings are treated with catnip. There are catnip treats. Liquefied spray versions of the herb exist. You name it and catnip has been applied to it.

Through the years in our Pet Nosh stores, we couldn't keep enough catnip in stock. Our most popular catnip items were so very originally called "Catnip Balls." They consisted of loose catnip—a very fresh and potent version of it—wrapped in rather pedestrian pieces of fabric and held together with minuscule pieces of yarn. We purchased them directly from a man who harvested a bumper catnip crop on his property. He made a nice living selling his catnip balls and freshly farmed loose catnip directly to retailers like us. We priced the balls at two for a dollar and could never keep enough of them in stock. While they appeared amateurishly manufactured, our customers loved them because their cats got such a big kick—literally—out of them. You, too, can farm catnip and sell it in a variety of places.

How Much Does It Cost to Start This Kind of Business?

If you can afford a pack of seeds, you can get started. What you do when you have a product ready for the market will determine the further size of your initial investment.

What Qualifications Do You Need for This Kind of Work?

If you can plant seeds, you can be a catnip farmer. Obviously, you need a piece of soil to plant them in. A backyard lawn and/or garden spot will do. The more space you have for the farming, the better your catnip yield and prospects for building a profitable business. You can grow your own product, harvest it, and sell it. There is a robust and perpetual demand for catnip and catnip products, particularly when the herb is freshly grown and fast brought to market. If you fancy creating catnip playthings, they don't have to be anything fancy. We sold thousands of mundane-looking cat toys that were essentially catnip raviolis—catnip-filled centers surrounded by crudely stitched together pieces of cloth. It's the quality of the catnip that counts.

How Can You Grow Catnip?

Catnip is a perennial plant, which means that it will come back year after year providing the winters aren't too severe. Catnip can grow just about anywhere in temperate climates with full sun, adequate moisture, and reasonable soil. In other words, you can raise it from seed in most locales in the United States where there are gradually warming spring and summer seasons that last several months.

Catnip seeds can be purchased at most garden centers or in garden catalogs. Be careful not to make the mistake of buying the ornamental catnip plant, which is a completely different animal from what we are talking about. Catnip plants can grow three feet or taller and their spread is ten to fifteen inches, so each seed should be planted approximately ten to fifteen inches apart. Catnip's leaves are light green, slightly furry, and have scalloped edges. The stems of the plant are hollow. You can begin harvesting your catnip as soon as the plants exhibit signs of flowering.

What you do then is cut off the stems roughly eight inches from the ground. Strip off all the leaves from the cut stems and place them in three- to four-inch high trays. The leaves can be stacked one on top of the other. Provided they are in a dry area with sufficient air circulation—and, very importantly, out of the reach of curious felines—the catnip leaves will get brittle and crumble to the touch in two to three weeks. And there you have it—catnip, a coveted pet product.

If you are a catnip aficionado, you very likely have purchased a Cosmic Pet product or two. Cosmic Pet is the world's leading seller of catnip and catnip accessories. A man named Leon Seidman founded the company as the Cosmic Cat Corporation in 1975. What made him start a catnip business in this quieter time before pet food and supply superstores and hotels existed for the four-legged? His inspiration: a fussy cat, who regularly sniffed his nose at store-bought catnip. This indifferent reaction from his feline boarder prompted Seidman to head to the woods for wild catnip, which his four-legged friend adored. Seidman eventually saved the seeds from the plants he brought home and started growing the herb himself. He gave friends and acquaintances samples of his harvest, and they fawned over the freshness and cat appeal of his homegrown catnip. Seeing how popular it was with one and all led to the founding of a business that would fast grow into an international sensation. Check out **Cosmic Pet** @ CosmicPet.com (888-226-7642).

How Do You Find Customers?

Depending on your ambition and, of course, the space you can allot to the farming of it, you could peddle the fruits of your labor, as it were, to any number of retailers and wholesalers in the trade. You could attend cat shows and pet products shows and acquire customers. Craft fairs with your catnip creations would be another market for you to conquer.

Geese Away Geese Police Franchise

When Canada geese are airborne, they are undeniably one of nature's wonders. Their synchronized flight patterns and accompanying chatter are impeccably choreographed. When a gaggle of geese is spotted effortlessly gliding across a lake or pond, it is a serene spectacle worthy of a snapshot.

Yet, increasingly, this oft-sighted species of waterfowl run afoul of homeowners, businesses, and park visitors in both urban and suburban settings. Be they on college campuses, sprawling golf courses, cemetery grounds, or in Mr. Smith's front yard, Canada geese are wont to make themselves right at home, even when they are unwelcome trespassers.

During nesting time, this class of bird fancies nothing more than feasting on succulent green grass, molting, and—alas—excreting waste and more waste. When these brassy birds come calling, lush green lawns often become brown wastelands blanketed in feathers and excrement. And, once Canada geese have settled in, it's not an easy task evicting them.

Herein lies an entrepreneurial opening you can drive a truck through. With mixed results, myriad products—chemicals, streamers, balloons, flagging—and methods—very loud noises—have endeavored to nudge Canada geese to someplace else—*anywhere else*. But not a single one of them has met with the success of employing border collies to do the job.

Foremost, it's important to keep in mind that federal law protects Canada geese, as do always-vigilant animal rights' groups. This means that **geese away** businesses must always utilize humane methods to accomplish their missions. When suitably trained, border collies chase the uninvited birds away without ever biting or harming them.

Border collies are herding dogs by nature. Once upon a time, the breed was busy driving livestock—from sheep to pigs to, yes, geese—to the marketplace. Needless to say, their workload was sharply downsized with the invention of the motor vehicle. But, fortunately, a new career has emerged for these intelligent and antsy canines, as well as for two-legged entrepreneurs interested in the invigorating business of geese relocation.

Geese relocation works with border collies and their wolf-like glare, called the *eye*. Viewing the nimble canines as predators, the eye frightens the birds, which usually fly away. Geese that cannot fly for whatever reason are herded—unharmed in the process—to an area off the property under geese evacuation. Generally speaking, the dogs are let loose up to four times a day. After several weeks of this kind of harassment, the geese typically have gotten the message and moved on to more tranquil locales.

A single goose can excrete one to two pounds of waste a day. While goose droppings may be *au natural*, they can pose serious health risks. The birds' excrement has, on occasion, carried salmonella, E. coli, and other bacteria. In and of itself, this less than sanitary picture is enough to generate a demand for geese away businesses that can humanely relocate the birds to environs where the two-legged don't regularly frequent.

How Much Does It Cost to Start This Kind of Business?

On paper this is the simplest of business concepts: dogs chase birds away. That's all there is to it. But, as you might imagine, in practice, it is anything but simple. A geese away business can be extremely profitable in areas where problems exist (an average of $300 to $600 per week per job can be had). However, starting one is not as straightforward as purchasing or adopting a border collie and running an advertisement in the local paper.

The key that unleashes a successful geese away endeavor is both suitably trained dogs and a properly established business with all the protections that a corporate structure affords, including necessary insurance. It is imperative that you learn the ropes before jumping into this commercial venture, or, most definitely, you risk getting strangled. When working with living creatures—on both ends in this business—you assume an added burden *and* responsibility. That is, every aspect of your business must be conscientiously conducted—you can't in any way, shape, or form injure the dogs *or the birds*.

David Marcks, founder of **Geese Police** @ GeesePolice.com is the father of geese away businesses. As a golf course superintendent in the 1980s, he witnessed up close and personal what geese problems entail. To make a long story short, Marcks put his restless pet border collie to work—*and it worked*. More than two decades later, he oversees a multimillion dollar business, which includes franchise operations of the Geese Police in several states. Marcks' advice to prospective entrepreneurs in this field: Educate yourself on the nesting behavior of geese, as well as the unique personalities and idiosyncrasies of border collies. In other words, knowledge of animal behavior is vital to the success of all geese away enterprises. The Geese Police have the imprimatur of both the United States Humane Society and People for the Ethical Treatment of Animals (PETA)—no small achievement.

Getting a business like this off the ground—in a small way—costs in the neighborhood of $2,500 to $5,000. This figure includes working with a respected handler of border collies and all of the legal paperwork, requisite insurance, etc.

What Qualifications Do You Need for This Kind of Work?

The geese away business is not an entrepreneurial endeavor that can be done on the fly. It requires a commitment that begins with a thorough education on animal behavior—Canada geese and border collies—and continues with the right and proper training of the dogs. This prologue to the actual operating business will take some time. If you want to be on profit terra firma tomorrow, this isn't the business for you.

How Do You Find Customers?

In this business, customer sites run a wide gamut and can be:

- ★ Residential backyards and front yards
- ★ Playgrounds
- ★ Public and private parks
- ★ Golf courses
- ★ Pubic buildings
- ★ Airports
- ★ Cemeteries
- ★ Schools/Universities
- ★ Corporate greens

Canada geese settle down in a wide range of places with this common denominator: green grass and, typically, a lake, pond, or some kind of nearby watering hole. When you discern where problems exist, let the overseers of these various geese haunts know what you can do for them. Send them fliers or, better yet, personal letters explaining exactly what you do. Ask them to call for a chat or to request a demonstration. Personally pay them a call.

Appreciate that this kind of business is something that you have to see to believe. Mere assurances won't always do the trick. When you've established yourself in a geese away business, your references will speak very loudly—but until then….

> If you are thinking, "Why do I need border collies? I can chase away the geese myself"—perish the thought. Getting together a group of friends to run the birds out of town won't work. Sure, the geese will take to flight, but they'll be back. Canada geese won't vacate their nesting areas for just anybody or anything. It's only something they view as predatory that will do the trick. That is, the birds fear being some creature's repast. Canada geese are highly intelligent and know that two-legged animals aren't out for blood, so they will return again and again—and you'll end up looking pretty foolish in the process.

Holiday Pet Merchandise Seller

What retailer doesn't look forward with breathless anticipation to the holiday season? Now that pets are interwoven in the family circle, they are logically entitled to all the perks and benefits of this eminent status—and this includes presents at Christmastime, as well as their fair share of the festive spoils in the season of goodwill.

It would hardly be a fool's errand to focus your entrepreneurial ingenuity and financial resources on pet-themed holiday merchandise and pet-themed holiday merchandise alone. After all, Christmas merchandise is an industry unto itself. The sheer amounts of Christmas stuff for pets that we sold every December was staggering. And so much of our holiday line of products were preordered long before the jingle bells sounded and the halls were decked with boughs of holly. We couldn't afford to be caught short when demand for cat, dog, bird, and other pet gifts went through the roof. Selling holiday merchandise is actually an all-year affair. Consider life as a **holiday pet merchandise seller** and capitalize on these astonishingly green business fields.

In fact, we relished nothing more than buying holiday-inspired products, be they entire Christmas displays or single items. Through the years, we sold countless red stockings full of pet goodies, playthings, and tasty treats. We sold dog toys that resembled snowmen, candy canes, Christmas trees, and Old Saint Nick. We sold all kinds of fashions, including colorful holiday collars festooned with bells. We couldn't keep enough stock of things expressly packaged and marketed for the festive season. Almost anything we placed on holiday-themed display racks went out the door, regardless of the particular nature of the merchandise for sale. You might not think there's a big demand for fabric reindeer antlers for dogs, but during the holiday season there is. And, keep in mind that you don't have to limit yourself to stuff expressly for the furry and four-legged. Pet-themed holiday merchandise for the homo sapien goes over real big, too. Things like pet-related Christmas tree ornaments and toppers, as well as holiday decorations, are always snatched up in the hustle and bustle.

For insight into the appeal and assortment of pet holiday merchandise, scope out **Jacqueline's Originals** @ JacquelinesOriginals.com (203-426-9169). You can also buy wholesale from this distinctive company, which features a vast array of charming pet products for people. You'll find everything from cat Christmas tree toppers to dog wreath pins here. In addition, Jacqueline's Originals sells a wide range of breed-specific items from statues to sweatshirts.

How Much Does It Cost to Start This Business?

There are many possibilities to weigh in this field of endeavor. Hence, your initial investment needs will vary considerably depending on exactly what route you travel down. You could sell pet holiday merchandise the same way you would sell other pet products. You could also create or harvest from other sources an alluring mixture of holiday items and prepare attractive display racks for them. Then follow this up with preorders for fully stocked displays. This method of operation would keep your startup costs low. That is, you wouldn't need to purchase huge inventories of products until you were assured of the business.

What Qualifications Do You Need for This Kind of Work?

When selling any kind of merchandise, it certainly helps to be cut from the salesperson's cloth. However, all you really need is the courage to go out among the people and offer your product to them. If what you're selling has genuine appeal to others, you are in business.

How Do You Find Customers?

There are many pet-specialty entrepreneurs who make not too shabby livings selling display racks of merchandise. That is, they sell entire displays of this, that, and the other thing. More times than not, in-store displays of products boost their sales. The consuming public is automatically drawn to things that appeal to, above all else, the eye. Pleasingly packaged and displayed merchandise is a marketing home run. The right displays of merchandise are powerful sales tools that sell products more quickly and in greater quantities than they otherwise would; that is, if the merchandise was sold on an individual basis and placed on shelves or hung on pegboards.

During the holiday season, eye-catching display racks of merchandise—specifically packaged for the merry moment in time—turn over the stuff faster than you can say, "Jack Rabbit," or, more fittingly, "Jack Frost." When you settle upon the right product line—or, perhaps, just one product—

organize sample displays and bring them to pet trade shows or directly to retail shops. Take orders for the entire displays. You'd be surprised how many you could sell—and well in advance of Christmastime.

Whether you are going to a trade show or straight to retailers with your pet holiday merchandise, you'd be wise to go with the right kinds of displays. There are many businesses that sell display racks for just this kind of thing. You'll encounter all sorts of counter and floor displays at **A Virtual Display Mall** @ AVDM.com (209-962-1226). Lots of trade shows and retailer rack specialties can be seen at **Displays2Go** @ Displays2Go.com (800-572-2194). For some interesting wire rack displays, visit **New England Wire Products** @ DisplayRacks.com (800-254-9473).

Santa Claus Lane

There are innumerable wholesale sources of pet-related holiday merchandise. Just peruse a pet trade magazine or attend a pet trade show and you'll see what we mean. Even the general gift shows are chock-full of pet-themed items, including ample holiday materials. There are also many independent entrepreneurs out there—creators of all sorts of pet-inspired merchandise from jewelry to glassware to candles.

In addition, if you are so talented, you have the option to establish your very own pet holiday merchandise line. If you are a gifted artist, fashions designer, inventor, or craftsperson, you could create your very own holiday products. Even if you have what you deem a winning idea, but feel you can't make it happen yourself, take it to somebody who can. For example, you could have an idea for a line of pet-themed holiday coffee mugs. You don't have to manufacturer them yourself. There are businesses that can make them up for you—ditto pet holiday collector plates, pet holiday buttons, pet holiday jewelry, etc. You could fill up your own Christmas stockings for cats and dogs and market them. The possibilities in this pet holiday merchandise arena are limitless.

Doggie Summer Camp

For pet owners who can't conceive of leaving their pets in even the most luxurious of pet hotels with every imaginable courtesy, there are doggie summer camps. This is yet another slice of the pet-specialty service field where entrepreneurial ingenuity is filling a widening niche. These summer camps are vacation hot spots for society's most committed couples: dog owners and their best friends. In other words: No more separate vacations!

Doggie summer camps can be found snuggled in places like the Green Mountains of Vermont, the picturesque Lake Tahoe in Nevada, the country-side of St. Helen, Michigan, and overlooking the wending Hudson River in upstate New York. Each and every one of them offers a vast spectrum of fun things for both people and their pets to do together, while, of course, commingling with like-minded souls in atmospheres of solitude and leisure. Maybe it's your destiny to organize and operate a **doggie summer camp**.

How Much Does It Cost to Start This Kind of Business?

This is a very expensive business undertaking. As with most of the business opportunities chronicled on these pages, the amount of investment capital needed is based on what you want to get out of it. Yes, you could organize a doggie summer camp and schedule just a couple of weeks of activities. There are doggie summer camps that host dogs and dog parents in a couple of unique sessions each year, such as a week for one group and then another week for a new crowd. In this scenario, you would need to find suitable property and rent it out for just the two-week time frame, thus minimizing your initial invest-ment. But, by the same token, you also limit your full profit possibilities.

A ballpark estimate for initiating a more wide-ranging doggie summer camp is $100,000 and up. Considerable investment is required to rent a location that sufficiently accommodates significant numbers of people and pets. Foremost, you have to pinpoint an appropriate dog-friendly site. This isn't a simple undertaking. The property must be at once sprawling and replete with amenities to comfortably service and entertain both the two-legged and four-legged. If there is no onsite lodging on the property, you have to coordinate your campsite with suitable sleeping quarters in close proximity. A whole lot goes into running a doggie summer camp.

Then there are the ample insurance issues that come attached to this kind of business. When multiple canines and canine parents congregate for weeks at a time in a particular locale, you have to pay the insurance piper to make it happen. *What if there is an accident? What if a canine takes a chunk out of somebody's arm or leg? What happens if two dogs get into a scrape and are injured?* The list of potential mishaps could go on. But the larger point here is that operating a doggie summer camp demands that you do your homework and fully protect both yourself and your clientele.

What Qualifications Do You Need for This Kind of Work?

As with just about every pet-themed business concept, it certainly helps to know an awful lot about pets. This is a no-brainer. But in the doggie summer camp business, you also have to have strong organizational skills. Successful doggie summer camps are highly choreographed events. That is, they furnish those in attendance with a roster of daily activities. It's the furthest thing from a business that runs on autopilot. In other words, you don't just lease property, put out the welcome mat for dog parent and dog, and then say, "You're on your own." On the contrary, you are charged with being a ring-leader. Your guests will expect you to be into everything that's going on.

How Do You Find Customers?

If you have both the requisite resources and the gumption to launch a doggie summer camp, you've unquestionably got a substantial marketplace in which to forage for customers. While doggie summer camps exist in a variety of diverse locales, there are not too many of them in the overall scheme of things. That is, dog parents interested in this sort of thing—vacationing with their pets in a special camp environment—don't have a whole lot of options from which to choose. The key that unlocks success in this inimitable business is the *adventure* that you will offer prospective campers.

Doggie summer camps have to be real happenings in really nice places. So what exactly goes on at these camps? Let's take a gander at one such vacation stopover for pets and their people. It's called Dog Days of Wisconsin. For those on the fence about vacationing with their canines in a summer camp environment, Dog Days of Wisconsin asks them to complete this short quiz:

1. Do you wish you could get away from it all *and* take your dog along?
2. Do you like to relax and chill out during the day?
3. Do you want to take your dog camping but feel tolerated instead of welcomed at campgrounds?
4. Do you like to try new and exciting canine activities but can't find a place?
5. Do you like to keep busy all the time and do lots of things all day long?
6. Do your coworkers look at you funny when you start telling those "I'm so proud of him or her stories" when the him or her is a dog?
7. Do you like to have lots of choices of things to do and down time?

"If you answered *yes* to any of these questions, then Dog Days of Wisconsin Summer Camp is just what you are looking for," says the camp's brochure. Now, whether doggie summer camps are what you are searching for as an entrepreneurial endeavor is another kettle of fish. As already underscored, there's a great deal involved in this kind of business. The foremost hurdle to leap over is the property. The camp has got to be a place that can facilitate things like swimming lessons (for canines, of course), freestyle dancing classes (for both dogs and dog owners!), and agility training (pooches only).

In other words, the doggie summer camp has got to be big and supply both pooch and person with a wealth of things to do in an environment conducive to camping in the great outdoors. And, on top of everything else, many of these vacation havens furnish their guests—both two-legged and four legged—with an education. That is, there are pet care experts around to lecture and train the assembled.

To appreciate what doggie summer camps are all about, visit their websites. **Camp Gone to the Dogs** @ Camp-Gone-to the-Dogs.com is a Vermont vacation unlike any other for canine and canine parent. **Dog Days of Wisconsin** @ DogCamp.com and **Canine Country Camp** @ GlenHighLandFarm.com are two more doggie summer camps to investigate. Better yet, why not vacation at a doggie summer camp. If this is at all feasible, it's always the wisest route to take before opening up a business—any kind of business. See for yourself what it's like—what the business entails from dawn to dusk. You might be surprised at what you discover.

Honey Loring is the owner of Camp Gone to the Dogs. "I founded the camp because I wanted to be able to vacation with my dogs," she says. "I'm lucky that there are a lot of people like me who eat, sleep, and drink dogs," Loring adds, citing her business's ever-growing popularity since its rather inconspicuous inception in 1990.

How does Camp Gone to the Dogs come to pass? Every year between the months of June and September, the camp gets rolling in bucolic locations in the state of Vermont. From camp session to camp session, it is an entrepreneurial undertaking that is not confined to a particular piece of property. Recent camps were held at The Mountaineer Inn in the town of Stowe, and a larger one at Marlboro College—with its 250 acres—in scenic Marlboro. There are between thirty to fifty activities for dog owners and their dogs to participate in each and every day. "You can do everything, or nothing at all," notes Loring, who encourages relaxation above all else. Depending on the particular camp session, pet care experts are often on hand conducting workshops on issues that matter to dog owners, such as grooming techniques and obedience training.

Camp Gone to the Dog's owner relishes the publicity her pet-specialty business gets each year. "Media people come out here and they film our fun stuff, like tail-wagging contests and kissing contests, but this is what we're all about, loving our dogs and all dogs." The most successful pet entrepreneurs are known to contact local newspapers and television stations. They inform these media outlets of the ABCs of their businesses and what events and such are on the docket. Any free publicity that comes your way is worth its weight in gold.

Somewhat different in approach from Camp Gone to the Dogs, Dog Scout Camp in St. Helen, Michigan, patterns itself after the Boy Scouts of America. Its motto is: "Let us learn new things that we may become more helpful." The canines who accompany their masters to this doggie summer camp can earn merit badges in various activities, including search and rescue, agility, backpacking, operant conditioning (a type of behavioral training), and water safety. One of Dog Scout Camp's most popular features is its sprawling sand lot, in which the canine species are given free access to dig holes—until they hit China, if they have a mind to. For the human animal, there are lectures on subject matter ranging far and wide from doggie massage methods to healthy canine nutrition to pooch painting. Seriously, if you opt to assist your dog in completing a piece of artwork, it will be matted for you—ready for framing—to take home.

The cost of attending Dog Scout Camp is $650 for both human and beast. But it's well worth the price of admission, particularly if a four-legged camper gets certified a scout, which one can upon passing a final exam at the end of the festivities. A dog that is a scout in good standing, is automatically a better citizen, capable of doing so many more things to assist both two-legged parents and society at large.

Dog Scout Camp @ DogScouts.com (989-389-2000) not only runs one of the country's largest and most successful doggie summer camps, it also offers interested parties the opportunity to host mini-camps in their necks of the wood. While there are doggie summer camps in different parts of the country, there is ample room for more of them in the vast geographic space that is the United States of America.

Once you have the location and adventure schedule all plotted out, you have to let the world know about your camp. Many dog parents will travel a fair distance to attend a doggie summer camp with a lot to offer. Advertise in pet-themed publications. Run advertisements in newspapers in the surrounding area. Establish a website that provides all of the particulars: dates, costs, lodging, and event rosters. Champion your credentials and those who will be working alongside you in running the camp. Accentuate the safety measures you have in place—onsite or nearby veterinary care, etc. Get rolling!

Cricket Farmer

Mother Nature works in mysterious ways. For instance, the most melodious of insects is also the preferred repast for countless herps—reptiles and amphibians—and for some baby mammals as well. And, yes, there's money to be made in successfully breeding these coveted bugs. You can be a **cricket farmer**.

How Much Does It Cost to Start This Kind of Business?

You can commence cricket farming with a very small investment. You need, of course, the accoutrements of breeding: food, nesting materials, and appropriate cages or containers. However, to test your wings as a cricket farmer,

227

you wouldn't require much of a monetary outlay. Over time, you could grow your business and make further investments in its expansion. That is, after you realize some successes in the A to Z breeding procedure and acquire some loyal and repeat customers. There are some very big bug enterprises out there that didn't get to where they are now overnight. There truly is a potent and unrelenting demand for crickets.

Aside from various pet reptiles, amphibians, and some tiny mammals, you can also peddle your cricket crop to fishermen. Large, full-grown crickets make great bait. There is also a range of cricket sizes to satisfy pets of varying dimensions. Many reptiles are capable of taking big, hearty bites, and so 5/8" crickets are the most in-demand of the chirping bugs. There are also petite-sized crickets—baby crickets—known as pinheads: 1/8" and 1/16". Certain infant insectivores relish these little munchies. A guiding principle for determining a pet's insect supper is that the bug be approximately half the width of the herp's head.

What Qualifications Do You Need for This Kind of Work?

You need all the facts on raising crickets, and you should adhere to the right and proper script to maximize your cricket breeding and to make a profit along the way. The general consensus is that if the twittering insects have adequate food and water, and are kept at the right temperatures—80 to 85 degrees Fahrenheit is an accepted range—they will breed like rabbits or, better yet, crickets.

Aside from learning what you need to know about nesting materials, their preferred diets, and what cages and equipment are required to facilitate hearty cricket breeding, there are other factors to mull over before leaping into this business venture, such as:

★ **Noise.** Crickets have got a lot to say. And they especially like saying it in the dark of the night. So, you have to determine where all of your farming activities will transpire, and whether it'll disturb you or your loved ones. (Raising crickets in the bedroom might not be the best idea.)

★ **Crickets are wily insects.** The shrewdest among them are known to escape now and again from their various confines.

★ Large congregations of bugs—any bugs—generate **odors** from their droppings as well as the hustle and bustle of day-to-day living. Bugs have got to go, too, and it stinks.

Essentially, if you can handle this downside of breeding crickets, you are cricket farmer material.

Cricket farming is not an entrepreneurial figment of the imagination. Visit **Ghann's Cricket Farm** @ Ghann.com. This international seller of crickets, worms, cages, food, dietary supplements, and myriad supplies was established in 1952. Check out, too, **Millbrook Cricket Farm** @ MillbrookCrickets.com. This company sells crickets, mealworms, superworms, and waxworms, the diets for millions of household pets who happen to be herps. Lastly, drop by **Fluker's Cricket Farm** @ FlukerFarms.com (800-735-8537), which sells crickets, mealworms, and assorted reptile products. Each one of these farms also supplies visitors to their websites with copious cricket care advice.

How Do You Find Customers?

Attend reptile and other pet shows. Make contacts and more contacts. Sell to individual pet owners who feed crickets to their pets. Approach appropriate retailers who sell the bugs, or perhaps, who should be selling them. Establish yourself as competent and a farmer of a fine product—and then, most assuredly, your business will take flight.

Aquarium Plant Farmer

Live plants in aquarium setups genuinely enhance their appearances. They add a natural quality to fish tanks that cannot be equaled. People who build and maintain aquariums often choose this living vegetation over the plastic alternatives. With this demand so firmly rooted, there is a need for **aquarium plant farmers**. In fact, in the A to Z of the aquarium business, aquaculture specialists are not always easy to find.

How Much Does It Cost to Start This Kind of Business?

To get your feet wet as an aquarium plant farmer, a small outlay of dollars will suffice. You could test your mettle in this area with under $1,000 up-front investment. You will need aquarium tanks, seedlings, lighting, filtration, and other aquarium plant accoutrements such as fertilizer. Take baby steps and prove to yourself—and your initial clientele—that you can grow healthy and attractive plants. Invest more when you are ready to expand your crop and are supremely certain that it will be a bumper one.

What Qualifications Do You Need for This Kind of Work?

If you know your stuff vis-à-vis aquarium matters, you are a prized human resource that can write your own entrepreneurial ticket in a very lucrative commercial field. There's a ton of technical minutiae that comes with the territory of aquarium plant farming. You have to be learned in areas ranging from proper lighting to the proper temperatures for optimum growing. You have to have a handle on filtration and fertilizing matters. Among many particulars, you have to be an algae buster, too.

How Do You Find Customers?

Bring your crop yields to retailers who sell tropical fish. Attend aquarium-related and pet-themed trade shows and secure both retail and wholesale accounts. Advertise in aquarium magazines and sell your plants directly to consumers.

> To fully appreciate the width and breadth of the selling opportunities and market for live aquarium plants, there are a couple of websites worth surfing over to: AquariumPlants.com and FreshwaterAquariumPlants.com. At these two cyber portals, you'll also encounter invaluable information on what goes into raising healthy and attractive aquarium flora. Check out too **Drs. Fosters & Smith's Live Aquaria** @ LiveAquaria.com. Here you'll encounter a mother lode of tips and techniques on this underwater brand of plant farming, including information on the myriad benefits of live plants to overall aquarium tank water quality and fish health and wellness.

Dog Star

Most dog owners consider their canine companions one-of-a-kind talents. They believe that their pets are true originals with looks that could kill and the most special kinds of aptitudes. Some of these aficionados of the furry and four-legged canine species also look upon their pets as prospective stars of stage and screen. That is, they feel their particular pooches have what it takes to be brightly shining **dog stars**. Are you of this mind?

How Much Does It Cost to Forge This Kind of Career?

This rather unusual undertaking is pretty much cost free, with the exception of membership fees in a professional organization such as the **Dog Actors Guild**.

If you believe your canine is movie star or model material, you might contemplate joining the **Dog Actors Guild** @ DogActorsGuild.com (212-414-9597). Membership certainly has its privileges. The foremost benefit is that your dog's picture is immediately in front of the movers and shakers in the industry—producers and directors on the hunt for animals with genuine star appeal. Another couple of options worth checking out in this field are the **Hollywood Animals' Animal Actors Agency** @ AnimalActorsAgency.com (323-665-9500) and **Hollywood Paws** @ HollywoodPaws.com (888-781-7827). These two organizations have the welcome mats out for all kinds of pets, including gifted felines.

What Qualifications Do You Need for This Kind of Work?

The key that can unlock doors for you and your budding thespian on four legs is a proper upbringing and a first-class home life. In other words, the big shots on the prowl for the canine stars of the future desire, above all else, well-trained animals with even and predictable temperaments. Since the competition in this particular bailiwick is dog-eat-dog, as it were, it behooves you to determine whether or not your canine soul mate is truly disposed for a career in Hollywood or life as a glamorous model.

Before you venture down this yellow brick road, ask yourself several questions:

★ Is my pooch properly trained to eliminate in the great outdoors rather than on the living room rug?

★ Does my best friend sit on command?

★ Does my canine comrade serenely stand at attention while getting groomed?

★ Can my dog stay home alone without suffering from separation anxiety and tearing apart the house?

★ Does my pet welcome the company of strangers without excessive barking, jumping, and other inappropriate or aggressive actions?

★ Is my dog sensitive to loud noises, such as thunder and firecrackers?

The answers to any and all of these questions will tell you whether or not you have a companion animal armed and ready for a life in the limelight. For instance, dogs that shake, rattle, and roll during thunder and lightning storms are probably not going to appreciate being in the hustle and bustle of a Hollywood existence. And, too, canines that growl at any foreign faces who come into their inner circles are not likely to win over the hearts and minds of talent scouts, even if they are sights for sore eyes. The bottom line is that to be a shining dog star, your furry compatriot has got to be properly trained and temperamentally suited for a decidedly different kind of life.

How Do You Find Work for Your Canine Companion?

For starters, join an organization that is committed to finding work for the gifted on four legs. Going it alone in this highly competitive field doesn't often yield fruit.

Pet Cemetery Proprietor

Consider this sliver of text part and parcel of the last mile in pet-themed entrepreneurship. Right now we are calling on America's vast and varied pet cemeteries. According to the International Association of Pet Cemeteries & Crematories (IAOPCC), there are more than 600 pet cemeteries in the United States. Pet burial grounds are quite often associated with veterinary hospitals, kennels, grooming and training outfits, as well as animal rescue and shelter operations.

There are, however, many independently owned and operated pet cemeteries. There are even a few that exist in places you wouldn't expect to unearth them. St. Andrew's Episcopal Church in New Providence, New Jersey @ StAndrewsChurch.org (908-464-4875) maintains a section of its grounds as a pet cemetery. It invites pet owners of all religious affiliations, or none at all, to bury their pets in its peaceful and picturesque locale. Ah, you think that church property and the interment of pet remains rings a little peculiar to the ear. Well, St. Francis of Assisi, the patron saint of animals and the environment, wouldn't think so. Perhaps you are interested in becoming a **pet cemetery proprietor**? It certainly is an entrepreneurial undertaking that is off the beaten path. But since death is one of only two guarantees in life—the other being taxes—there's really nothing extraordinary or uncanny about owning and operating a pet cemetery.

The **International Association of Pet Cemeteries & Crematories (IAOPCC)** @ IAOPC.com (518-594-3000) says that independently owned pet cemeteries must be appropriately deeded. The customers—bereaved pet parents—must feel completely confidant that their animals' remains will rest in peace for the foreseeable future. In other words, they should know with some degree of certainty that Donald Trump isn't going to come along and build a skyscraper on the cemetery grounds. IAOPCC also emphasizes that pet cemetery owners should always maintain a care fund, which their human counterparts do, to guarantee that the necessary funds are in the kitty, so to speak, for the ongoing upkeep of the property. For further information on pet cemeteries and all that goes into their startups and ongoing operations, peruse the association's website and its various links.

As youngsters growing up in the late 1960s and early 1970s, the book's authors couldn't believe that pet cemeteries actually existed. In those days of yore—before pet parenting assumed center stage—they were truly considered places that only a miniscule number of pet-owning eccentrics would contemplate patronizing. One pet cemetery in particular fascinated us to no end. It was located on the well-traveled Central Avenue in Hartsdale, New York, about fifteen miles north of our Bronx home. Whenever we passed by it during the dog days of summer, its manicured lawn and neat and colorful rows of begonias and marigolds caught our attention. We noted that its spiffy appearance trumped the not-too-far Gate of Heaven human cemetery, where we occasionally visited deceased relations.

Subsequently we learned that this eye-catching burial ground, the Hartsdale Canine Cemetery, established in 1896, lay claim to being the oldest in the entire country. (Archaeologist Dr. Stewart Schrever has since exhumed a burial site in Green County, Illinois, which he believes interred pets. He dates his find at 6500 BC. Regardless, the Hartsdale Canine Cemetery maintains the distinction of being the oldest *operating* pet cemetery in the United States.) The inscription inside the cemetery's gate, which, despite its name, welcomes dearly departed felines, reads: "In 1896, a prominent New York veterinarian, Dr. Samuel Johnson, offered his apple orchard in rural Hartsdale, New York, to serve as a burial plot for a bereaved friend's dog. That single compassionate act served as the cornerstone for what was to become America's first and most prestigious pet cemetery."

The present reality is that—just like most pet-specialty businesses in the new millennium—pet cemeteries are getting both more notice and more business. It stands to reason that in this era of conscientious pet parenting, more owners—*parents*—of cats and dogs are seeking out proper burials and lasting memorials for their deceased animal companions. Burials and memorials, that is, with all the solemnity, dignity, and longevity of their human equivalents.

How Much Does It Cost to Start This Kind of Business?

Foremost, if you want to own and operate a pet cemetery, you need a chunk of property. Sorry, but there's no way around this. The land, by law, must also be suitable for hosting a cemetery within its confines for as far as the eye can see. If you haven't been shopping around for a piece of real estate lately, you might be surprised that land doesn't come cheap nowadays. Of course, so much of the cost is rooted in the physical location of the piece of earth under consideration. Perhaps you already own appropriate space for a pet cemetery—that would be nice!

Keep in mind, too, that you cannot lease or rent property for a legitimate pet cemetery. The land must be owned outright by a proprietor, proprietors, or an established cemetery corporation. Before interring their deceased pets, your clientele are going to want to know all about the enduring prospects of your cemetery as a business entity. In other words, they wouldn't want to see the burial grounds cast asunder when the land is sold to the highest bidder for development purposes.

Many pet cemetery businesses also perform cremation services as well, which are popular. So, if you want to do this business right and thoroughly, you will need crematory equipment, which is costly. You will have to purchase all of the necessary insurances and acquire the requisite operating permits, but this is true for all substantial business endeavors. If you don't already own the necessary land, anticipate an initial investment of at least $100,000 to get the cemetery ball rolling in the right direction.

What Qualifications Do You Need for This Kind of Work?

Aside from the obvious and ample investment needs, owning and operating a pet cemetery is a decidedly layered undertaking. Foremost, you need a solid entrepreneurial head on your shoulders and a long-term commitment to running a business with both present and future obligations to your customers. In this type of venture, it sure helps to have an empathetic and compassionate spirit, too. You really have to appreciate that your customers— today, tomorrow, and the tomorrow after that—will be bereaved pet owners who require a bit of succor along with your myriad burial services.

How Do You Find Customers?

Considering the small aggregate numbers of pet cemeteries in existence, it wouldn't be too difficult to attract business via the traditional routes of advertising.

As a pet cemetery proprietor, it would also be wise to align your business establishment with nearby veterinary hospitals and as many other pet-themed enterprises as possible. You want word of mouth in pet-parenting circles to start spreading the news that a reputable pet cemetery exists as a real option for them.

Pet Identification Tag Maker

No matter where you call home, your city or town very likely requires that all of its canine residents be properly licensed. This isn't to suggest that everybody who cohabitates with a dog complies with these licensing bylaws—but millions of people do. Years ago, the dog license was seen as a lost canine's best hope of reuniting with his or her owner. That is, because the licenses sported identification numbers, they could be cross-matched via the county clerk's office, or whoever housed the records of dogs and their respective owners. But, really, a dog license doesn't suffice any more as *the* identification tag. The convoluted process of wading through bureaucratic rigmarole to locate a lost dog's apprehensive parents is pretty silly, when, in fact, the same dog could be wearing a comprehensive "return to sender" identification tag.

Nowadays, growing numbers of dog parents purchase the genuine article: full-fledged identification tags, which they attach to their best friends' collars, in addition to their licenses. Cat owners also purchase identification tags, particularly for those felines let loose in the great outdoors. These inclusive tags include such fundamental information as:

★ The pet's name

★ Owner's name, address, daytime and evening phone numbers

★ Owner's e-mail address

There is money to be made as a **pet identification tag maker**.

237

How Much Does It Cost to Start This Kind of Business?

What you need to call yourself a pet identification tag maker in good standing is a piece of machinery to do the work. You could purchase or lease one for a reasonable sum—below $5,000.

What Qualifications Do You Need for This Kind of Work?

There are many employees in retail pet food and supply superstores who operate pet identification tag machines without any snafus. In other words, you don't need to be a Rhodes scholar to do the job.

Visit **Lucky Pet** @ LuckyPet.com (800-543-8247) and uncover a pet tag company like no other. Lucky Pet offers its customers a vast selection of pet identification tags from stainless steel to brass colored to die-cut plastics in all shapes and sizes. It's a pet ID heaven and quite a revelation. You certainly can appreciate the width and breadth of this business opportunity. For an additional fee, Lucky Pet extends to its clientele an *Owner Alert* pet recovery service, in which registered pets are given a unique number to complement their tags. This number comes attached to a 24-hour toll-free hotline, which enables operators to immediately access an abundance of information about a lost pet, including a medical history and the owner's whereabouts at any given time.

How Do You Find Customers?

For starters, you can bring your pet identification tag machine to flea markets and pet-themed shows. You can sell them via a website. You can partner with retailers and veterinarians in the trade and give them a percentage of every sale. The bottom line is that these tags are in continuous demand and will always be coveted pet products.

The Digital Age

If you are going into the pet identification tag business, consider where technology has taken us. Yes, even the ID tag will never be the same. The renowned L.L. Bean Company of Freeport, Maine recently sold the latest in pet identification tags via both its stores and catalogues. This particular ID tag enables you to, digitally, place up to forty lines of information in it, and it's still just an unobtrusive little tag hanging from your cat's or dog's collar. This tag, however, sports an LCD face, which will identify your pet in a style befitting the Information Age.

Of course, you don't have to sell anything so elaborate as an electronic ID tag to realize profits in this field. Many pet food and supply retailers have machines on the premises, which will stamp out fine-looking identification tags, replete with pets' names and all their owners' contact information—and all in a matter of seconds. And there's no reason you can't do the same for your clientele.

For an engraver of pet identification tags—just like the one you see in retailers—check out **iMARC Engraving Systems** @ iMarcEngraver.com (888-99-iMARC). This outfit leases and sells an identification tag engraver that does the job on everything from metals to plastics. It's been reported that employees in the aforementioned retail stores have no trouble operating it. This means that it is very simple to use.

CHAPTER IX
The Virtual Truth: Online Pet Business Opportunities

eBay Pet Merchandise Seller

If you don't call home the planet Neptune, you are more than likely aware of the wonder and possibility of selling things on eBay. In fact, every single hour of every single day finds visions of eBay riches dancing through the heads of people the world over, who feel their attics and basements are chock-full of overlooked valuables that will surely make them a mint on this online auction behemoth. We are not here to encourage or quash these dreams of impending eBay gold strikes, but to elucidate on exactly how you can be an **eBay pet merchandise seller** and earn some serious dollars in the process. How much you earn is entirely up to you.

The beauty of selling on eBay is that it places your merchandise in front of potential buyers all across the country (and, indeed, the world) in a matter of minutes. Of course, a successful end game entails you getting as many people as possible to view what you are selling on your eBay auction pages. Simply understood, the eBay model is rooted in marrying buyers with sellers who have what they want. Optimally speaking, when you market pieces of pet merchandise on eBay, you want to pique the interest of men and women expressly looking for these very things. For example, let's say you place a piece of cat furniture on the eBay auction block. There are registered eBayers who are simultaneously combing the auction site for just that. These feline enthusiasts type "cat furniture" in the auction site's search apparatus and are transferred to a comprehensive listing of the current eBay sellers of cat furniture. In a nutshell, that's how eBay works and how it can work for you.

To get your auction business up and running, visit **eBay** @ eBay.com. The company website is replete with information on everything that you need to know to start selling stuff right now. On the comprehensive eBay site, you'll encounter copious tips and techniques on how to maximize your selling experiences, including the importance of writing thorough descriptions of each and every one of your featured items. This online auction enterprise has grown in leaps and bounds since its rather inconspicuous inception more than a decade ago. It now offers sellers the option to pitch merchandise as *Buy It Now*, circumventing the time constraints of the traditional auction approach. Hey, you can even run your very own eBay store.

How Much Does It Cost to Start This Kind of Business?

The listing fees on eBay are rather minimal. So, aside from the cost of the inventory of products—what you intend to sell—this is pretty much the sum and substance of your up-front investment. In other words, you make the call. Ultimately, you give eBay a small percentage of the final value of each item that sells, but all of this comes on the backside of successfully completed auctions. Overall, it's a pretty fair deal considering that you are afforded access to a user-friendly, far-reaching auction site that attracts millions of visitors to it each and every day. This isn't to imply that it's simple to complete transactions on eBay and make oodles of money, because it's not.

Over the long haul, profitable eBay selling involves a concerted business commitment to see auctions through from start to finish.

Selling on eBay entails a litany of particulars from picturing your merchandise on auction to describing every item in very precise detail to determining fair shipping rates to answering occasional queries from interested buyers to ultimately completing the transactions in the bright light of day. Never lose sight of the fact that after the auction sales are done deals, you are responsible for shipping the genuine articles, as it were, just like in all other mail-order businesses.

What Qualifications Do You Need for This Kind of Work?

You don't need any special qualifications to sell things on eBay. The key to unlocking your success in this venue is a full appreciation that what you are doing comes attached to real responsibilities. That is, you have to approach eBay selling as akin to operating a real business—because it is just that. Sure, you have to own a computer and know how to operate the machine, because selling things on eBay necessitates filling out the cyberspace equivalent of forms. You've also got to put a picture or pictures of your merchandise on the auction page, which you can upload from your computer hard drive. So, yes, there is a degree of know-how required to sell on eBay, but you don't have to be a technical genius or anything like that.

After registering with the company, eBay will scrupulously lead you through all the logistics in getting your merchandise up and in front of prospective buyers. What you must be fully prepared for is literally dealing with real people and real problems. Sorry, this is not an autopilot business undertaking, as all too many people surmise. Yes, even in an Internet-driven business, you've still got to deliver the goods—always—and this doesn't occur by osmosis. In fact, it is your brand of customer service that will establish your reputation—one that'll persuade more and more eBay buyers to bid on your stuff with confidence.

Feedback

On eBay, both buyers and sellers are offered the opportunity to leave feedback for their trading partners. That is, they can say positive or negative things about the business experience. As a seller, you naturally want to accrue positive feedback ratings from the folks who win your auctions—your customers. You accomplish this feat by being honest in describing your merchandise, fast in shipping it, and swift and frank in answering any questions or concerns that come your way. And this is critical: If a customer is dissatisfied for any reason with the merchandise he or she receives, you make proper and prompt amends. This consistently conscientious approach to your eBay selling will fast shape you a strong reputation backed up by a bulwark of positive feedback, which will make your future auctions both appealing to more people and more profitable.

You can find pet merchandise to sell on eBay at wholesalers and closeout dealers. Try **Dollar Day\$** @ DollarDays.com (877-837-9569). Also check out WholesaleDir.com and search the Pet Accessories category for a listing of wholesalers and other sources of products. To achieve maximum success selling pet merchandise on eBay, try to unearth unusual items not being sold by others. There are many possible suppliers of pet merchandise ranging from individual crafters to inventors to local retailers.

How Do You Find Customers?

On eBay, you essentially find customers by being in the right place (or places) at the right time. That is, you want to list your merchandise in proper categories and attract buyers who want to bid on, or immediately purchase, what you are selling. For example, you want your rawhide bones listed under *Pet Supplies* and not *Sporting Goods*. Many buyers look for very specific things when they comb through eBay auctions. Fortunately, countless others get swept up in those "gotta have that" impulse moments, which is always good for business.

Aside from correctly classifying your merchandise, you should also describe it in precise detail. It's only fair that buyers know exactly what they are bidding on. Moreover, many eBay buyers chance upon auction pages based on particular search words that are found in product titles and descriptions. So, the reality is that a briefer than brief description of your merchandise doesn't aid your business cause in the least.

In addition to the aforementioned basics of selling on eBay, sellers have many options that can increase each auction's visibility, from bold headlines to colorful page borders to subtitles. You can even optimize your eBay auction listings for Internet search engines. This means that people searching the Web could encounter a link to your eBay auction, without being on the actual eBay website. Of course, you have to pay eBay additional fees for these promotional boosts, but—depending on what you are selling—it's sometimes worth it.

Online Pet Newsletter

The World Wide Web and its seemingly infinite outreach offers innovative and entrepreneurial-minded persons a never-ending stream of ways to make a buck. Nowadays, it's practically a necessity for businesses to erect websites, even when the Internet itself assumes a backseat role in what they do. On the other hand, there are many businesspersons who earn their greenbacks solely from transacting within the boundless frontiers of cyberspace.

Countless pet-themed businesses utilize the vastness of the Internet to find customers for their merchandise and services. But, aside from selling merchandise or hands-on services to pet parents, there are other ways to harness the energy of virtual reality. Launch an **online pet newsletter**, or some sort of informational cyber portal. It is an entrepreneurial pathway that is at once doable and rife with moneymaking potential.

If an online pet newsletter is done right and is given ample time to blossom and get noticed, it can be a real income producer for you. In other words, if you inaugurate an online pet newsletter, it's got to be truly informative and/or unique in some demonstrative ways. To attract the interest of large numbers of pet parents, you have to set your newsletter apart from the run-of-the-mill stuff that is omnipresent. And, even when you establish something of real value, you've still got to tap into your targeted demographic. You have to draw as many people as possible to your website—and this will take some time. As the old saying goes: Rome wasn't built in a day. An online pet newsletter has to be given a fair shake to win over the hearts and minds of pet owners. Getting the surfing masses to know you exist in the first place is job one.

How Much Does It Cost to Start This Kind of Business?

The cost of initiating an online pet newsletter is essentially the cost of constructing a website. If you are proficient in all of the particulars that go into building a functional and user-friendly website, monetary outlays and investment requirements can be kept to a bare minimum. If you require the talents of a professional in this field, it'll you cost you $1,000 to $2,000, depending on the kind of website you have in mind.

Never lose sight of the fact that in order to generate profits in this decidedly creative business undertaking, you will—in the end—need to sell things. That is, you might choose to sell subscriptions to your informational newsletter. You could also sell advertising space on your website. In addition, you could work with various businesses as their affiliates. This would enable you to earn small percentages of everything that is purchased from them via links on your website. Of course, to earn income through any of these routes, you have to furnish the pet-parenting public with something of value.

If you foresee building a subscription base, you must supply pet owners with a product worthy of a subscription price. Unless you have the critical website traffic to make it worth their while, potential advertisers aren't going to be breaking down any virtual doors to promote within your online pet newsletter. Finally, in order to generate any significant affiliate income, you will obviously need a regular flow of visitors both checking out and spending some time on your website.

There are hundreds upon hundreds of businesses on the Internet that work with affiliate partners in an effort to drive more and more traffic to their websites. Affiliate partnerships operate by you placing other businesses' banner ads or links on your website. When somebody visiting your site clicks on a given link and places an order from that particular business, you get a percentage of the sale. The precise amount of the commission earned is determined upon registration with the company that offers the affiliate opportunity. Amazon.com works with the most affiliates on the Internet. For instance, you could link various pet care book titles directly to Amazon and get a percentage of any sales generated from your website. Check out Affiliate-Program.Amazon.com for the details on how you can earn up to 8.5% of the purchase price. Pet-specialty businesses that offer affiliate opportunities are many and range from **Veterinary Pet Insurance** @ PetInsurance.com to **Botanical Dog** @ BotanicalDog.com (843-864-9368), which will give you 10% of all sales generated from their banner link on your website, to **Pet Nutrition Products (PNP)** @ PetNutritionProducts.com (866-4PET-HEALTH).

What Qualifications Do You Need for This Kind of Work?

If you are capable of being your own webmaster, you need only the requisite skills inherent in erecting and operating a website that can withstand the massive influx of visitors that you anticipate generating. If you have somebody else doing this all-important work for you, then you obviously don't need any special qualifications in this area.

We are defining this business opportunity as an online pet *newsletter*. A quality newsletter has got to be more than miscellaneous sentences strung together in a haphazard way. It certainly helps if you are learned and, at the very least, a passable writer. Or, should you use the writings of others in your newsletter—*e.g.*, various experts on pet care matters—make sure that their contributions meet certain quality standards. And, if you have to, hire an editor. It's imperative that you do everything humanly possible to make your website stand out from the pack. Let's face it, there's no more sorry spectacle than a website awash in typographical errors and poor grammar. Insist that your online pet newsletter be the genuine article—at once informative and lucid. Make your website professionally shine in all areas from appearance to functionality to content. An all-around professional job will ensure that your chances of success are much greater than if you approached the online pet newsletter with less than the absolute reverence it deserves.

How Do You Find Customers?

You could have the best website in Cyber Town—eye candy and erudite to the core—and still not get any hits on it, save perhaps for the few family members and the couple of friends that you instruct to check it out. The harsh reality of virtual reality is that people won't likely stumble upon your website by chance. There are certain things you need to do to lure visitors and customers to your creative and business undertaking. Foremost, maximize your position in search engines. Link your online pet newsletter with other pet-themed websites. Pass out business cards with your web address prominently featured on it to as many pet people as physically possible. Finally, you could pay for advertising on websites that reach what you deem your demographic. Eventually, you could advertise your virtual newsletter in pet-themed periodicals.

Online Pet-Dating Network

We'll leave the contentious debate on the subject of global warming to scientists. What concerns us here is the colder and colder world that we live in—metaphorically speaking. Sociologists from A to Z are pretty much in accord on this one. And courtesy of the frosty, more impersonal climes of the present times, it's a darn good thing that there are felines, canines, and other companion animals around to warm things up a bit.

It's a fact—more and more people are finding companionship with creatures on four legs and with feathers. They are in some instances substituting these relationships for the harder to unearth and certainly more complicated two-legged varieties. But the reality is that people still need people, and what better way to connect soulmates with one another than via a mutual passion for a particular kind of animal friend. In other words, there are cat lovers who would love to hook up with other cat lovers; dog lovers who would like nothing more than to meet with fellow dog lovers; bird lovers who would appreciate flying away with like-minded bird lovers; reptile lovers who would fancy chewing the fat with reptile-loving members of the opposite sex—you get the point.

This discussion could only be heading to one place: the entrepreneurial possibilities inherent in an **online pet-dating network**. That is, you bringing together a community of persons with comparable interests in the wild and wooly world of pets. In other words, you run a dating service for pet lovers to meet with one another—if they so desire—and, after that, who knows? And no, this opportunity isn't about pets dating one another.

There are several online businesses in this field of endeavor for you to check out. For starters, drop by DateMyPet.com, which, as its name reveals, focuses on the art of matchmaking with an obvious pet twist and connection. An attention-grabbing quote on this website reads: "90% of single women believe that how a man treats his pet indicates how he treats a love interest." A more general online dating network is eHarmony.com, which has mushroomed in both size and notoriety. While not pet-themed, it is nevertheless the quintessential model of success in cyberspace's love connection business. Meticulously scrutinize the goings-on of these outfits and others. Understand how they operate from soup to nuts, paying close to attention to their terms and conditions of service, how they promote themselves, who advertises on their sites, and so on.

How Much Does It Cost to Start This Kind of Business?

This is a business endeavor that entails a highly efficient and ultimately comprehensive website. You could start it on the cheap, but to do it right and build it up, you are going to have to develop a database of customers. You will only attract clientele in this business with clientele—people who need people are the requisite bait. This means that you are going to have to advertise and promote your site in as many ways possible to get it noticed. If you are thinking long-term and earning profits, you'll need a minimum of $5,000 to get things up and running. Of course, this ballpark investment figure could be a whole lot more—that's what that oft-spotted plus sign means. It all depends on your business plan, what you want to do, and in what time frame you want to do it.

What Qualifications Do You Need for This Kind of Work?

Foremost, it would help to be highly literate in computer ABCs as well as website building. Of course, you could hire somebody or some outfit—or partner with a computer geek—to run the whole technical shebang for you. Before wading into an online pet-dating network business, you should know very precisely what you are getting into. This isn't a traditional business concept. In other words, you must fully understand how this kind of "selling" works, and exactly what your responsibilities are to your customers. The simplest advice, which applies to every business undertaking, is to do a heaping helping of due diligence, scrupulously studying the models of successful businesses in this intriguing field of matchmaking.

How Do You Find Customers?

You want to get people to visit your website—lots of people. You can promote your network on pet-related pages in cyberspace. Get in those search engines and get highly ranked. Look outside and consider running ads in pet-themed magazines and periodicals. Once you start getting hits on your site and your database achieves some serious depth, you have an evolving business that will attract advertisers who will pay you for the privilege of promoting their products or services on your dynamic website and virtual love nest.

Pet Merchandise Catalogue: Mail & Online

During the formative years of our Pet Nosh business odyssey, we published a catalogue called *Kitty B. Goode*. It showcased a diverse range of whimsical gift items for cat consumers and, despite its rather exclusionary appellation, for dog consumers as well. At that moment in our business timeline, we didn't stock in our stores—for lack of a better description—upscale merchandise. We introduced the catalogue to the buying public in what could best be described as the infancy of pet parenting.

In those days gone by, our locations were more mom-and-pop than super-store in content and design. We concentrated our retail resources on maintaining good prices on wide varieties of pet foods and accessory products. And, let's just say, ceramic cat banks and kitty kimonos didn't yet fit into our merchandise scheme. However, in a full-color catalogue mailed to pet consumers, they were right at home. Just as we did those many years ago, you too could launch a **pet merchandise catalogue**, utilizing both traditional mail and the power of the Internet.

How Much Does It Cost to Start This Kind of Business?

Today there are certainly more printing options than when we produced the Kitty B. Goode catalogue, and the technology is a far cry from what it was twenty years ago. There was no sophisticated digital picture taking and printing techniques in the late 1980s. What all of this means is that you can now shop around for the best possible printing deal with the least amount of hassles. And, if you own the right equipment, you can employ digital photography to snap pictures of the merchandise that you eventually select for your catalogue. We literally mailed the physical items featured in our catalogue to a color-printing outfit, which both photographed the stuff and printed the catalogues for us. To get a serious pet merchandise catalogue off the ground—at least one where you can potentially realize a profit—you would need a $5,000 to $10,000 initial investment.

Keep in mind that you will not only have to print the catalogues, but mail them to prospective customers. So, there are mailing lists to purchase and postal considerations to weigh—bulk-mailing permits, etc. Last but not least, a beginning inventory is necessary to get the catalogue business ball rolling. It needn't be a humungous one. But if you are planning to mail catalogues to potential buyers and sell online, you certainly want to have the featured items in stock and at the ready for shipment.

What Qualifications Do You Need for This Kind of Work

The good news surrounding a pet merchandise catalogue business is that you can do it all from the comforts of home. This means no additional rental and utility costs—no overhead. Naturally, you need sufficient space for your preliminary inventory of products. You should also be proficient in properly packing boxes for mailing. Conscientious shipping will save you a ton of headaches down the road. Foremost, you want your merchandise to arrive at its intended destination in one piece and undamaged. You also want it to look like it was packed by a bona fide business entity, not a hodgepodge conglomerate consisting of family, friends, and neighbors utilizing yesterday's news and worn-out socks for padding purposes. In fact, you should have your mailing system firmly in place at the onset, including the method of shipment you intend on using—USPS, UPS, FedEx, etc. Determine your shipping and handling rates and make certain they are fair and reasonable based on the actual costs of packing materials and the postage.

> To mail catalogues, it might be in your pecuniary best interest to secure a bulk-mailing permit from the **United States Postal Service (USPS)** @ USPS.com. This would enable you to send out a whole bunch of them at mailing rates below standard first-class mail prices. Of course, you'll have to learn the ABCs of the bulk-mailing system, which entails a lot of sorting and banding based on zip codes, states, and such. But it's simple enough and well worth the additional work required, particularly if you are mailing thousands of pieces. For the shipping of merchandise, you have options beyond the post office. There is **United Parcel Service (UPS)** @ UPS.com and **FedEx** @ FedEx.com to consider. There are also postage and mailing stores all around, which you could partner with to make all of your shipping issues less convoluted and worrisome.

Of course, the heart and soul of this business undertaking is ultimately the merchandise selected, pictured, and sold through the catalogue. How and where do you find distinctive merchandise that will appeal to the pet-parenting public? Then there is the not inconsiderable task of getting your catalogues into the physical hands (or seen online by the actual eyes) of this consumer demographic. For instance, mailing your pet merchandise catalogues to the non-pet-owning population wouldn't generate much business. Simply put, you would have better success sending your catalogues to subscribers of *Cat Fancy* and *Dog World* magazines than you would mailing them to subscribers of *U.S. News & World Report* and *Time* magazine. And you'd pay a lot more for the latter. Granted, among subscribers to any and all magazines are also pet owners, but this should be as precise a science as possible.

Renting mailing lists doesn't come cheap. Therefore, the names therein should be fastidiously correlated to exactly what you're attempting to sell, or you're throwing good money at bad results. The reality of direct-mail solicitations is that you will get only a sliver of responses from even the best-matched lists. In other words, if you send out 5,000 catalogues, don't anticipate getting orders from 4,500 people. If you get fifty orders, consider yourself off to a very good start.

In the catalogue business, renting appropriate mailing lists with the names and addresses of potential customers is often a profitable road to venture down. There are many mailing list brokers around. What you must do is find one that has what you want—consumers of pet merchandise. This demographic could consist of subscriber lists of pet-specific magazines and periodicals. It could be lists of member names in pet-specific organizations and clubs. To get a handle on some of what the mailing-list business has to offer, visit **Mailing Lists Direct** @ Mailing-Lists-Direct.com (866-314-5228) and **Century List Services** @ CenturyList.com (877-585-LIST).

How Do You Find Customers?

Once you have the physical pet merchandise catalogues in hand and a corresponding website presence, you are in essence open for business. The aforementioned mailing lists—targeted to your audience—can ignite a spark under your fledgling business. But don't assume a catalogue business should limit itself to direct-mail solicitations. Take your catalogues and your merchandise to pet-specific shows and events. Ask if you could appear at pet-specialty retailers, or, at the very least, leave your catalogues with them. If you are not selling competing merchandise, this could be acceptable. Leave your catalogues at veterinarians and at grooming businesses—with their permission, of course. Find out where local breed clubs meet and any other pet organizations. Tell them about your business and hand over a bunch of catalogues.

Our Kitty B. Goode catalogue business didn't simultaneously materialize on the World Wide Web, for a very good reason—there was no such thing as the Internet at the time. Nowadays, there is no excuse for you not to operate a catalogue business in the bright light of day, as well as in virtual reality. More and more people are buying things over the Internet. You'd be surprised how many people will order online these days before they would write out a check, or use their credit card information, then seal an envelope, put a stamp on it, and drop it in the mail. We live in a super-fast age. Even if interested parties receive your catalogues in the mail, they might not place orders unless they can do it via their computers and immediately.

To do a pet merchandise catalogue right and proper, you have to have a distinct phone number and accept credit cards. More often than not, your customers will place orders via the Internet or over the phone with their credit cards, rather than mail payment to you in the form of a check. There are many pathways to travel down in securing the capacity to accept credit cards. Do ample research here to get the best deal possible, as it is a very competitive field. Outfits that offer merchant credit card services include Charge.com (800-706-3724) and **Cardservice International** @ CardService.com (800-456-5989).

The Merchandise Safari

We already mentioned that the heart and soul of your pet merchandise catalogue business is—no surprise here—the merchandise. You don't want to fill your catalogue up with products that can be readily purchased in pet food and supply superstores and Wal-Mart. Instead, you want stuff in there that transcends these corporate behemoths and their coldly bottom-line product acquisitions methods. Simply stated, the odds are better that you'll succeed in the pet merchandise catalogue business by distinguishing yourself with products that consumers don't ordinarily encounter in their daily travels.

The most obvious places to start building your catalogue business are pet industry trade shows and general gift shows, which are ubiquitous in all parts of the country. Attending these events are sellers of every imaginable product. These get-togethers will furnish you with a wide range of possibilities—*i.e.*, stuff that is not likely to find its way onto the shelves of Wal-Mart. If you are not yet convinced of the potency and entrepreneurial potential of the pet care trade, just visit general merchandise gift shows and count the numbers of pet-related products sold there.

If you cannot attend industry trade shows and gift shows, get hold of trade magazines, such as **Pet Product News**, **Pet Age**, and **Pet Business**. There are all sorts of merchandise advertised for entrepreneurs just like you. And, need we say it: Comb the Internet, which is replete with intriguing websites featuring pet products and gift items that are not found in too many places.

AFTERWORD
The Sky's the Limit

An advertisement in *The New York Times* for the trendy Burberry Company features one of its models bedecked in the latest fashion. Only this model is a real dog—and its canine coat is on sale for $225. A Hammacher-Schlemmer catalogue arrives in the mail broadcasting its mission statement on the front cover: "Offering the Best, the Only and the Unexpected for 155 Years." Inside are a medley of offbeat products, some dubbed for "Pet Lovers," including the Non-Slip Pet Ramp at $189.95, which enables pets with dysplasia or osteoarthritis to smoothly navigate in and out of things without injuring themselves or experiencing undue pain. Priced at $129.95 in the very same catalogue is the Lightweight Pet Stroller, the ideal contraption for pet owners who fancy taking their small dogs and cats with them on shopping trips and other errands.

As demonstrated time and again throughout *101 Best Businesses for Pet Lovers*, the humanization of pet products and pet services are revolutionizing the trade. This compelling commercial reality arms entrepreneurial-minded men and women with the tools to succeed beyond their wildest dreams on the pet business frontier. Opportunities abound for those with the quirkiest business ideas. More conventional thinkers can thrive in pet-specialty retailing. Pet service providers of all stripes can write their own tickets. Stay-at-home moms and others can convert their lairs into manufacturing assembly lines. Inventors can fashion the next must-have pet products.

In fact, many prognosticators consider the business of pets the closest thing there is to a recession-proof slice of the economy. The sky's the limit in the pet care trade. And when the sky's the limit, it behooves you to reach for the sky.

APPENDIX A
A Crash Course in Marketing

Not every particular in this section will be applicable to your chosen pet business undertaking. Nevertheless, its purpose is to furnish you with a mother lode of ideas on how to promote and jumpstart an entrepreneurial endeavor—whatever it happens to be. So, take an idea, or multiple ideas, and tailor them to suit what you are doing and what you want to accomplish.

Successful businesses are constantly innovating—trying all kinds of things to distinguish themselves from the competition and bring customers to their doorsteps. In the highly competitive business of pets, it's imperative that you reveal to the world, as it were, what you have to offer and why it is different—and, in fact, better—than what others are offering. As this entire book demonstrates beyond a scintilla of doubt, the pet care marketplace is rapidly expanding, as are the numbers and types of businesses servicing pet owners and their companion animals. But, alas, this also means that many pet-inspired businesses are falling by the wayside. To increase your odds of success, it behooves you to promote and promote some more.

Once you have a pet product or pet service to sell that sufficient numbers of consumers genuinely need or otherwise covet, your success on the business frontier rests principally on getting yourself noticed. That is, you need to draw attention to your business by promoting it in every conceivable way. Job one is getting potential customers to know that you are there to serve them.

Then, both your short-term and long-term mission is to leave a positive and lasting impression on them.

Event-Driven Marketing

Event-driven marketing fosters what we call the *promotional multiplier effect*. For example, Pet Nosh launched what has now become a holiday tradition at myriad pet-specialty retailers all across the country: pets sitting atop Santa's lap for a photo opportunity. When we first ran this promotion more than twenty years ago, it was considered a rather bizarre event to say the least.

Nevertheless, all of us working at Pet Nosh in those days gone by understood that the pet owners who brought their many and diverse animal companions to our store for the free photo weren't the shy and retiring types. On the contrary, we knew they were going to show the picture to everybody and anybody. Their pets sitting on Santa Claus's very busy lap were guaranteed to be conversation pieces over the holiday season and long thereafter. In other words, a lot of people were going to see the pictures and learn of their origin. *You got that picture at Pet Nosh? What's a Pet Nosh? Where's Pet Nosh? I'll have to check the place out.* Flapping tongues are the most cost-efficient advertising around. When a simple thing called *word of mouth* is out there singing your praises, you've accomplished your promotional objectives.

Apart from our annual Santa Claus visit, we embraced an assortment of imaginative promotional events to get us noticed and get us business, such as:

★ **Midnight Madness Sales**
Even though these sales occurred prior to the midnight hour (9 p.m. to 11:30 p.m.), they were winners every single time. We would advertise them well in advance and get people out and in the shopping mode after traditional business hours. We'd have searchlights in our parking lots flooding the skies above. Many passing motorists, who didn't know what was happening at our

stores, would stop by just to satisfy their curiosities. We initially utilized these unusual sales as springboards for our new livestock departments (promoting mainly fish-related merchandise). Eventually, the after-hour extravaganzas featured a more wide-ranging mix of products for all pet owners.

The larger point is that these store sales transcended the norm. They got people talking about them beyond mere bargains—and, yes, there were plenty of them. Look for the midnight "red dot" and save. This kind of notoriety is what you want in any kind of business. It's one of the things that will distinguish you from your less dynamic competition.

★ Morris the Cat and other celebrities visit Pet Nosh

We live in a celebrity-obsessed society. Even stars on four legs appeal to us. The famous and finicky feline, Morris of 9Lives, dropped by our multiple store locations during his campaign for president in 1992. You didn't know he was a presidential contender? Well, while the coddled cat comfortably and rather imperiously sat on a director's chair, his entourage passed out hundreds of campaign pins promoting his candidacy to Pet Nosh customers. Our patrons were invited to pose for pictures with the precocious TV star. Again, this event generated that all-important buzz that distinguishes businesses from the pack.

On another occasion, we had two-legged pet expert and syndicated radio talk show host Warren Eckstein appear in one of our stores. He attracted a considerable following of his admirers, many of whom had never set foot in Pet Nosh before. Eckstein fielded pet-related questions from the assembled. Sure, we had to handsomely recompense the man for showing up, but it brought us some new customers and added to Pet Nosh's budding reputation as a happening kind of place.

★ Halloween Fashion Shows

We also sponsored Halloween fashion shows for pets, offering all sorts of prizes to the winners and, as they say in the trade, their people. Of course, local media was always alerted of these curious affairs, and we often got free publicity for them. For starters, a write-up in a newspaper or even a penny saver alerts people that you exist. It never ceased to amaze us—particularly when we operated several superstores on heavily trafficked thoroughfares—how many people didn't know we existed. Never assume that the whole world knows you are open for business.

Newspaper stories, a photo of an atypical store event, or—better yet—a television mention are invaluable promotional fodder. Send out press releases to media outlets. It's a win-win marketing move. Tell the media that you are the new kid on the pet business block. Notify the press of the products you carry or services you provide. Always seek out free publicity for your business's goings-on—big or small. The media is continually looking for interesting feature stories.

★ Customer Seminars

Depending, of course, on the exact nature of your business, hosting seminars or learning fairs for your clientele is a smart move. At Pet Nosh, we sometimes gathered experts from specialty fields in the trade—nutrition, veterinary medicine, training, grooming, etc.—and advertised the store events as simultaneously fun and educational. *The business of pets is remarkably interactive.* Customers appreciated these opportunities to consult and kibitz with knowledgeable persons in the pet care sphere.

Seminars of learning are good for business because, in the big picture, they pump up sales. That is, you get more people into your place of business, including many first-time customers. More of your products or services are discussed. And, yes, more purchases are made. Educated consumers are your best friends.

★ The Woodcarver Cometh

Early in the Pet Nosh timeline, we invited a gifted woodcarver to display his talents in one of our stores. He specialized in domestic pets. Carving away for hours, he sat at a table for all to see. Our clientele were encouraged to chat with him about his craft and order, if they so desired, individually carved statues of their beloved cats and dogs.

Again, the woodcarver appearance complemented the Pet Nosh shopping experience. It created a buzz of something transpiring in the store other than a humming cash register. It behooves you to routinely augment your business enterprise with happenings—things out of the ordinary or supplementary to the norm. Pet-specialty retailers, in particular, are afforded infinite possibilities to stir the pot to draw attention to themselves. The woodcarver visit was a small thing, easy enough to set up, and it delivered what we wanted.

★ Free Lunches

The late economist Milton Friedman once remarked, "There is no such thing as a free lunch." However, in business environments, giving your customers a free bite now and again is, well, good for business. Our most widely attended promotions often included freebies of some sort.

For example, we frequently had salespeople from assorted manufacturers dispensing free samples of their products. Sometimes these handouts consisted of entire bags of food and whole cans. Aside from pet-related giveaways, we occasionally offered our customers complimentary hot dogs, freshly popped popcorn, and ice cream bars. Most retailers can tell you that there is a human gene of sorts that relishes getting something for nothing, whether it is a sample sliver of cake from the bakery or a tube of new toothpaste that arrives in the mail. So, why not provide your customers with a little relish?

We literally doled out tons of free samples of cat and dog foods in our first few years in business. Many of our customers switched brands because of

263

these giveaways—they switched to both healthier foods for their pets and foods that, yes, made us more money. These kinds of win-win scenarios are what you want in business. But we never, ever, applied the hard sell. We just furnished our customers with a broad range of choices and some freebies along the way to help them make up their own minds.

In addition, we also ran some intriguing quasi-free promotions. One was dubbed *Trash for Cash*, in which we asked our clientele to bring in their empty bags of supermarket brands of cat and dog food. We would then exchange them for trial sizes or small bags of premium pet foods that were not available in mass merchandisers. The Trash for Cash concept resonates with people and can be repeatedly tweaked to suit your distinct business needs. This promotional pathway encourages people to sample new products that they wouldn't otherwise try.

In the dog-eat-dog business milieu of today, all kinds of enterprises offer all kinds of free stuff to consumers. These freebies often go beyond merchandise and include things like flu shots, blood pressure checks, and events such as pet adoptions. The bottom line is that the right types of promotional events stir the business pot. Whatever pet business you call your own, we'd recommend that you begin stirring right now and never stop. Pet Nosh fashioned a reputation through the years as more than just a place to purchase pet supplies. We accomplished this mean feat by being bold and different from the outset. Our stores were seen as appealing stopovers for pet consumers—places that appreciated and respected their idiosyncrasies, as well as catered to their every whim.

Traditional Marketing

Once you establish yourself as a legal entity open for business, you will be inundated with advertising alternatives. New businesses in town are descended upon by hordes of salespeople—each one, of course, pitching the most cost-effective and productive advertising opportunity on Mother Earth. Beyond the more colorful and creative promotional avenues that we've already touched upon, there are the traditional and, in many instances, necessary advertising roads to drive down, including newspaper ads, direct mail, fliers, cable television, and radio.

★ Newspaper Ads

Select newspaper ads often worked wonders for Pet Nosh, particularly when we advertised specific products at bargain-basement prices. We regularly ran sales on cat foods and dog foods, priced at below what we paid for them. We found that these *loss leaders* brought us new customers—both individuals who had never heard of us, and others who knew we existed, but until then didn't care that we did.

All that glitters is not gold. Keep this maxim in mind when considering your advertising alternatives. Scrupulously avoid throwing money into advertising that'll get you no return on your investment. It's so easy to do. Before paying for any advertising, or running any kind of promotion, ask yourself these two questions in the context of your business: *Who am I? What do I do?* When you can honestly answer these dual queries, you'll understand where your advertising dollars can be best allocated. Then, of course, you must weigh whether the advertising under consideration will reach your consumer demographic, and if it will reach sufficient numbers of them to make the cost worthwhile. When you are fully satisfied that your target audience is in your sights, it's now time to decide "the how" and "the what" to advertise. There is nothing gained in locating your customer base and then offering them something they don't want, or a muddled promotion that misses its mark entirely.

Since we initially considered the supermarkets our main competitors, we aimed our advertising howitzers at their customer base. We conducted sales on merchandise that people customarily bought there—commercial brands of pet food and basic supplies. Often what supermarket shoppers discovered when they entered a Pet Nosh store for the first time was that we had everything they needed for their pets—and at very competitive prices too. Of course, the convenience of purchasing in large quantities, wide selections of items on the shelves, and carryout service on top of all that were additional selling points.

★ Direct Mail

Direct mail is yet another formidable promotional option to ponder. Over time, we built up a substantial customer mailing listing and inaugurated a VIP program. It is always beneficial to get your clientele's names and addresses and, via periodic mailings, keep them abreast of what you have to offer and how you differ from the competition. Send them coupons and sale announcements.

Co-op advertising is also worth looking into. We had measurable success with co-op coupon ads mailed to targeted zip codes in and around Pet Nosh store locations. (This entails your specific advertisement getting mailed in concert with noncompetitive businesses' advertisements at significantly cheaper rates than the aforementioned individual mailings.) We always offered a variety of coupons that ran the gamut of our consumer demographic. That is, there was always something for cat owners and something for dog owners. Depending on the season, we often featured coupons for cheaply priced bags of wild birdseed. Eventually, when our stores brought in livestock—fish, birds, reptiles, and small animals—we recognized the importance of these consumers to our business with coupons aimed at their needs and wants. Co-op mailings are very effective for pet-specialty businesses of all kinds, including dog walking, doggie daycare, pet hotels, dog washes, etc. This brand of advertising is particularly helpful in bringing customers to your door for the first time.

★ Flexible Fliers

In the beginning, there were fliers…lots of fliers. When we assumed ownership of Pet Nosh in the waning months of 1979, the very first promotional move we made involved a simple flier. On it, we broadcast the existence of our home delivery service. We were extremely aggressive in going after home delivery customers. We sought clientele in the area of our Little Neck, Queens store and for miles in every direction of it. But we didn't stop there.

At the time, the Pet Nosh ownership resided in the borough of the Bronx and commuted to work, as it were. So, we spread our wings—and our fliers—further still, carpeting apartment building hallways near our homes, as well as in other densely populated spots between where we lived and where we operated our retail business. Our first delivery vehicles were our cars—their trunks and interiors were regularly crammed with cat and dog supplies.

An interesting footnote here: When we circulated the fliers in our home borough, we noted on them that the merchandise would be delivered from "our Bronx warehouse." This, alas, was a white lie—we had no such place. Nevertheless, we reasoned that customers on our home turf would be less apt to order from us if they thought we were merely a mom-and-pop store from a faraway borough of New York City—Queens. We are not advocating any such deceit—truth in advertising is always best—just recollecting how our young business minds worked in those days of yore. We considered every possibility—including consumer psychology—as we tried to win over customers and get a leg up on our competition.

A flier campaign is an advertising vehicle that can be effortlessly waged by placing them on car windshields in parking lots and along streets. Fliers can be affixed to telephone polls and put in mailboxes or on front porches. Given that our target customers were principally supermarket shoppers, we repeatedly blanketed supermarket parking lots. A targeted flier effort is cheap, easy to organize, and quite often productive.

★ Television

Nowadays, the state of television—with its hundreds of cable channels—makes it possible for small businesses to affordably advertise on the boob tube. Pet Nosh ran advertisements on local cable stations. In fact, we got enough positive responses from them that we went into reruns. One of our TV spots featured a Chihuahua named Scrabby. The diminutive canine had been selected as our company "mascot" in an in-store contest that we ran, with one of the prizes being this prestigious appearance on the small screen. Granted, our commercials on A&E, Nick at Nite, and the Discovery channel didn't win us any Emmy awards, nor are they archived in the Museum of Broadcasting, but television is such a powerful medium that it shouldn't be overlooked as a promotional possibility.

★ Radio

We also ran radio ads in our last few years in retail and were pleasantly surprised at the positive reception. "I heard your ad on the radio when I was coming home from work." Like cable television, radio advertising is something worth exploring. Talk radio programs, in particular, are more popular than ever. Get your ad on a show, or in a particular format, that reaches your consumer demographic.

> Whether you are offering your customers merchandise or services (or a combination of both), offer them gift certificates, too. The purchase of a gift certificate is a sale, but it very often brings a potential repeat customer to your business door. For starters, the redeemer of the gift certificate might just buy more than its monetary value. And, after patronizing your business and enjoying the experience, this customer may return again and again. And that's what you want. Make it known that you have gift certificates for sale.

In addition, we once had a local radio station's deejay broadcast live from our superstore in Paramus, New Jersey. Both Pet Nosh and the radio station reaped some positive publicity from this unusual promotional pairing. The deejay and his associates doled out all kinds of freebies festooned with the station's call letters to our customers. In the big picture, it generated more of that buzz that we've been harping on.

Don't Shun the Small Things

Promoting your business venture needn't be a complicated or imposing undertaking. There are, in fact, countless small things that you can do to effectively market your business. Small things that can add up to very big things.

When you are walking or driving along a thoroughfare lined with retail businesses, what catches your eye? Store signs? Attractive window displays? Bunting flapping in the wind? Die-cut sandwich boards outside of stores? To get your business noticed, a simple move like hanging balloons outside your front door can attract customers. When you see something that breaks up the monotony, your eyes are automatically drawn to it. Remember that once you capture your potential customers' two eyes, then maybe you can get their two legs to walk through your door or inquire about your service.

We once commissioned a local artist to paint our original company mascots (pre-Scrabby the Chihuahua) onto our first delivery truck. It was a cartoon depiction of a cat and dog, which we named Tyler and Nash. On one side of the truck, Tyler held a gun to his head with a word balloon coming out his mouth that read, "Get me to Pet Nosh or else!" (This was before political correctness reigned supreme. Today, we would likely receive complaints about such a "violent" depiction on a delivery truck out on the open highways for all of the world's children to see.)

Anyway, Tyler and Nash existed in animation only until we purchased a custom-made dog costume and brought the canine half to life. You'd be surprised how many Pet Nosh employees volunteered to wear the costume and stand alongside busy traffic holding balloons and waving to passersby. From their perspective, it beat packing shelves and punching up sales on a cash register. The costume cost us $300 and we got years of use out of it.

We put Nash the dog among the people whenever we had a mind to—during store sales, distinctive promotional events, or on busy weekends. Nash handed out balloons to kids and candy to kids and adults alike. Who can resist such a spectacle? Consider your reaction to the human lobster in front of a seafood restaurant, the walking pencil at the office supplies' store, or the colossal Dunkin' Donuts' coffee mug inviting you in for a piping hot cup of java. At the very least, you pause and reflect on what you are looking at.

Smart businesspersons love kids. Depending, of course, on what explicit pet business you are in, welcoming parents and their young offspring into your shopping experience is usually a smart move. We had PBS's popular purple dinosaur Barney visit Pet Nosh. Believe it or not, we weren't pitching a Barney brand of dog food or anything like that. We had face painting and clown visitations specifically targeted to kids. An astute businessperson understands that youngsters bring their parents with them 100% of the time. And, the word is out, many adults like to shop! Something as simple as renting a helium machine, which we also did, and giving out balloons to children kindles positive publicity and a good feeling all around.

All the News That's Fit to Print

Throughout our seventeen years in business, we periodically published customer newsletters. Even when we were very small potatoes, we projected Pet Nosh as being bigger than it actually was. That is, in a newsletter format, we ran feature biographies on our store managers and recounted the history of the company's founding. While the company story wasn't quite the epic proportions of Microsoft or McDonald's, it always helped to exude confidence and display a little grandeur, because perception is reality in business. Our original newsletters—from the pre-computer era—were crudely done on a typewriter and printed on sheets of white paper and then stapled together. But they worked in both entertaining and informing our clientele.

Never be afraid to tell your customers about yourself and what you have to offer them in products and services. Connect with them on a human level, as well as business level. You can accomplish this one-two punch with a simple newsletter. Also, depending on the exact nature of your business, you can sometimes get your suppliers to pay for the entire newsletter's production. For a fee, let your vendors promote their merchandise with advertisements in it. Allow a particular manufacturer to sponsor it entirely.

Customer VIP Programs

When Petco purchased our chain of superstores, then-CEO Brian Devine identified three Pet Nosh particulars that he wanted to immediately incorporate into his business model: Special Ordering, Book Departments, and a Customer VIP Program.

With computerization, it is now rather simple to track what individual customers purchase, how much they purchase, etc. With some form of VIP program in place, you repay customer loyalty to your business. And, in today's increasingly competitive pet marketplace, rewarding your customer base is indispensable. It'll keep them coming back to you because they are, in essence, invested in your business. In other words, when they faithfully buy things from you and receive discounts or freebies (the rewards) for doing so, why would they want to shop elsewhere?

The Virtual Truth of Marketing

When Pet Nosh got rolling, there was no Information Superhighway and hence, no emailing and no website presences. We were first assaulted with such earth-shattering technological advances as the fax machine. And mere faxes revolutionized the way Pet Nosh conducted business! In our first decade in business, the Pet Nosh team spent hours upon hours reading orders over the phone. Placing an accessory order with hundreds of different products meant having to recite hundreds of individual code numbers and corresponding quantities. Suffice it to say, this ate up a whole lot of time that could have been better spent. But what choice did we have? That's the way it was done.

Anyway, that was then and this is now. Computers exist in the majority of today's homes and most of the citizenry is, at the very least, Internet literate. For this reason alone, businesses should mine this promotional bailiwick. Even a minimal website that functions as an e-newsletter can sweeten your bottom line. Make your site an information portal, both fun and educational. Use it to keep your customers abreast of cutting-edge product or service news, sales, and upcoming events. Any way you can, stay in contact with your clientele. Naturally, you have to promote your Web address. However, as a way to keep your customers informed in the new millennium, it's a no-brainer courtesy of its minimal operating costs (after an initial start-up investment). There is no more cost-efficient method to communicate en masse than via an emailing.

In all of your advertising—whatever the costs or methods—ask yourself the same question: "What am I looking to get out of it?" Set clear promotional goals. Whether you produce a flier or don a lizard costume and march back and forth in front of your place of business, carefully consider your objectives. Who are you trying to reach? What amount of business will satisfy you from your promotion? Never do anything without a target in sight that you'd like to hit.

APPENDIX B
Professional Associations & Informational Websites

About Knitting @ Knitting.about.com

About Sewing @ Sewing.about.com

About Veterinary Medicine @ VetMedicine.about.com

American Pet Products Manufacturers Association (APPMA) @ APPMA.org

American Veterinary Medical Association (AVMA) @ AVMA.org

Animal Transportation Association (AATA) @ AATA-AnimalTransport.org (713-532-2177)

Aquatic Community @ AquaticCommunity.com

Association of American Feed Control Officials (AAFCO) @ AAFCO.org

Association of American Veterinary Medical Colleges @ AAVMC.org (202-371-9195)

Association of Authors' Representatives @ <u>AAR-Online.org</u>

Association of Pet Dog Trainers (APDT) @ <u>APDT.com</u> (800-PET-DOGS)

Association for Pet Loss and Bereavement (APLB) @ <u>APLB.org</u>

Association of Professional Animal Waste Specialists @ <u>APAWS.org</u>

Avian Publications @ <u>AvianPublications.com</u> (800-577-2473)

Birds n Ways @ <u>BirdsNWays.com</u>

BirdShows.com @ <u>BirdShows.com</u> (901-878-1307)

Book Market @ <u>BookMarket.com</u>

Bow Tie Press @ <u>BowTiePress.com</u>

Center for Veterinary Medicine @ <u>FDA.gov/cvm</u> (888-INFO-FDA or 240-276-9300)

CraftAndFabricLinks.com @ <u>CraftAndFabricLinks.com</u>

Craft Yarn Council of America @ <u>LearnToKnit.com</u>

Dog Actors Guild @ <u>DogActorsGuild.com</u>

Doggie View @ <u>DoggieView.com</u> (866-DOG-VIEW)

Don Debelak @ <u>DonDebelak.com</u>

Drs. Foster & Smith on **Live Aquaria** @ <u>LiveAquaria.com</u>

Drs. Foster & Smith @ PetEducation.com

Entrepreneur.com @ Entrepreneur.com

Equissage @ Equissage.com (800-843-0224)

FedEx @ FedEx.com

FindLaw for Small Businesses @ SmallBusiness.FindLaw.com

Hollywood Animals' Animal Actors Agency @ AnimalActorsAgency.com
(323-665-9500)

Hollywood Paws @ HollywoodPaws.com (888-781-7827)

Home Sewing Association @ Sewing.org (412-372-5950)

**Independent Pet and Animal Transportation Association International
(IPATA)** @ IPATA.com (903-769-2267)

International Association of Animal Massage Therapists @ IAAMT.com

International Association of Pet Cemeteries & Crematories (IAOPCC)
@ IAOPC.com (518-594-3000)

International Directory of Dog Waste Removal @ Pooper-Scooper.com

International Professional Groomers (IPG) @ IPGCMG.org (847-758-
1938)

Invention Home @ InventionHome.com (866-THINK-12)

League of Animal Artists @ AnimalArtists.org

Massage Awareness @ MassageAwareness.com (561-383-8205)

The Merchant Account Guide @ TheMerchantAccountGuide.com (866-219-4838)

National Association of Dog Obedience Instructors (NADOI) @ NADOI.org

National Association of Professional Pet Sitters (NAPPS) @ PetSitters.org (856-439-0324)

National Dog Groomers Association of America (NDGAA) @ NationalDogGroomers.com (724-962-2711)

New York Institute of Photography @ NYIP.com (800-445-7279)

Pet Age @ PetAge.com

Pet Business @ PetBusiness.com

Pet Food Institute @ PetFoodInstitute.org

Pet Groomer @ PetGroomer.com (800-556-5131)

Pet Product News @ PetProductNews.com

Pet Sitters International (PSI) @ PetSit.com (336-983-9222)

Photography.com @ Photography.com

Publishers Marketplace @ PublishersMarketplace.com

The Reptile Information Network @ ReptileInfo.com

T.H.F. @ THFPublications.com

United Parcel Service (UPS) @ UPS.com

United States Patent and Trademark Office @ USPTO.gov (800-786-9199)

United States Postal Service (USPS) @ USPS.com

U.S. Small Business Administration (SBA) @ SBA.gov (800-U-ASK-SBA or 800-827-5722)

VeterinarySchools.com @ VeterinarySchools.com (800-940-0080)

WhereTechsConnect.com @ WhereTechsConnect.com

Writers Net @ Writers.net

APPENDIX C
Additional Reading

Dr. Pitcairn's Complete Guide to Natural Health for Dogs and Cats, Richard H. Pitcairn, DVM, PhD and Susan Hubble Pitcairn (Rodale, revised edition, 2005).

How to Start a Home-Based Pet Care Business, Kathy Salzberg (Globe Pequot, second edition, 2006).

The Law (In Plain English)® for Small Business, Leonard D. DuBoff (Sphinx Publishing, second edition, 2007).

Opportunities in Animal and Pet Care Careers, Mary Price Lee and Richard S. Lee (McGraw-Hill, 2001).

Pet Sitting for Profit, Patti J. Moran (Howell Book House, third edition, 2006).

Specialty Shop Retailing: How to Run Your Own Store, Carol L. Schroeder (Wiley, 2002).

The Small Business Owner's Manual: Everything You Need to Know to Start Up and Run Your Business, Joe Kennedy (Career Press, 2005).

The Small Business Start-Up Guide, Hal Root and Steve Koenig (Sourcebooks Inc., fourth edition, 2005).

Start & Run a Creative Services Business, Start & Run series, Susan Kirkland (Self-Counsel Press, 2005).

Starting on a Shoestring: Building a Business Without a Bankroll, Arnold S. Goldstein, PhD (Wiley, fourth edition, 2002).

Start Your Own Pet-Sitting Business, Startup series, Cheryl Kimball (Entrepreneur Press, 2004).

The Stone Guide to Dog Grooming for All Breeds, Ben Stone and Pearl Stone (Howell Book House, 1981).

1001 Ideas to Create Retail Excitement, Edgar A. Falk (Prentice Hall Press, revised edition, 2003).

Ultimate Homebased Business Handbook: How to Start, Run and Grow Your Own Profitable Business, James Stephenson (Entrepreneur Press, 2004).

ABOUT THE AUTHORS

Joseph Nigro's success story unfurled under the vast umbrella of the pet care industry. In 1979, at the age of only 19, he and business partner Rich Covello purchased a mom-and-pop pet food and supply store. Located in the New York City borough of Queens, it was aptly named Pet Nosh. Approached by the Petco Company in 1996, Joe and his partners agreed to sell their Pet Nosh stores to the retail behemoth for millions of dollars.

Nicholas Nigro is a veteran of the pet care business. Wearing a variety of hats in the trade, he labored in every imaginable capacity through all seventeen years of independent retail chain Pet Nosh's existence.

INDEX

B

C

Q

R

S